family North

Mount Lebanon Cedar Boughs

Original Poems

family North

Mount Lebanon Cedar Boughs
Original Poems

ISBN/EAN: 9783744710909

Printed in Europe, USA, Canada, Australia, Japan

Cover: Foto ©Thomas Meinert / pixelio.de

More available books at **www.hansebooks.com**

MOUNT LEBANON

CEDAR BOUGHS

ORIGINAL POEMS

BY

THE NORTH FAMILY OF SHAKERS

As from Mount Lebanon of old
   Were quarried stone and cedars brought,
With precious gems and finest gold
   To be in God's great temple wrought;
So, from the mountain heights of praise
   Where heaven's sweet blessings ever rest,
To light, uplift and cheer life's ways,
   We bring our treasured gifts the best.

BUFFALO
THE PETER PAUL BOOK COMPANY
1895

PRINTED AND BOUND BY
THE PETER PAUL BOOK COMPANY,
BUFFALO, N. Y.

Affectionately
to our spiritual kindred of the Household of Faith
and in earnest service to yearning souls
in the wide, wide world, this
volume is dedicated.

INTRODUCTION.

THE world has been told by many witnesses that the Shakers, through integrity and industry, have peace and plenty in their beautiful homes; but has it been adequately declared that they are a progressive people without creed, superstition or traditional asceticism; that the broad, genial warmth of their lives has its ripples of mirth, its sparkles of wit as well as the spiritual and mental clearness "that grows brighter and brighter unto the perfect day."

It is through the solicitation of friends that we present this collection of poems to the public, that they may be enabled to obtain at least a slight glimpse of our inner life; a life that is as sweet to us as it is incomprehensible to the world generally.

Not infrequently do we meet with discerning souls who have lucid views of the truth, and of the beauty enjoyed here in our mountain home; from such we draw the incentive to put forth these unpretending efforts, few of which were ever intended to go beyond our own borders. We labor with our hands and with our hearts to bring the higher conditions of happiness to each other, and most gladly extend the good thus acquired to all who can receive or appreciate it.

Art may weave a coronal of roses, and simplicity entwine forest boughs, but their work will not admit of comparison, therefore we hope to be exempted from the severer standards of criticism, and to find acceptance through the sincerity that does not attempt to teach, except as the tree teaches, by gathering the elements of growth and spreading its branches for *what they are*, even as we send forth our Cedar Boughs.

CONTENTS.

		PAGE.
Dedication		3
Introduction		5
The Cedars	C. De Vere	13
Our Mother Ann	C. C. Vinneo	14
The Saviour on the Mount,	M. J. Anderson	16
Blessing		19
A Gift	C. Allen	20
"I Bide My Time"	A. R. Stephens	21
Peace and Plenty	A. White	22
War of the Rebellion	C. De Vere	23
Glorious Cross	L. S. Bowers	26
Right Shall Triumph		27
Strengthen Me	L. Staples	27
The Money Changers	C. C. Vinneo	29
True Greatness	M. J. Anderson	30
Health	L. S. Bowers	30
The Last Day of Slavery	C. De Vere	31
Conquering Legions	M. J. Anderson	32
Lost—Saved		34
Overcoming		36
Life's Problems	C. De Vere	36
The Hindoo's Request	M. J. Anderson	38
Praise	A. R. Stephens	40
Not All a Dream	C. De Vere	40
Inspiration	A. R. Stephens	42
'Tis Victory	F. Staples	43
Exaltation	L. S. Bowers	44
The Rose and Golden-Rod	M. J. Anderson	45
Tenderness	A. R. Stevens	46
The Old Apple Tree	M. J. Anderson	47
Home	S. J. Burger	49
Lincoln and Stanton	C. De Vere	50
Idealize the Real	L. S. Bowers	53
Beautiful Rivers	M. J. Anderson	53
A Desert Spring	A. R. Stephens	55
Zion's Soul Communion	C. De Vere	56
Memento Mori	L. S. Bowers	58
The Poet Whittier	C. De Vere	58
The Future is Ours	A. R. Stephens	60
Heart Lessons	C. De Vere	61
Two Wheels	Lydia Staples	63

		PAGE.
The Bird Craze	M. J. Anderson	63
A Plea For the Turkey	C. C. Vinneo	65
The Jews Gathering Manna	C. De Vere	66
No Time to Lose	A. R. Stephens	67
"Give Us This Day Our Daily Bread"	M. J. Anderson	68
Faith	M. E. Lane	69
Hope	A. R. Stephens	70
Love	L. S. Bowers	70
Sympathy with Friends in the West	C. De Vere	71
Truth	M. J. Anderson	73
The Cry of the Suffering	C. C. Vinneo	74
The Millionaire's Daughter	C. De Vere	75
Sympathy	M. J. Anderson	78
True Goodness	A. R. Stephens	79
"How Swift the Shuttle Flies"	M. J. Anderson	80
Forgiveness	C. C. Vinneo	80
Silence	A. R. Stephens	82
Renewal	C. Allen	82
Press On	A. R. Stephens	84
Gethsemane	C. C. Vinneo	85
The Last Night of Jesus on Earth	C. De Vere	86
Perfect Through Suffering	A. R. Stephens	88
Be Calm	M. J. Anderson	89
Sunrise Around the World	M. J. Anderson	89
Spring's Frolic	C. De Vere	92
A Snow Storm	M. J. Anderson	94
Human Progress		95
The Slaves of Poverty	C. C. Vinneo	98
The Factory	M. J. Anderson	100
America's Working People	C. De Vere	102
The Ohio Temperance Crusade		105
The Nineteenth Century		107
New Life	C. Allen	109
To the Music Maker	C. De Vere	110
The Wood Thrush	C. C. Vinneo	112
The Waters	C. De Vere	114
To My Little Sister	C. C. Vinneo	115
Wonderment		117
Acrostic	M. J. Anderson	120
What is True Life?	L. S. Bowers	121
To-Day	C. De Vere	122
War and Peace	M. J. Anderson	123
Columbian Liberty and Peace Bell	C. De Vere	125

		PAGE.
The Angel Choir	A. R. Stephens	126
Love's Ministry	M. J. Anderson	128
Life Without Love	L. S. Bowers	131
My Little Bed		131
Pockets	M. J. Anderson	134
The Robbin	C. C. Vinneo	135
Welcome to June	L. S. Bowers	136
A Picture	C. C. Vinneo	138
A Triplet of Sonnets	M. J. Anderson	139
Carnations	C. C. Vinneo	141
Autumn	S. J. Burger	141
Stars That Twinkle	J. Robe	142
Reply of the Stars		145
Peace Offerings at the World's Exposition	C. De Vere	152
"At Last"	M. J. Anderson	154
Bryant	S. J. Burger	155
Hazel Blossoms	L. Staples	156
The Daisies	L. S. Bowers	156
Wheat	C. C. Vinneo	158
A Happy Mood	A. R. Stephens	158
The Meadow Lark	S. J. Burger	159
God is Everywhere	L. S. Bowers	159
Physical Resurrection	C. De Vere	160
Teach Me To Trust	A. R. Stephens	162
The Mountain Lake	C. C. Vinneo	162
Lord, Increase My Faith	A. R. Stephens	163
The Circle of the Year	C. De Vere	164
January	L. S. Bowers	166
February		166
March		167
April	M. J. Anderson	167
May	L. S. Bowers	168
June	M. J. Anderson	168
July		169
August	C. C. Vinneo	169
September		170
October	L. S. Bowers	170
November	L. Staples	171
December		171
Year of Life		172
The Crow's Lecture	C. De Vere	173
Contentment	M. J. Anderson	176
The Bird Legislator	L. S. Bowers	177
Guest-Angel	M. J. Anderson	179
Truth	C. Allen	179
Reverence	M. J. Anderson	180

		PAGE
Solemn Thoughts	S. Wayne	180
Immortality	M. J. Anderson	182
Unborn Poetry	F. W. Evans	182
Look Upward	J. M. Lincoln	183
Beautiful Day	M. J. Anderson	183
Sunrise	A. R. Stephens	184
Day Dawn	C. De Vere	185
Night Falleth	C. De V.	187
In the Moonlight	L. S. Bowers	188
Land of Our Dreams	M. J. Anderson	188
Waking Thoughts	A. R. Stephens	189
The War in Egypt	C. De Vere	190
Shaker Homes	S. Wayne	192
Christmas Day	C. C. Vinneo	193
A Mother's Love	C. Allen	195
Bless and Curse Not	A. R. Stephens	197
Gift of Friendship	M. J. Anderson	197
Go Find Thy Friends	C. C. Vinneo	198
Language	M. J. Anderson	199
Funeral Day		200
America in Shame	C. De Vere	202
Inward Peace	M. J. Anderson	205
A Financial Panic	C. De Vere	205
Comparison	L. Staples	208
Monopoly	C. De Vere	208
The Home That We Have Found		210
Adieu	M. J. Anderson	211
Courage	A. R. Stephens	214
Maternal Spirit	A. White	215
A Mother's Love	L. S. Bowers	216
Our Beloved Mother	C. C. Vinneo	216
Our Roll Call	S. Wayne	218
The Increase	C. De Vere	219
The Victor	M. J. Anderson	220
Self Denial	C. De Vere	221
Resignation	L. S. Bowers	222
The New Year	L. Staples	223
Lengthening Days		223
The Dead Year		224
The Frost on the Pane	A. R. Stephens	224
Our Water Works	C. De Vere	226
Thanksgiving	M. J. Anderson	230
What Hath the Struggle Availed?	C. C. Vinneo	230
Thy Will Be Done	S. J. Burger	232
The Churches of Our Land	C. De Vere	233

		PAGE.
Speak, Lord, to Me	A. R. Stephens	234
The New Flag	C. De Vere	235
The Milennial Time	C. C. Vinneo	237
True Wealth	M. J. Anderson	239
Reliance	L. Staples	240
Words of Cheer	C. C. Vinneo	241
Poet and Prophet		242
Communion	C. Allen	242
Nothing New	M. J. Anderson	244
Heavenly Light	M. A. Burger	247
A Prayer for Rain	C. C. Vinneo	247
After the Rain	M. J. Anderson	249
Lillies of the Valley	L. Staples	250
The Tube Rose	M. J. Anderson	250
To the Five-Finger	L. Staples	251
The Calla Lily	M. J. Anderson	251
The Purple Pansy	L. Staples	252
The Snow Flower	L. S. Bowers	252
Blighted	M. J. Anderson	253
Fallen	C. De Vere	254
A Lesson	L. Staples	257
Motherland	C. De Vere	257
The Famous Hutchinson Family	C. De Vere	260
Life's Treasure	C. Allen	262
Alone	M. J. Anderson	263
Adoration	L. S. Bowers	265
The Pilgrim and the Mile Stone	C. De Vere	268
Grateful Thought	M. J. Anderson	269
Unrest		270
Two Lessons From Egypt	C. C. Vinneo	272
William Cullen Bryant	M. J. Anderson	274
Bethesda	C. C. Vinneo	274
The Humming-Bird	L. S. Bowers	275
Hygeia	S. J. Burger	275
Compensation	L. Staples	276
Death of the Pharisee	C. De Vere	276
The Rainbow of the Morning	C. C. Vinneo	279
The Groves	L. S. Bowers	280
Psyche	M. J. Anderson	280
Faith	A. R. Stephens	281
By the Sea	L. S. Bowers	281
Wrecked	M. J. Anderson	282
Forgiveness	A. R. Stephens	283
Patience	C. C. Vinneo	283
My Conclusion	L. Staples	284
To Our Honored Father	C. De Vere	285

		PAGE.
Duty	A. R. Stephens	287
A Tribute of Affection	C. De Vere	288
Holy Stillness	A. R. Stephens	291
Elder Richard Bushnell	C. De Vere	291
Fields of Heaven	M. J. Anderson	293
To Our Father	C. De Vere	293
Pleasure	M. J. Anderson	295
Joined the Immortals		296
Grateful Tribute		296
Day and Night	L. Staples	298
Not Dead	A. R. Stephens	298
Motherhood	C. De Vere	301
The Memory of Our Own Dear Mother	L. S. Bowers	302
"We Rise to Call Her Blessed"	A. R. Stephens	304
In Memoriam	M. J. Anderson	305
Rest in Peace	F. Staples	307
The Reward of a Dedicated Life	C. De Vere	309
Crossing Life's Tide	E. Offord	311
Recompense	C. C. Vinneo	312
Youthful Petition	C. Allen	313
Culmination	L. Staples	315

MOUNT LEBANON CEDAR BOUGHS.

THE CEDARS.

O WHENCE are they? we knew them first
   In the full grandeur of their prime,
As if their seedlings had been nursed
   In fields beyond the realms of Time.
Or when he ground the rock to feed
   The crystal filter of his hours,
Did he turn surplus grains to seed
   Endued with such gigantic powers?
Mayhap strong winds from heaven blown,
   When earth was in her misty youth,
Set firm the cedars in the stone
   As symbols of enduring truth.
What if the soil around was dry,
   By hidden springs their roots were fed,
And to the love-bestowing sky
   The beauty of their branches spread.
Their leafy temple raised to God
   Before great Israel's hosts were born,
Had shrouding-veil, the welkin broad,
   And altar-flame, the smile of morn.
An earthly king essayed to rear
   A miracle for all the arts;
They felt no rivaling human sneer,
   But gave the best gifts of their hearts.
Aloft, magnificent they stood
   Where legions knelt with hearts of fire;

Their very shadows casting good,
    Their voices crying "come up higher."
They twined a chaplet evergreen
    Around a coronal impearled;
They made Mount Lebanon the queen
    Of all the mountains of the world.

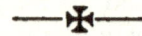

OUR MOTHER ANN.

I SEE her by the forge fire's light,
    A guileless, thoughtful Quaker child;
The glowing embers burning bright,
    Her meditations have beguiled.
Sweet lessons from the Holy Writ,
    That on her heart impression made,
Before her fancy swiftly flit,
    In colors that will never fade.
Afar she sees the falling rain
    On Noah's lonely struggling ark;
Then views the cities of the plain
    That would not to the warning hark.

The youth that was to Egypt sold,
    The infant hid where rushes sigh,
And he whose innocence was bold,
    That softly answered, "Here am I."
Then comes the vision of that birth
    Whose music seems her soul to thrill,
When angel hosts sang, "Peace on earth,"
    God's glory, "and to man, *good will.*"
One, on his Father's business bent,
    Sat with the Doctors of the Law
To question them, with mind intent
    On truth that they but dimly saw.

In him it was a quickened seed
   That yet would yield its hundred-fold;
'Twas his to fill its utmost meed,
   And still a higher life unfold.
And when that youth returned to grow
   In favor with both God and man,
The past to him was all aglow
   With types of God's great future plan.

But *she*, whose childhood now we trace,
   Rose like a star above the sea,
To usher in the day of grace,
   The Heavenly Mother's majesty.
Stern sat the ages in their pride,
   And boasted of each noble son,
For they of *daughters* were denied,
   'Till man's great prowess should be won;
And 'till he proved his power to *fail*,
   In all attempts to free the race,
And knew that he could not prevail
   'Till *woman* held her rightful place.

Earth needed *dual* heart and brain
   To learn the song that heaven sings;
To echo the melodious strain,
   From harps that chime a thousand strings.
It needed hands that God could teach,
   To deal with priestcraft and with sin;
The temple's inmost vail to reach,
   And there disclose the ghoul within.
It needed one whose gentle soul
   Could sorrow with a tender grief,
Of whom the Christ could take control,
   And make a fountain of relief.

And she was called in early days,
   Not by loud thunders from above,
But by the "still small voice" that stays
   Among the elements of love.

Sweet in her lowly home she grew,
    Beneath the watchful angels' care,
And spoke far wiser than she knew,
    And prayed the soul-redeeming prayer.
No human heart could her sustain,
    Though like a fruitful vine she clung,
Or lonely wept and strove in pain,
    While yet her wondrous life was young.

When persecution's demon-band
    Made dark the pathway that she trod,
She turned her eyes to freedom's land,
    For she was serving freedom's God.
O had that land in *part* received
    The saving truth her spirit bore,
No war nor slavery would have grieved
    Its vast domain from shore to shore.
But on its soil the tree of life
    Was planted, and beneath its shade
We have a home with blessings rife,
    A home her faithful children made.

THE SAVIOUR ON THE MOUNT.

PRESSED by the mulitudes that thronged his way,
    And clamored for a miracle or test,
Who sought the things that lasted but a day,
    Nor cared for truth his inner life had blessed.

The lowly Jesus went his way apart,
    And his disciples followed him apace;
They knew the springs that welled within his heart
    Would flow to them in streams of living grace.

His steps were bent unto the favored spot
    Where he was wont to seek a calm retreat,

While cares and trials all, his soul forgot,
   Where heaven and earth in close communion meet.

The sunny beams upon the mountain broke,
   The olive-trees with glistening dews were sweet,
Among their branches gentle murmurs woke,
   And snowy blossoms fell before his feet.

Fair emblems of the precious words, that came
   Unsullied from the lips of him who spake
To those who loved to hear, and name the name,
   That bore the power the slumbering soul to wake.

Beneath the olive's shade, whose glossy leaves
   Droop peacefully above his Christ-like brow,
The golden threads of life divine he weaves,
   In which beatitudes refulgent glow.

The shimmering gleams that 'lumed the shady bower
   Were faint, compared with truth's bright piercing darts,
That God had placed within the archer's power,
   To slay the foes that lurk in human hearts.

He sat not there, with Pharisaic mien
   Propounding logic of a mystic creed;
But, with a spirit self-subdued and clean,
   He ministered according to their needs.

A flood of inspiration thrilled his soul,
   And thought expanding found expression free;
The Christ-anointing held supreme control,
   And gave his spirit heavenly liberty.

Before all men, then let our light shine forth!
   That they may see our works are just and true,
And glorify the Father, who hath wrought
   A work which will create all things anew.

He came not to destroy the written law
    But one more perfect to impress within,
Souls unto truth and righteousness to draw,
    Thus save them from the blighting power of sin.

He gave to them the simple, golden rule,
    More potent than the conquering Roman state,
The fires of passion to assuage and cool,
    And *love* its motor, to subdue all hate.

They bowed their hearts in sacred reverence,
    While he in simple faith taught them to pray;
A prayer so full of trust, yet so intense,
    'Twas like the glory of a new-born day.

Fair lilies of the valley robed in white,
    Knew not the cankering care of mortal needs;
Yet he who, trusting, dwells within *His* light,
    Our heavenly Father blesses, clothes and feeds.

And thus he crystallized the gems of worth,
    In illustrative parable outwrought;
While mighty principles which move the earth,
    Were to the understanding clearly taught.

Some marveled at the doctrine, strange and new,
    That Jesus taught the people day by day;
His wondrous system rose before their view,
    And all their old traditions swept away.

The Messianic kingdom they had planned
    Came not with regal pomp, nor glittering show;
The Prince of Peace went forth through Judea's land,
    The seeds of everlasting life to sow.

He healed the sick, the lame and blind made whole;
    Demoniac spirits from his presence fled;
Superior forces acting through his soul,
    Restored to living consciousness, the dead.

How beautiful upon the mountain's height
    The Master in his earnestness appears !
All crowned with halos of prophetic light,
    That circle 'round the centuries of years.

BLESSING.

ONLY an acorn that fell by the wayside,
    Only a tiny seed hidden from sight,
Only a crystal drop lost in the flowing tide,
    Only a star shining out in the night.

Lo, the great oak a broad shelter is weaving,
    Many fair flowers shed sweetest perfume,
Bosom of ocean are mingled drops heaving,
    Numberless planets the dark sky illume.

Thus be our life into purpose expanding,
    Small in beginning yet good in intent,
Noble and useful and truthful in standing,
    Spreading in blessing as days are well spent.

Ever the rich and the precious seed sowing,
    Gray wastes shall blossom and deserts shall smile,
Kindness and care on the needy bestowing,
    Reaping a harvest of pleasure the while.

Better to swell the bright billows of gladness,
    Though we have only a little to give,
Rather than drain the last dregs of life's sadness,
    Only for love let us labor and live.

Though in the galaxy faint is our gleaming,
    Still will our glory be made to appear,
Ever with steady light so be our beaming,
    God marks the orbit of each circling sphere.

A GIFT.

WHEN night had drawn her sable folds,
    And slumber brought the gift of rest,
A thought that memory sweetly holds
    Upon my spirit was impressed.

It seemed a friend had beckoned me,
    Who stood in silence and alone,
Her eyes were fixed so searchingly
    I almost feared to hear her tone.

She spake in words of living flame
    Against the hidden life of sin,
Until their power in me became
    A quenchless fire to burn within.

My hand in hers was firmly clasped,
    My spirit bowed beneath her word,
And eagerly each sentence grasped
    As though an angel voice I heard.

And then like sheltering wings outspread
    Her love and mercy covered me,
The truth had brought no fear or dread,
    But joyous life and liberty.

I knelt to render gratitude,
    And bless the hand which bore the rod,
My soul was humbled, and renewed
    Its consecration unto God.

And as I rose, a gladsome song
    Of triumph thrilled the tranquil air,
It rolled in cadence clear and strong,
    Its melody was sweet and rare.

It bore the boon of inward peace
    Which seals the conqueror's holy strife,
The prophecy of rich increase
    Of glory in eternal life.

I felt that in that simple dream
   Dear angel guardians neared my soul,
To teach how good the truth will seem
   If we but yield to its control.

I'll bless it when it scourgeth me
   And leads me to acknowledge wrong,
And in its glorious liberty
   My spirit shall be brave and strong.

O precious truth, I'll cleave to thee,
   My every act and inmost thought
Guided by thy light shall be,
   Till in thy power my life is wrought.

"I BIDE MY TIME."

"I BIDE my time," O lesson sweet,
   In patience e'er to wait;
God's mercies like fair autumn flowers
   May often blossom late.

What though to-day my feet must tread
   Dark Alpine vales of woe,
Perchance to-morrow's sun will shed
   Its brightness where I go.

If all life's streams with joy would flow,
   Our hearts were always glad,
That rarest bliss we'd never know
   Of being sometimes sad.

"I bide my time" in patience strong,
   In hopes that ne'er abate;
God's promises to those belong
   Who daily work and wait.

"I bide my time;" through shade and shine
　I wait for God's decree,
Assured that in his own good time
　There's something sweet for me.

PEACE AND PLENTY.

THERE cometh a time when sorrow
　　Shall darken the earth no more,
When Peace, with her snowy pinions,
　　Shall rest upon every shore;
When the fear of war and carnage,
　　No more the heart shall seize;
But the notes of joy and gladness,
　　Be borne on the gentle breeze.

There cometh a time of sowing
　　The seed of the kingdom new;
It falleth alike on many,
　　As falls the evening dew.
In the true and honest-hearted,
　　Rich soil for an increase,
It shall ripen, and the harvest
　　Be fruits of an endless peace.

There cometh a time of reaping
　　The true from the false and vain;
The fan of the Lord shall sever
　　The chaff from the precious grain;
And the golden sheaves be gathered
　　To Christ the living head;
Souls in peace and love cemented
　　Shall eat of the living bread.

There cometh a time of weeping
　　Unknown to the earthly mind,

A sorrow that works repentance
   Ere rest shall the spirit find;
When the books of memory open,
   The sea gives up its dead,
Shall the song and word of triumph
   Be sung and by thousands read.

Rejoice in the past and present,
   Rejoice in the time to come,
The wilderness soon shall blossom,
   Earth's desert places bloom;
And the ransomed turned to Zion
   With everlasting joy,
While the horn of peace and plenty,
   Shall follow their blest employ.

WAR OF THE REBELLION.

THE angels brought the high command
   To "*Make Columbia's children free,*"
They sought the noblest of the land
   To hew a path for liberty.
They called the justice-loving *Friends*
   Whom they had taught in silent hours,
To give the country's eyes a lens
   Through which to scan her crushing powers.

They thrilled the cords in woman's heart,
   Drew sympathy from every tone,
Until she made that cause a part
   Of all the wrongs that were her own.
Where e'er a generous nature glowed,
   Where e'er was breathed the gift of song
The floods of inspiration flowed
   In burning waves against the wrong.

Where e'er the thought was clear and brave,
    These angel messengers were found
In earnest pleading for the slave,
    Whose limbs and heart alike were bound.

The hearth, the pulpit, and the press
    Were all invoked to lend their aid;
The lowly heart was claimed to bless
    The efforts that the mighty made;
Until there rested in the air
    An element like subtile flame,
A pressure as of mingled prayer,
    Yet who could tell from whence it came?

O, even in our little day,
    How great the struggle that arose
To banish *slavery* away—
    That *monster* of all household foes.
With glass reversed, we view it o'er,
    And strive to fix it on the past;
And yet the fearful guise it wore
    Will haunt our memories to the last.

The angels shook the nation's gates,
    And blew their trumpets long and loud,
Until the crime-encumbered states
    · Rebelled with spirit fierce and proud;
And Sumter's gun that woke the land
    Sent echoes to the unseen realm,
Which brought a *war*-like spirit-band
    To take the nation's broken helm.

O paradox in human life!
    The hands that sought the captives' weal
Were nerved, amid that blinding strife,
    To dye with kindred blood their steel.
Yea, those whose hearts for *freedom* felt,
    And strove by righteousness to win,
Because in Babylon they dwelt,
    They were partakers of her sin.

The work the angel spirits did
  Seemed lost below that passion blaze;
And yet their aim was only hid
  To be restored in after days.
Those legions of the earthly plane
  Performed their work with dauntless rage,
Achieved with speed a precious gain,
  But brought a loss that none can gauge.

We pass beyond the broken homes,
  The ties that can not be replaced,
The hearts where never sunshine comes,
  The unapprized external waste,
And think of what the nation lost
  In weight that talent might have earned,
Of what her reeking altars cost,
  While souls were scarred and bodies burned.

O loathsome fields! O prison pens!
  Be ye no more the nation's shame;
With you all vindication ends,
  For violence in freedom's name.
Henceforth must legislation stand
  The only arbiter of right;
For God has called this glorious land
  To be redeemed from battle's blight.

There but remains a vail of days
  Till woman's servitude shall cease;
I see her, through its shining haze,
  The star-crowned guardian-friend of Peace.
For she who gave the bondman aid
  While cruel shackles were her own,
Shall yet, in council halls, persuade
  That love and wisdom are but one.

GLORIOUS CROSS.

GLORIOUS cross of Christ! what power in thee lies,
   Virtue sought and treasured through thee never dies,
Heights of truth's eternal glory rise to view,
   When by thy righteousness we strive life's journey through.
Days that live but now in story tell of thee,
   Name Thy name, but know not of thy purity.
Carved on palace walls and temples and still tombs,
   Carved to last perhaps ages through earth's glooms;
But not in symbols dull and olden art thou known,
   With the true cross is Christ's presence fully shown.
Shown by working soul's salvation from all sin,
   Known, by giving through each trial peace within.

Talisman against all evil—blessed cross!
   Be my whole life's impulse, leading from all loss.
Leave thy mark upon my forehead there to shine;
   That control of thought and feeling may be mine.
Set thy seal upon my spirit through the light,
   And when fades the time of sunshine keep the night.
O, I seek thee not for glory nor for crown,
   Though a blessing through thee surely cometh down,
But for good thou workest in me that my soul
   Loosed from tetherings may attain its perfect goal.

RIGHT SHALL TRIUMPH.

THE battle wages and the foe is strong,
    The air is wild with strife's confusing din,
    But God is mighty and the right must win.
The weak, down-trodden of earth's surging throng,
Who've borne their burdens patiently and long,
    With deep pulsations of true joy within,
    Will hail love's triumph and the death of sin
In stirring music of a glad new song.
Yea, time is coming when all unjust gain,
    Tyrannic force, and blinding creeds shall fail;
When purity and peace will life sustain,
    E'en to earth's border-land the truth prevail.
Arise! with resurrective thought, God works with you,
O let His power make your spirits true.

STRENGTHEN ME.

TAKE from my heart O Lord, all vain desires
        Through faith denied,
And may it as my soul to Thee aspires
        Be purified.

Leave not mine eyes to seek mid pleasures throng
        Those flowers loved best,
For 'neath the rose and in the crimsoned wrong
        Sharp briers rest.

But spotless lilies, emblemed angelhood
        In snowy dress,
Are safe, upon the bosom of all good
        To closely press.

Lead Thou my feet in pleasant ways of life,
    By waters still,
They in the safety of thy blessing rife
    Will do Thy will.

Make mid Thy altars-gifts my hands to feel
    For heavy task;
Forgiveness as upon its steps I kneel
    Is all I ask.

Teach me from wisdom's book in language meek,
    My thoughts to raise,
And to Thy holy name my tongue shall speak
    Continual praise.

Help me to pray, to ask in faith's clear light
    For conquering power,
That legions may not daunt my purpose right
    In sorrows hour.

Make me though deaf, in trying times to hear
    The truth's grand psalm,
To Thy soft whispers may I bend the ear
    In storm and calm.

'Twas once I sought the cross that pleasure wore,
    Her pearls to wear,
But now, the cross of Christ that Jesus bore,
    I too will bear.

And if I may, through struggle in Thy strength
    More perfect be,
My fruit of consecration shall at length
    Be brought to Thee.

THE MONEY CHANGERS.

SMITE with thy hand of wrath, O God of nations,
    The bold blasphemers at our country's shrine,
O'erturn the tables with their vile creations,
    And give the judgment that alone is Thine.

Tear down the veil of fraud that blinds the people;
    Drag mammon from the altar and the throne;
Let Thy swift warning sound from dome and steeple;
    Break Thou the gods of brass, of wood and stone.

At the States' senate where the great assemble,
    Behold the cunning, malice, greed and thrall;
O send the message that will make them tremble,
    The weird and awful writing on the wall.

And in the hour of revelry and splendor,
    Condemn the wicked for their deeds of shame;
Call up a saint, as did the seer of Endor,
    Who'll dare to speak Thy message, in Thy name.

The war is on, and right is ranked 'gainst error,
    But error holds its legions manifold;
And blinded men in ignorance and terror
    Defend the kings of silver and of gold.

In Thy rich earth are wretched people dying,
    Unknown to pity and unwept with tears;
While man-made schemes like ruined forts are lying
    Along the blood-stained pathway of the years.

The hand of Pharaoh holds the poor, like cattle,
    His heart of evil will not let them go,
O come, and lead Thy chosen on to battle,
    And strike the note that leveled Jericho!

TRUE GREATNESS.

NOT in the pomp and circumstance of state,
    Not in its war-like heraldry of fame,
Its pride of power and striving for a name,
—Ambition's lust and greed insatiate—
Are found the qualities that make men great.
    No conquering strength its lauded heroes claim
    The beasts of passion to subdue and tame,
And graceless heart-wilds to regenerate.
True greatness forms the soul's sun-belted zone;
    Where virtue grows to heaven-exalted deeds,
    Where good all direful evil supersedes,
    And love expands to meet all human needs;
Where righteous works for errors past atone,
And mortal want and misery are unknown.

HEALTH.

A PEARLY brow that tells of holy thought;
    A ruddy cheek, and eye with sparkling light;
Strong, well knit arms that love to do the right;
A heart that times life's motion as it ought,
And crimson blood from healthful substance wrought.
    Free lungs that heave with pure air day and night,
    These make of mortal life a sweet delight.
Health, priceless health, a boon from heaven brought.
In sacred writ, we learn that God made man
    In his unblemished image, strong and whole,
But sin, usurping power, has marred the plan,
    Destroying even beauty of the soul.
But God has yet dominion, and we can
    Through righteousness, regain the perfect goal.

THE LAST DAY OF SLAVERY.

I WATCHED the gray clouds in the sky
   And thought upon this mighty day,
Till my hushed soul could hear the cry
   Of hearts that had not power to pray.
My spirit roamed that sunny clime
   Where nature wears her richest dress,
And wept to see man's darkest crime
   Imbosomed in such loveliness.

If for a moment Hope might shine,
   Then cringing Fear's dark breath would rise;
And so these wearying thoughts of mine
   Were like the dim clouds in the skies.
Ah! life at best on Labor's plane
   Hath little that the soul can crave;
But Slavery's unremitting pain
   Is ended only in the grave.

Long, long each gold and azure morn
   Hath mocked the slave beneath his gloom.
Will Freedom's advent come with dawn?
   Will God destroy the man-made doom?
Thus eagerly my spirit longed
   To pierce the misty veil of Time,
And see if God would help the wronged,
   And prove his justice all sublime.

But ah! that veil concealed full well,
   Although it seemed a thing of air
That left sincerity to swell
   To God in waves of humble prayer.
O must the bond-man still be bound?
   Will Freedom's hand not touch his chain?
And must soft wind still bear the sound
   Of agonizing groans in vain?

Are not the sins of earth ripe yet?
 Or must her fields wear deeper red,
And shall gaunt famine coldly set
 His seal on many a blameless head?
I hear the Nation's great heart beat
 With new dependence on Thy power;
I see Thy Truth with Error meet,
 I feel the struggle of the hour.

The angel choirs around me swell
 The happy song of Jubilee;
And Destiny with deep-toned bell
 Proclaims a suffering people free.
Thus e'er the signal cannon spoke,
 Before the nation's loud acclaim,
Before the pen's resounding stroke,
 Emancipation's message came.

CONQUERING LEGIONS.

THE world is in commotion, and human hearts are stirred
With passions strong upwelling, and sense of hope deferred.
Great wrongs are yet prevailing, and the battle must be fought
With weapons that are tempered at the glowing forge of thought.

In fires of agitation and the living flame of zeal
Is wrought the bar of justice and truth's incisive steel.
Nerved be the hand with fortitude these mighty powers to wield,
Till earth's usurping minions to righteousness shall yield.

To noble tides of feeling throbs the pulse of yearning
    hearts;
Who strive for the uplifting a truer life imparts;
Thro' sway of truth and reason, with a deep and fervent plea,
Come forth the marshalled toilers with a cry of liberty.

Adown the shadowy vistas of the ages dim and vast
We hear the muffled treading of armies that have passed,
Through time's unceasing war between the evil and the good
The contest wages ever till the right is understood.

Led by the conquering legions who will make no compromise,
O may the suffering millions, in freedom's name, arise,
To strive above the sordid love of kindred, class or clan,
And follow Him whose kingdom is the brotherhood of man!

  Wake unto action in the glorious strife;
  Every soul to duty press where the wrong is rife;
  Sheath all weapons carnal, armed with godly might
  He alone shall conquer whose life is in the right.

LOST—SAVED.

LOST! lost! in the by-way turns
    That meet in the downward road,
When the soul the narrow highway spurns
    Which upward leads to God.

Lost! but a little slip at first,
    Then many a footfall down,
Till the fair of earth with sin accursed
    Miss virtue's shining crown.

Lost! in the drunkard's shadowy path,
    First drawn by the sparkling bowl
To enter the way of sin and wrath
    That ruins body and soul.

Lost! how the tempting gleams of gold
    Set honesty aside,
Till by degrees the heart grows bold
    In the stronghold of its pride.

Lost! in the vain and fruitless chase
    For honor, and wealth, and fame,
Where glory wrapped in selfhood base
    Proved but an empty name.

Lost! through the storm of passions wild
    Which led the feet astray;
Unconsciously, through wrong beguiled
    They passed on the downward way.

Lost! for an awful dearth and blight
    Rests on the wayward heart,
Who, turned from a knowledge of truth and right
    Walks from all good apart.

Lost! there are stealthy, subtle foes
    Who bind their chains around,
Till habits formed, their power disclose
    And the helpless soul is bound.

LOST—SAVED.

Lost! to a sense of blushing shame
   With a conscience seared and scarred,
Rises no holy incense flame,
   From out that vessel marred.

Lost! O! shall we think for aye
   Are sealed their fate and doom?
That through the blackness gleames no day
   Their dark haunts to illume?

Saved! saved! from the depths of woe
   And endless misery;
Saved, though fallen ever so low
   Each human soul will be.

Saved! there are blessed angels sent
   From glorious spheres above,
Who cause the erring to repent
   Through the pleading voice of love.

Saved! when the steps shall be retraced
   With a purpose to do right;
Through sorrow alone is sin erased,
   Or the spirit robes made white.

Saved! for eternal justice grand,
   Rules all above, below;
Unchanged and true God's laws shall stand;
   "We'll reap just what we sow."

OVERCOMING.

"SELF is the lord of self" good Buddha taught,
    Who else could rule o'er all man's passions base,
  Subdue each foe, all wrong with good displace,
And find the joy of life through virtue wrought.
Devata just and true have many sought,
    Yet know not that within must dwell his grace,
    Supreme uplifting of our mortal race,
That breaks the prison bars of sinful thought,
    And gives the soul a God-like liberty.
Released from all inordinate desire
By passing through truth's crucible of fire,
    The spirit from all pain and sorrow free
    Finds rest, and peace and immortality,
The goal to which our trusting hearts aspire.

LIFE'S PROBLEMS.

WE stand within our life's bewildering thrall
    And musing, watch the gray tide rolling hither,
As swift the changing light and shadows fall
    We ask two questions, "Whence, O! whence and whither."
The snow hath melted which our dear ones trod,
    We saw it drip from lap of spring away,
There is no shade of them on flowery sod,
    The earth forgets her children in a day.
But soon we find on prehistoric rock
    The foot-prints of a race to Time unknown;
Where is the key this mystery to unlock,
    This guarded secret of the ages flown?
We know that orbs have burned from out the sky,
    That stars have come to shine in heaven's dome,

Yet our own destinies all hidden lie,
  If exiles or if pilgrims, where is home?
We ask the sea-shell if it knew our birth,
  Yet uninterpreted its words remain;
We ask the morn, was it of heaven or earth?
  She smiling answers, but alas! in vain.
We fall in tears beside the shrine of prayer
  Where soul-humility is altar-stone;
Life keeps her lamps of revelation there,
  And there to us her oracles makes known.
Our lips say, "Teach us," in that hour of trust
  When copious tears like showers of rain come down,
And lo! new hopes are blossoming from the dust,
  And reason hath the sunshine for a crown.
We question not, from whence, with anxious brow;
  We see the whither by the inner light;
This bridge of sighs, this throbbing, swaying Now
  Becomes a stepping-stone secure and bright.
Not where philosophy hath mountains piled,
  Not where research her daring car hath driven,
But where the lowly violets lure the child
  We find the pathway to the gate of heaven.
The brave simplicity that still must win
  Will seek the pure, the beautiful through prayer,
Perceive God's love and having entered in,
  Behold life's problems more than answered there.

THE HINDOO'S REQUEST.

In India it has been a custom, from time immemorial to burn the dead. The Ganges—the largest river in Hindostan—is the Hindoo's sacred stream in which they freely bathe, and before which, they perform their devotions. To die with one's face toward its waters is deemed by the trusting and reverential Hindoo a great blessing conferred on the soul. Their burial Ghauts are walled inclosures along the banks of the river, within which they rear their funeral piles; for the wealthy, sandal and spice wood are used. Friends bring rice and fruit which are placed in the coffin. Priests perform the last duties with a solemnity becoming the scene, first anointing the head and sprinkling the body; then, during the process of burning, they walk slowly around the pyre, "chanting prayers of consolations" and peace. Quite in contrast to Western custom, the mourners dress in pure white.

"FRIENDS and kindred, I am dying,
    Death's cold hand is on my brow,
And alone, my heart is sighing,
    That the change is coming now.

"But I ask you, yet to bear me
    To the Ganges sacred stream,
Where my fathers have before me,
    Dreamed earth's last and sweetest dream.

"I would gaze upon the bosom
    Of those waters clear and bright,
Cast upon the tide some blossom,
    Emblem of immortal light.

"While I view the sky above me,
    And the palms outspreading wide,
I will think of those who love me,
    And my time in patience bide.

"Take me at the day's first dawning,
    Place me on the verdant sod,
And without a thought of mourning,
    Leave me to commune with God.

"Where the winds and waves,—low moaning—
　　Death's soft requiem shall sing,
And the angel harps intoning,
　　Heavenly harmonies shall bring."

*　　*　　*　　*　　*　　*

Soon beside the flowing river,
　　On his humble mat he lay,
Where his soul went out forever
　　In the golden light of day.

And the last faint words were spoken
　　In a spirit true and calm;
"Hope and trust are still unbroken,
　　I shall yet be one with Brahm."

For the ancient faith had taught him
　　Reabsorption of the soul,
And a holy life had brought him
　　Perfect power of self-control.

Thus at rest, unto the mortal
　　Friendly offerings were brought,
As they bore him through the portal
　　Of the high-walled burial Ghaut.

Kindly hands in preparation
　　Reared the scented funeral pyre,
And the process of cremation
　　Soon was wrought by ruthless fire.

Priests with solemn rites, attending,
　　Slowly paced around the pile,
Incense sweet from censers sending,
　　Chanting dirges all the while.

And the white-robed mourners tarried
　　Till the last gleam died away;
Then in earth was ashes buried,
　　Dust to dust without decay.

PRAISE.

FOR the rich autumn days, the summer's rare treasures,
    That passed like a glad spirit's flight;
For the gift of our lives, their unfailing pleasures,
    We thank Thee, O Father of Light!

An unending chain of mercies eternal,
    From life's rosy dawn to its close,
Have filled all our days with blessings supernal,
    While joy like a fountain o'erflows.

We'll count the calm hours of sunlight and gladness,
    And walk where the hope-light appears;
We'll banish the clouds of sorrow and sadness,
    And praise Thee through smiles and through tears.

Then hear, Father, hear our songs of thanksgiving,
    Accept our sweet incense of praise;
Our voices shall tell in the courts of the living,
    The worth of our fullness of days.

NOT ALL A DREAM.

I DREAMED of a flowing river,
    That was fed from mountain and plain,
That came like a harvest giver,
    To gardens, and fields of grain.
Whatever it touched it brightened,
    For life was within its wave;
Whatever it washed it whitened,
    For in it was power to save;
But I dreamed that its waves, impeded,
    Shrank back to their little springs;
And the tide that the great world needed,
    Was circling in hand-breadth rings.

I dreamed that the angels planted
   A vineyard of God, below;
That unto the earth was granted
   The power to see it grow.
That up from her barren places,
   Her desert's extended scope,
Like music the echo chases,
   Came voices of joy and hope.
But I dreamed that the vineyard perished,
   That all but its roots were dead!
For strength, that its life had cherished,
   Like dew of the morning fled.

And I dreamed of a holy altar,
   Where Truth had kindled a fire;
A light for the feet that falter,
   A gleam for the eyes that tire.
Its radiance flamed with a glory,
   The dwellings around to fill;
And the earth was thrilled by the story,
   Of the city upon the hill.
But I dreamed that the altar tumbled;
   That its glow became a spark;
That its steps and its pillars crumbled,
   And its dwellings around were dark.

I dreamed a new song was started,
   That floated the wide world o'er;
That brought to the weary-hearted
   A courage unknown before.
'Twas the song of the Revelation,
   The song that the harpers sung;
Its theme was the *new salvation;*
   Its words were the *glad new tongue*.
But I dreamed that its numbers ended
   Ere their import half was told;
That the singers from heights descended,
   And covered their harps of gold.

Yea, I dreamed that the dual token
   Of Zion, was lost to sight;
And I wept, that a bond was broken,
   And quenched was a heavenly light.
Then I dreamed that our hearts, in union,
   Went out to the children of men—
That the swell of our love's communion,
   The river sent forth again.
By toil of our hands, united,
   The vineyard in beauty bloomed !
Devotion and truth relighted
   The city, our home illumed !
And the gift of deep inspiration,
   That flowed through Mount Zion's throng,
Was heard by each listening nation,
   And know as the *full new song*.

INSPIRATION.

MY soul was all aglow with holy thought,
   My heart aspired to reach life's vast ideal;
Night's curtain parted, shafts of light reveal
A hidden glory that the morn has brought,
So, inspiration chased the night and caught
   Infinities bright beams, my soul could feel
   Their glow; wearing hope's everlasting seal,
A clearer radiance from heaven I sought.
But hark ! faint voices from the ether space
   Break on the upper air, with glad surprise
I listen while they say, with chastened grace
   In daily ministries, O actualize
Thy burning thought ! then shalt thy being trace
   The hidden springs where God's deep fountains rise.

'TIS VICTORY.

THE power that yields to death and to defeat,
  Yields but the conquest to the nobler strife;
Forces repellent, mightier forces meet,
As fast recedes the ebbing tide of life.
But, vainly cowering 'neath the sway of doubt
We mark as death the power that sets us free,
'Tis but transition unto joys more real,
The triumph of immortal life to see.

O life! thou hero, haloed but with bliss,
And laureate with emblems of thy grace,
Thou'st smitten but the transient unto dust,
Entombed, the perishing receives its place.
While, 'mid the tranquil hush, the calm serene,
The spark that knoweth not decaying blight
Thy snow-plumed pinions bear from earth away,
To dwell amid unchanging scenes of light.

Why tread this vail as one of doubts and tears?
The mead is sure, the recompense is just.
O life! thy power calms turbulence and fear,
Divines the mission of exalted trust.
Thy thrilling touch the latent germs revived,
And hope's white blossoms swayed in balmy air;
Thy voice, a minstrel inspiration woke,
As floats its echoes down the aisles of prayer.

Clothed in the majesty of thine alone,
In dimless glory shines thy crown of light.
The chill damps of the misty tomb, O life,
Ne'er touched thy gleaming robes of spotless white.
No shadows linger e'er to veil or mar
Thy radiant form, in symmetry complete,
Love, from grief, tears the sable pall of fear,
And at thy bidding, casts it at her feet.

We view thee as an angel form of light,
Enrobed in vestments of immortal bliss,
And through the cloud-wreaths, view thee gleaming
    bright,
Transfigured in thy perfect loveliness.
Conferring but the boon, perpetual youth,
That knows no blight, no withering or decay;
As fresh, as bright, in emerald unfold
The buds of spring-tide to the west wind's play.

The conflict's o'er, the victory is won,
The struggling force with force is done,—'tis o'er.
The spirit greets the cheerful morning light,
And of earth's gloom and sorrow, knows no more.
For, mounting upward from earth's din and strife,
Disrobed but of its brief mortality,
Its gladsome song through arched dome portals rung,
'Tis spirit life and breath,—'tis victory!

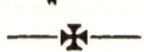

EXALTATION.

MY soul rejoices in the golden light,
    My thoughts are happy of the vaulted blue,
And O! my pleasure in the sparkling dew
That comes 'mid beauty of the starlit night
To earth and plant and flower a sweet delight.
    I feel transported with the sunset view
    For ages pictured, yet still grand and new.
O world of wonder to the mind and sight!
O God, Thou art our God, most high, most pure,
    Intelligent, beneficent, sublime.
Though graven heaps of stone Thy Name secure,
    Still Thou art He who ruleth every clime;
Who made the earth, whose fountains will endure,
    A monument to Thee till end of time.

THE ROSE AND GOLDEN-ROD.

AND is this our nation's chosen flower,
    The proud, proud rose with a velvet dress,
The perfumed queen of the regal bower
    That charms with an outward loveliness?

True sign of the royalty that rules
    With sovereign grace and gilded name,
Which springs from soil of the old world schools,
    From thrones where the lesser has no claim.

Shall we lean to aristocracy,
    And place on our hearts its emblem rare,
And plant in the new democracy
    Trees that its cherished blossoms bear?

Would we grasp the hidden thorn of power
    That lurks 'neath the beauty of the rose,
And pass unheeded the wayside flower
    That strength and safety alike disclose?

Through earnest struggle our fathers wrought,
    The seed of freedom was sown in pain,
Out of the battle by sword and thought
    A good was brought that should not prove vain.

The ground of this mighty continent
    Is pressed by liberty-loving feet,
A noble race that finds content
    In homes where honor and justice meet.

Over New England's mountain-towers,
    Over the Southland and fertile West,
They come in their march like the brave wild flowers
    That deck profusely our mother's breast.

From simple blossoms that beck and nod,
    O'er hills and vales of our country dear,
I would choose the stately golden-rod,
    A symbol to cherish and revere.

On the poorest spot of earth it lives,
  To sun and rain with bloom responds,
In thanks for the life that nature gives
  It lifts to the sky its shining fronds.

Fair type of the common people's aim,
  To mold their thought to a high ideal,
Through honest effort to rear to fame
  A temple whose base is true and real.

O, may the sun-crowned golden crest
  That waves on the homely earth-brown stem,
A signet be by the nations blest,
  Adorning our country's diadem.

TENDERNESS.

DOWN in the woodland's deep and solemn gloom,
    Where shadows quiver, green boughs interlace,
    And soft cool zephyrs tremble in each space,
The modest violets grow in purple bloom;
All wet with dews, exhaling rare perfume;
  We gaze into each bright uplifted face,
  They sweetly smile with soft and tender grace,
A glimpse of joy from worlds beyond the tomb.
They seem to wear an angel's aureole,
  Such as we see round pearly dew-drops shine,
  Their fragrance like an oracle divine
Breathes forth this word to every listening soul,
  "All life is rich that humbly seeks to bless,"
  O petaled message of Love's tenderness!

THE OLD APPLE TREE.

HOW memory's chain all golden-linked
   Girds well the cherished years,
Till pictured on their pillared walls
   Life's background reappears.
With many a vivid scene portrayed
   But none more bright to me
Than childhood's home and pleasant thoughts
   Of our old apple tree.

In walled enclosure safe it stood
   Where purpling grapes hung high,
Yet towered o'er all its leafy boughs
   Toward the kindly sky.
We shared the grapes but was there aught
   That grew so temptingly,
As wine-red fruit upon the boughs
   Of our old apple tree?

Scarce it is true, and rarely came
   The season that it bore,
We watched the blossoms of the spring
   And scanned our future store.
And disappointment filled our hearts,
   Instead of joyous glee,
When fair Pomona failed to bless
   Our dear old apple tree.

Its branching limbs o'ershadowed all
   The grassy lawn below,
Where we for play and romping sport
   Were oft forbade to go.
But no such stern restrictions given
   Curbed there our liberty,
We well enjoyed the pleasant swing
   In our old apple tree.

MOUNT LEBANON CEDAR BOUGHS.

We climbed the trunk, and quiet sat
    Within its chair-like arms,
Full many an hour to sew and read
    And share its quiet charms.
With nothing to disturb our peace
    And sweet tranquility,
While we were singing happy songs
    In our old apple tree.

Around the favored cottage porch
    The honey-suckle twined,
And flora's gems all beautiful
    Their redolence combined.
These met the city travelers' gaze,
    Bright gladsome sight to see,
But in a more secluded spot
    Grew our old apple tree.

An hundred years and more it stood
    This history to trace,
That once a rustic farmhouse stood
    Within that very place.
When city walls were closing round,
    'Twas very plain to see,
Not long would place be granted there
    For quaint old apple tree.

And lo! there came a time of doom,
    Its growth became less firm,
And in its grand old generous heart
    There burrowed ant and worm.
A nuisance to the housewife neat
    As all good folk agree,
And then that dread command was given
    To fell our apple tree.

To growing boys it seemed but fun,
    Their prowess to display,
As axe and hatchet did their work
    Upon that fatal day.

With tearful eyes one mourner viewed
    The scene regretfully,
For deep affection had enshrined
    That choice old apple tree.

With branches cleft, the trunk laid low,
    With wedges firmly driven,
And all its toughened fibers rent,
    By ruthless powder riven,
Consigned to flames its precious wood,
    Yet sweet the memory
That lives to bless fair childhood's dreams
    And our old apple tree.

HOME.

OUR Zion home is not adorned
    With pictured walls, or gold;
Nor in a glittering chain of pearls,
    Is all her glory told.
She bears the substance of sweet peace,
    The treasure of pure love;
Her power, truth and holiness
    That rule the heavens above.

Her walls are made of living stones,
    With brightness they're aglow;
They form the temple of the Lord,
    Where souls His truth may know.
And all who come beneath this dome
    May work for virtue's fame,
Gain the true riches through that life
    Which claims a blessed name.

O, happy home, what joys are thine!
    Who from thy courts would go
To be a slave to passions base,
    In wickedness to grow?

My heart will keep the sacred law
    That holds us in one band,
And feast upon the heavenly fruits,
    That grow in Canaan's land.

With dear companions I'll unite
    In consecrated toil,
And growing in the glorious light,
    Will till the gospel soil.
And when we leave this mortal shore,
    To dwell with saints above,
We'll breathe a prayer that holiness
    May bless the home we love.

LINCOLN AND STANTON.

STRANGE was their station, called to guide a strife
    That shook a continent from sea to sea;
To order death along the ranks of life,
    And wrap in flames the blessings yet to be.

'Twas theirs to speak the word of stern command
    That gave the inspiration to the hour,
As if they knew an earnest spirit band
    Sustained and aided every human power.

They struck with deadly shafts the monstrous crime
    That fiends had fortified with walls of lies;
They made it feel the weight of judgment-time,
    In crimson earth and more than crimson skies.

They made the wrath of man conduce
    To aid the plans of wisdom and of love,
To turn the raging passions into use,
    They sent the vulture to precede the dove.

'Twas theirs to make the red-mouthed cannon speak,
  And call the warrior to the gory field;
And it was theirs to screen the low and meek,
  And be for God, their guardian and their shield.

When storms of fury swept across the land,
  We sought protection only from on high;
They broke the cloud to show us mercy's hand,
  And bade us on the nation's heart rely.

In faith we prayed that duty might be done,
  That freedom might her heritage possess,
That peace and victory through terrors won,
  Should "come to stay," and banish all distress.

And is not prayer a focalizing power,
  To draw the fires of truth, to burn the dross?
Ah! well we proved it in that fearful hour
  When human vision saw but human loss.

'Twas not for party nor for section proud,
  That Zion's ardent supplications rose;
But that the land should be with right endowed,
  And God should His progressive laws disclose.

O day of grief! the Proclamation's page
  Shining with triumph that the world might feel,
Aroused the spirit of unconquered rage
  That stamped it fiercely with a sable seal.

Thus it became the *death decree* for him
  Who was an instrument of hosts unseen;
It was a passport through the valley dim,
  And through the gates that mighty forces screen.

We saw the tears that mingled near and far
  Wash from that seal the blackness of its face,
Until it beamed a brilliant rising star,
  A pledge of freedom to an injured race.

How thoughtfully our hearts recall that time;
  How place we Stanton close by Lincoln's side
Amid his toils, his sacrifice sublime,
  And 'neath the burdens of whose weight he died.

One balmful thought to which he oft referred,
  And drew its solace round his closing life,
Was that his heart compassionately heard
  The pleas of conscience to be free from strife.

They called him stern; no gentler soul drew near
  For tranquil respite from harsh hampering care;
No kindred heart e'er held our love more dear
  Nor felt the unction of affection's prayer.

Thus we remember him whose waving hand
  Had millions swayed as strong winds sway the sea;
Whose soul-integrity profound and grand
  Raised simple heart-life into majesty.

O, not with hero worshipers we bend,
  But honor those that met the nation's need,
That bore her through the struggle to the end,
  And made calamity to victory lead.

Stanton and Lincoln joined in Freedom's name,
  Alike intent to win her cause for earth;
But one had zeal that burned a solemn flame,
  And one had ardor flamed with solemn mirth.

IDEALIZE THE REAL.

'TIS earnest strife that wins the shining goal;
   'Tis glowing hope that lights the cloudy way,
  And life divine turns darkest night to day.
'Tis patience that brings comfort to the soul,
And holy thought holds passion in control.
   Sweet mercy cometh when we love and pray,
   And wisdom, when God's law our hearts obey,
By these is life made beautiful and whole.
E'en if thy duties lead in lowly lines
   These heavenly states thou mayest realize;
E'en if some obstacle thy power confines
   Within thy limits thou mayest upward rise;
But if thou canst not reach thy high *ideal*
With ceaseless love and care, *idealize* the *real*.

BEAUTIFUL RIVERS.

BEAUTIFUL rivers, like silvery threads
   Coursing their way over dark sandy beds,
Sweeping through valleys and circling the hills,
Gathering the ripples from thousands of rills,
Flowing from mountain, from rock and from dell
Ocean-bound waters with music to swell;
Brooklet and fountain and deep placid lake,
Greet the bright waves on your surface to break.

Beautiful rivers that gladden the earth,
Spirit of waters with joy gave you birth,
The smile of her face was impressed on your tide,
Beaming forever as onward you glide;
Joyously singing the song of the free,
Giving with pleasure your wealth to the sea:

Dancing, and glancing with sunbeams at play,
Never shall cloud on your sunny face stay.

Beautiful rivers, majestic and grand,
Blessing the desert of Egypt's fair land;
Waking the verdure 'neath tropical sun,
Flowering the sands where your golden streams run;
Filling the air with the moisture it needs,
Rising like incense of kind loving deeds,
Forming the clouds over mountain and plain,
Falling in copious showers of rain.

Beautiful rivers, that rolled on your way
Long before man saw the light of the day;
Long e'er the light gazelle sought you to drink,
Long e'er the wild races dwelt on your brink.
They who made hunting and fishing their aim
Came and passed on, yet *you* flowed the same.
Now, all along by your rocky bound course
Shrieks the shrill voice of the fleet iron horse;
Civilization, with quick pulse and heart,
Rears its bold front and its busiest mart.

Beautiful rivers, so calm in your flow,
Vessels of freight safely sail to and fro,
Gliding like nymphs o'er your broad open breast,
Ploughing the waves to a foam-beaten crest;
Thus through the means art and science can wield,
Men interchange the rich fruits of the field,
Commerce and trade, with their works of renown
Spread their white sails by the city and town.

Beautiful rivers, your murmurings sweet
Sing to my spirit of concord complete;
Ev'ry clear drop that may enter your tide,
Knows not the spirit that seeks to divide;
O, that life's current thus smoothly might roll
Free from the care that perplexes the soul,

Stirring its depths, till the whirlpool of strife
Sinks all the good that would gladden our life.

* * * * * *

'Tis by the side of some beautiful stream,
I would sleep my last sleep, and dream my last dream;
Waking to joy on the bright sunny shore,
To walk by the river of life evermore;
Leaving no trace of my pilgrimage here
Save in the hearts of the loving ones dear;
Ripples shall murmur a song soft and low,
As the tide of my life on forever shall flow.

---✠---

A DESERT SPRING.

A DESERT traveler, worn with dust and heat,
   O'er sandy stretches went his weary way;
  Dying with thirst he lowly knelt to pray,
That Allah kind would send the draught so sweet.
With eyes upturned, the smile of heaven to meet,
   He rose, when, sparkling in the noon-tide ray
   He saw a fountain rise to greet the day;
With gladdened heart, with faith and joy replete
He stooped to drink, and saw that waters gushed
   From out a rocky ledge where man ne'er trod;
And then his soul within grew still and and hushed,
   On arch above was carved the name of "God."
O, faith and trust such simple lessons teach,
God's blessings lie not far beyond our reach.

ZION'S SOUL COMMUNION.

IF I may kneel beside the waves of prayer,
    And kiss the shore;
In spirit kneel, for Mother's gift is there,
    I ask no more.
This gift hath all my life shall ever need,
    For Mother's love
Will downward to the Jordan waters lead
    Where broods the Dove.
What if the waves roll high, and I must swim,
    I will not quiver.
The land beyond, so bright, no storms can dim,
    I'll brave that River.
Prayer and repentance still are crested waves
    That hold the light;
Their union buoys the soul, inspires and saves;
    They know not night.
O kindred, blessed, yearning, toiling souls,
    My heart bows low;
I feel the mighty river as it rolls
    In holy flow.
Here on its banks the "tree of life" is found,
    Its fruits we share;
Across its depths, transparent and profound,
    'Tis yet more fair.
The call to waverers is, "Be not sad,
    Nor pause to doubt;
But seek the stream that makes the city glad;
    Woe is without."
Is there one child that Mother's love would win,
    That will not hear?
Is there one heart that would decide to sin
    Through lust or fear?
The voice of many waters answers, "Nay!"
    Each guileless one,

Turning in simple grace to learn to pray,
    "Thy will be done,"
Shall through the crystal current, see the world—
    Its awful state,
Where Eden's enemy in roses curled,
    For prey doth wait.
Then shall sweet lessons on the spirit crowd,
    By faith illumed;
Then it shall cry, "If I am longer proud,
    Oh! I am doomed!
Dear gospel kindred, now I know your worth,
    Help me to win
The life transcendent, far away from earth—
    I hate all sin."
So ran the meditation of the hour,
    When saints unite
To seek the increase of the spirit power,
    And error's flight.
To pray for every heart, in every need,
    From age to youth.
And that the earth make ready for the seed
    Of virgin truth.
O when I felt the perfume rising up
    From each pure shrine,
There was a joy within my spirit's cup
    Which seemed like wine.
That I might bring frankincense and sweet myrrh
    With Mother's few,
And make the sacrifice sought out by her,
    Was blessing true.
To have with them a humble place and name
    From sin removed,
Was more than gorgeous gifts of wealth and fame.
    Such gladness proved.
Dear ancients of the city, lingering pray
    Through twilight time,
Help Zion to accept the seven-fold day
    Of light sublime.

To be established in the truth revealed
    That strikes earth dumb.
God's missionary mountain unconcealed
    Whose word is "Come."

MEMENTO MORI.

EARTH-LIFE is brief, the whole but as one day;
    'Tis like the dawning of the golden sun
  Which, at its height, full half its course is run,
Anon how shortened grows meridian ray.
O happy youth, so blithesome, free and gay,
    Remember in thy morn, life just begun,
    The eve, when ill or well, thy deeds are done,
And fair or graceless thou shalt pass away.
The face, may sometimes inner life reveal,
    And deeds in part, the silent thought make known.
But in the world to come, no forms conceal,
    All undisguised, the soul is clearly shown.
Then live thy best, the change of death to feel
With consciousness that God thy life doth own.

THE POET WHITTIER.

AS desert travelers watch a star,
    Dear friends had watched his rolling years,
Deeming his inner life afar
    While he but held them as his peers.
They on the dusty, heated plain,
    Or 'neath the palm-trees cooling shade
Spoke of his heart's ennobling strain,
    His words of light that could not fade;

And marveled that when war was red,
   His pen undaunted by its breath
Crept through the lines, till slavery dread
   Was reached, unveiled and pierced to death.
They knew he had a poet's eyes
   To penetrate each opaque cloud,
And see the hidden prospects rise
   That mists of coming day enshroud.
A royal gift, a sage's mind,
   Whose realms of thought, O! who could trace;
It held the truths that angels find,
   He set them forth with hallowed grace.
A poet's spirit more than these
   They recognized with joy and pride,
And felt that nature's sacred keys
   In love to him she did confide.
And yet they said "his austere school"
   Had wrought for him its meed of harm,
Nor deemed that gentle Quaker rule
   Gave to his life its nameless charm.
They had the world's unbounded scope,
   Its heights, its depths, its utmost rim;
Unhampered fancy, flashing hope,
   But not the *substance* found by him.
The fear which is the love of God,
   The bond which is the Golden Rule,
The Holy Spirit deep and broad,
   Form not for souls an austere school.
Religion never was a creed,
   It is from heaven, a deathless flame,
A quickening pulse, a living seed,
   In every age and clime the same.
We, sheltered in our Zion home,
   Guess dimly at the bitter strife,
Where raging billows lashed to foam
   Mark progress to a better life.
We bless the workers of the world
   Who toil amid the breakers' roar,

With bright "Excelsior" unfurled
 And compass pointing to the shore.
To him who in the darkened hour
 Still raised the lily as a sign,
That right and purity had power
 Which must be pledged in heavenly wine.
Our Whittier, may we make the claim,
 When he his world-wide feelings gave
To hold man's brotherhood the same
 From reigning potentate to slave.
Unselfish, universal good
 From us, from him, uncramped must flow,
Till nations in one sisterhood
 Shall kinship and its blessing know.
Oft when the beacon fires we feed,
 Or lamps of faith revive and fill,
We feel the earth's great pressing need
 And God's great loving, saving will.
Above is Revelation's star,
 That heralds the advancing sun,
Beneath whose glory near and far
 That saving will shall yet be done.
And as we climb the path of light
 Our spirit's journey not alone,
Nor doubt we that the mountain's height
 Is God's Eternal Throne.

THE FUTURE IS OURS.

I STAND entranced upon the Mount of Vision,
 And watch the shadows slowly disappear;
I catch bright glimpses of that land Elysian,
 Where truth hath triumphed in its grand career.
The mists of time like darkening clouds impending,
 Are vanishing before the morning light;
I feel that God His heralders is sending
 To usher in the glorious dawn of right.

There have been those upon this earth of ours,
    Who tarry here, though numbered with the dead,
Their memories rise like incense breathing flowers,
    Whose fragrance last e'en when their life has fled.
From sordid gain and honor backward turning,
    They sought on earth a higher joy to find,
They nobly toiled, all selfish impulse spurning,
    They lived to God, to truth, and all mankind.

And now we see 'twas no Utopian dreaming,
    That fired their souls into a holy flame,
They saw the twilight through the midnight gleaming,
    We see the sunrise, and the darkness wane.
'Tis now for those who feel earth's needs and losses,
    Unflinchingly to keep God's laws divine;
To raise truth's standard 'gainst opposing forces,
    And speak the true word in the storm and shine.

The sins of earth, of ignorance and error,
    That long have chained the soul in thralldom's might,
Shall quail beneath truth's mighty power with terror,
    And vanish in the coming golden light.
O, bright the future as it flows toward us!
    Diffusing glory, sweeping sin away;
With radiant hope the heavens are beaming o'er us,
    Now is the dawning of the perfect day.

HEART LESSONS.

A LITTLE spark, the sky is full of stars;
    O mighty midnight! how can I be thine?
For e'en the mists send up their hiding bars,
    Lo! all the heavens flashed the answer—"Shine."

A hidden stream, in fissure dark I weep,
    Through rocky cavern, lost my feet must go ;
One chamber echoes, o'er its jags I leap
    And ocean bids me "Welcome" to its flow.

A fragile blossom on a giant tree
    Watches the shadows swaying on the ground ;
While sundrawn sap, while wind in every key
    Encircling press, its inner life to round.

A speckled lark upon a daisied sod
    With listening ear and russet, untried wing,
Stood mute amid the music poured to God
    Till sweet Aurora bade her rise and sing.

A pale rose murmured on a lonely stem,
    "How can I bless when thorns around me wreathe ;
The lilies give the lake its diadem ;"
    June climbed the thorns and softly wispered,
        "Breathe."

If star and stream, if blossom, bird and rose
    Can feel their destiny, and keep their sphere,
Does not faith's intuition still disclose
    The growth and action that we must not fear ?

A common round within a common space ;
    Can aught be common where God's glory falls,
With love that gives the burnished sheen of grace
    To hold the heart within the jasper walls ?

No life but hath its gleam to light the page,
    Its tides to freshen, and its fragrant flowers,
Its golden fruit, its cheering song to raise—
    O heart awake ! expand, diffuse thy powers.

TWO WHEELS.

TWO wheels there are, the ruts of one we trace,
    The other never leaves its wonted place,
One rolls amid the spoils of conquest won,
The other silent is when duty's done.
One meets the bloom in morning's early gray,
Returning, withered rose leaves strew its way;
One breaks the waters flow, then takes its curls,
And makes its silver tresses into pearls.
Which serves the most with use the world to grace,
The wheel that turns the mill, or runs the race?
God governs all, if in his love we rest,
Where wisdom rules in duty we are blest.

THE BIRD CRAZE.

A WOMAN whom fashion long held in her sway,
    Whose vanity naught could embarrass,
Was decked in rich silks and velvets all gay,
    And a beautiful bonnet from Paris.
A head-dress, you know to the feminine mind
    Is the principal point of attraction,
A part of adornment we frequently find
    That causes a mental distraction.
And here was the thought that filled her whole heart,
    The style was so sweet and becoming,
She knew that her friends would admiringly start,
    For the birds, you could almost hear humming.
Two dear little mates decked the front of the crest,
    With plumage the brightest and fairest,
And over the crown—like an inverted nest—
    Spread wings of a songster the rarest.

The ribbons that folded the coronet round
    Gave a touch and a grace most exquisite,
A bonnet more charming could never be found
    Though all the *beau monde* she should visit.

A change wrought by magic, comes over our theme,
    Which causes a simple digression,
This creature of taste had a wonderful dream
    Which made on her mind an impression.
She seemed to be dressed *a la mode*—cap-a-pie,
    For Sol's blessed southland preparing,
A journey most pleasant new beauties to see,
    Where nature a glad smile is wearing;
She was *there*, transported, delighted and thrilled
    For forests and groves were most charming,
Where sunny-hued songsters their blithe music trilled,
    No terror their wild haunts alarming.

But lo! fatal day, a behest to fulfill,
    The huntsmen, with powder and ration
Came fully prepared the dear minstrels to kill,
    To meet the demands of Dame Fashion.
Quick came the reports, and they fell to the ground
    Like innocent victims in battle,
In the midst of the slaying our dreamer was found
    Transfixed with the din and the rattle.
The birds flew around her and screamed in their fright
    Till their cries pierced her heart with a meaning
And turned into sorrow her days of delight
    The truth of the vision unscreening.

They spoke to her soul with a plaintive appeal
    "O indolent daughter of pleasure!
The pain that we suffer you surely must feel,
    For justice will mete her full measure."
All over the tropics, from sun unto sun
    The vandals are scouting and raiding,
And thousands of birdlings are slain one by one,
    Such cruelty God is upbraiding.

This work of destruction by unhallowed hands,
    Shall meet with a full compensation,
For blight and destruction shall rest on the land,
    And insects make great devastation.

She nodded her head: from dreamland awoke,
    But the vision she knew must be real,
A *horror* her head-dress now seemed to invoke
    In the light of a humane ideal.
She said, " I have learned a deep lesson from this,
    A vow I will make as a token,
The forfeit of life shall ne'er yield me bliss,
    May it never, O, never be broken!
My sisters, who thoughtlessly yield to caprice,
    Let us live for some nobler endeavor,
And weave for our brows the fair laurels of peace,
    And banish the bird-craze forever."

A PLEA FOR THE TURKEYS.

I SAW them first when with their mother, they
    Took scratching lessons, peeped a turkey song,
And wandered in the grass that turned to hay
    When summer sun grew hot and days were long.

Again I saw them in their youthful prime
    After the moulting days had swiftly passed,
And thought how dextrously old Father Time
    Had worked, to make their feathers grow so fast.

But months passed on, the festal time drew near,
    The turkeys grew in strength and size and weight;
But, oh, alas! I felt a sudden fear,
    And pity smote me as I mourned their fate.

I saw the gory execution block,
    And sharpened ax that told of days gone by
When man against his kind with cruel shock
    Condemned them by the guillotine to die.

But justice seemed to call for deeds of shame
    In those fell days when anarchy ran wild,
And truth and liberty bore all the blame,
    When slaughter bade worst foes be reconciled.

But in the death of these poor innocents
    Not even justice could approve the waste,
And mercy shocked, forsook the murderous tents
    Where men raised blood-stained hands and killed
        for taste.

And when I saw the dread dissecting knife
    Wielded by hands that nurse the infant race,
And not content with simply taking life,
    They mutilate the corpse,—oh, foul disgrace!

And then before the market-place in rows
    I saw the naked victims cold and pale,
And seemed to hear them say in dying throes,
    "Come cannibals, our bodies are for sale."

My heart sank in me, for in dream I saw
    Children and lords and ladies (?) sit and jest,
Yea, even judges of the moral law,
    And sport about the part they fancied best.

Oh pitiless! we send the Holy Book
    And missionaries where the heathen roam,
But in our folly blindly overlook
    The unconverted heathen here at home.

THE JEWS GATHERING MANNA.

'TWAS never painted, artists' brush would fail
    To reproduce a scene so vast and grand,
And brightest colors only blur and pale
    Before the light that fell upon that land.

The sunlight lying like a warp of gold
   Beneath a woof of diamond-glittering dew;
The rainbow pearly mist that upward rolled
   To form the clouds beneath the arch of blue.
And then a million of the crushed and poor
   O'er whom progressive angels anxious brood,
Bending to this first lesson to secure
   By equal labor, pure and simple food.
'Twas never pictured; pencil, voice nor pen
   Could ne'er portray it, for the world ne'er saw
In all the mighty host of gathered men
   So many governed by so grand a law.

NO TIME TO LOSE.

FOR THE CHILDREN.

"No time to lose," say the tiny buds
   As they catch the spring-tide's beam;
"We must open our calyxes green and gold,
   E'er our wonderful bloom is seen."

"No time to lose," say the blithesome birds,
   As they fly with straw and hay,
"Not even time for our sweetest song,
   Till the daylight turns to gray."

"No time to lose," say the busy bees,
   "In these golden sunny hours
We must sip the dew so pure and sweet
   From the cups of a thousand flowers."

"No time to lose," say the working ants,
   "We're always busy, you know,
We gather our store in the summer days
   Ere the winter brings the snow."

"No time to lose," say studious girls,
  "While our school-days glide away
We'll fill our minds with every good,
  Nor our moments waste in play."

Then we will learn from the buds and flowers,
  From insects,—the ants and bees;
Lessons of industry, patience, trust,
  Nature is teaching us these.

———✠———

"GIVE US THIS DAY OUR DAILY BREAD."

O TRUSTFUL prayer! by earnest heart expressed,
  The simple utterance of a common need;
A want, awakened in each human breast,
  That seeks for some sustaining power to feed.
Christ taught his true disciples thus to pray—
  While by his gentle hand their souls were led
To trace the shining paths of wisdom's way—
  "Lord, give to us this day our daily bread."

Along the centuries' broadening aisles,
  Whence come the precious truths of long ago,
We see the sunbeams of those golden smiles,
  That flood the earth with an eternal glow.
The bud and blossom of the passing years,
  Their harvest fruitage in our pathway spread,
To this blest prayer the answer now appears.
  "Lord, give to us this day our daily bread."

While millions in the fated Orient
Have yielded to starvation stern and gaunt;
While plague and scourge, on direful mission bent,
Have filled the sunny South with woe and want,
Our home—among the hills that God hath reared,
Where timely showers and gentle dews are shed—
Has not by scorching heat and drought been seared,
For we have shared each day our daily bread.

Thus while we ask, O ! let us not forget
That constant blessing, like a silvery stream
In peaceful flow, our hearts' desires have met,
Till all life's toil and duties pleasant seem.
Ah ! in the consciousness of doing right,
The crystal sea of perfect truth we tread,
And, dwelling in the glory of its light,
Receive from angel hands our daily bread.

And now within this sacred, calm retreat,
Once more our gifts on Nature's shrine we lay ;
O ! may their perfume rise like incense sweet,
And mingle with our orisons to-day.
While we commune from all the world apart
As did that Judean band, with Christ their head,
Likewise we pray with fervency of heart,
"Lord, give to us this day our daily bread."

The fruits of union and the sweets of love,
The harvest-yield of friendship's precious seed,
The ripened sheaves that peace hath stored above,
These shall supply our spiritual need.
And for the mortal we would seek for wealth
That springeth from earth's rich and fruithful bed,
The food that giveth lengthened life and health,
Give us this day, O, Lord ! for daily bread.

FAITH.

WHILE on the sea of life, what faith is mine,
    I walk upon the wave, nor fear the tide ;
  When earth-born ebon clouds arise and hide
The azure sky, like Bethlehem's star 'twill shine
And lead the way to perfect light divine.
    'Tis like the form of Christ when storms betide,
    It whispers to the soul, "O e'er abide
In God, and kneel at Truth's pure, sacred shrine."

The voice of doubt speaks not of holy peace,
   Nor of the gifts we covet as the best.
  Thus while I hold this light within my breast
My soul shall know no failing, but increase
In that pure way whose blessings ne'er will cease,
   Not e'en when passing life's severest test.

HOPE.

BEYOND the mists are verdant sunlit ways,
   Beyond the clouds are sun-kissed mountain heights,
  Beyond the night, the morning's cloudless lights,
Beyond the winter's storm the song-bird's lays,
The spring-tide fragrance and the perfect days.
   O list, creation's chorus of delight,
    For life is born of death, as day of night,
It hath its harvest too, its meed of praise.
Then come, bright hope, with rainbow tinted wings,
   Sing like a bird of promise glad and sweet,
Sing to our hearts of pure and holy things;
   For grief, joy, loss and gain, each heart must meet,
The honey and the gall, yea all time brings,
   Our lips must taste to find life most complete.

LOVE.

LOVE born of God! what power is more divine?
   Transcendent excellence! O what compares
  With this great sovereign good? What soul declares
A holier power? it will all hearts refine;
Unlimited, no boundaries confine.
   Possessing all, the light of truth it wears,
   Unceasingly, surpassing gifts it bears,
In it all true and sacred things combine.

Pure love is watchful, tho' it slumbers, does not sleep,
   Fatigued, but not exhausted, long endures.
Who sows to love, the fruit of love will reap,
   And treasures which its blessedness insures.
Expand O heart, its power transforming feel,
God's love in thee will God alone reveal.

SYMPATHY WITH FRIENDS IN THE WEST.

WRITTEN FOR BRETHREN AND SISTERS OF SOUTH UNION, KY.

WHEN traitors to their country's cause
   In fraud and treachery grew bold;
When sacred bonds were snapp'd like straws,
   And Judas bargained as of old;
We pray'd your little stricken band
Might firmly for the Gospel stand.

And in the hour when war's dread storm
   Built round your home a wall of fire;
When wild reports of ev'ry form
   Rush'd forth like phantoms filled with fire,
We turn'd our hearts to God in prayer,
   That He would keep you in His care.

We watch'd the showers of shot and shell,
   'Mid lightning's flash and cannon's roar,
And thought there must be *peace in hell*,
   For earth her own confusion bore;
And humbly bent our hearts to pray
That God the fearful scourge would stay.

When neither friendly man nor law
   Could yield protection or relief,
The Lord, who all your peril saw,
   Raised up the fierce guerrilla chief.*

---

* Morgan.

Thus human wrath in our own days,
Was turned by miracle to praise.

When clouds and sorrows deepened fast,
   Doubt spread a curtain o'er the land,
As fold on fold was thickly cast,
   We saw through it the Lord's own hand,
And prayed that in that hour of night,
Your dwellings might be filled with light.

And when the bondmen's smother'd cries
   Came like the voice of moaning waves;
When earth's red bosom burst with sighs
   And gave her bleeding children graves,
We pray'd that, in that matchless woe
The Lord would ev'ry wrong o'erthrow.

And ever and anon there came
   From you, brave words of faith unmoved;
We knew the Lord the hearts would claim
   Whose true dependence he had proved;
With tears we bow'd to God in prayer
To give you strength to do and bear.

Though still the hour is wild and dark,*
   And persecutions lash your home,
The guarding hosts your sorrows mark,
   And they will turn the waves to foam;
While earnestly our spirits pray
That God may speed the better day.

---

*The South Union Society is now threatened by the *Ku Klux Klan* for employing freedom.

During the progress of the war the Shaker societies passed through a peculiar experience. Those of them located in the State of Kentucky (Pleasant Hill and South Union) were for years in the power of the Union and Rebel armies alternately. And, although they fed the hungry, and clothed the naked, and nursed the sick of both the contending forces, thus "giving aid and comfort to enemies," yet the officers of either army restrained, as far as possible, the depredations of the rank and file.

They suffered and lost immensely in person and property, but not

As from the fount unceasing streams
　　Flow to the valleys far away,
As through the gloom the morning's beams
　　Tunnel and gild the path of day,
Our anxious hearts o'erflow to bless
Our gospel kindred in distress.

Thus, thus is Christ united found,
　　His life-blood all true members feel;
In joy or sorrow they are bound,
　　And stamp'd with *love*—the heavenly seal.
So, join'd, we ever will move on,
And watch and pray to still be one.

TRUTH.

CURBED be the spirit that would dauntless be
　　In the fierce strife of crushing out the truth,
The light of age, the guiding star of youth,
The priceless pearl of life and liberty.

Dark would be earth had Truth no victory won,
　　Still, dull monotony would beat her round,
　　While spirits wrapped in stoic sense profound,
Would, like the glacier, coldly spurn the sun.

　　　　*　　*　　*　　*　　*　　*

unto death, or entire destruction of the temporal or community organization.

　The frequent communications to the more favorably situated societies of the East, graphically detailing the scenes through which they were constantly passing, excited one continued state of fear and alarm among the brethren and sisters, leading to the most fervent prayers to the *God of Christians* for their protection and safety. The following lines, just written to those long-tried Western Shakers, will be understood when it is stated that Morgan, the guerrilla chief, was especially friendly and protective to them.

Shine on, O glorious Truth! forever bright;
  Pursue thy course e'en to the nether sphere,
  Till superstition's altars disappear,
And error quails, and cowers in trembling fear.

Till crumbling thrones their tyrant-sceptres yield,
  And bear instead the trident of the right,
  Love, Justice, Mercy, triple power of might,
These conquest gain, upon thy battlefield.

THE CRY OF THE SUFFERING.

THE earth hath need of prophets in this day,
  Who will not down, and will not quiet be,
Who fear not creeds, nor danger, nor delay,
  But speak the truth for God's humanity.

"New times demand new systems and new men,"
  Then why embalm the old ones long since dead?
Why set the boundary to a law, and then
  Condemn the hungry when they fight for bread?

Earth's cry of suffering rises like the cloud
  That hung so darkly over Sinai,
While Israel stood below, a faithless crowd,
  And Moses caught the tablets from the sky.

Borne on the lightning and the thunder peals
  We hear the echo of man's strife with man,
While patient Justice to our souls reveals
  The curse that lingers in oppression's plan.

Strong manhood languishes in fetters, cast
  At the fierce forge of its necessity
And then is branded, and condemned at last
  To prison cells. Who says that man is free?

Who talks of virtue? When the man is starved
   Can conscience hesitate and question law?
Nay, it must sin and see its tombstone carved,
   Nor raise a voice to justify its cause.

Ah! where is virtue, when our womanhood
   Must sell its birthright for a crust of bread?
Must tread its feet upon the soul of good
   And heap the coals of shame upon its head?

And where is virtue when the children dear
   Must learn with care the youthful ruffian's art?
And with the strife for money boldly sear
   The early promptings of an honest heart?

The haughty may condemn with words of pride
   The humble victims of their craft and hate,
But though delayed, 'twill never be denied
   The justice that must come though ne'er so late.

And it will come, the promises are sure,
   God's voice we hear above the strife and din,
The triumph comes to spirits who endure;
   And goodness will erase the blight of sin.

THE MILLIONAIRE'S DAUGHTER.

A PROPHECY.

SHE came before him in the simple guise
   That decks the floret of the field and wood,
But never fairer to his world-worn eyes
   Had seemed the beauty of her maidenhood.
Yet missed he not sheen pearls nor vesture rare,
   Till heavy tears with sudden rush came down,
As summer cloud-gems start the dreamy air
   When darting lightnings pierce the noonday's crown.

Awaked he then to note the boding change,
  The utter absence of the girlish pride,
The earnest manner, the emotion strange,
  E'en folly's ostentation cast aside.
"Why greet with tears," he said, "and why this dress;
  In my long absence Fortune's wheel went round,
And only stopped at mountains of success,
  It was enough, my hopes were more than crowned.

"I may not guess my wealth, 'tis deep and high,
  Its girt is in the years I shall not see,
Its gold horizons toward thy sunset lie,
  For all my plans, my aims are but for thee."
"Alas!" she cried, "appalling is success
  That takes calamity to any heart,
That from the wheel, the rack-wheel of distress
  Flings dismal ruin as its counterpart.

"You question, whence this knowledge of the moil,
  Your daughter's mind should never touch its rim;
You kept her far from groveling hords of toil,
  Whose hands are smirched, whose savage souls are grim.
Finding by chance a truth-illumined page
  I soon disguised, stood smitten mid a throng
Where want and slavery in every stage
  Had crushed the weak and galled the brave and strong.

"Yet they portrayed less sharply than I felt,
  Their souls had *lamps*, my soul had *sheets of flame;*
I could have there to any beggar knelt,
  And asked forgiveness for my sin and shame.
O, father! they impeached such men as you
  Whose force united might reclaim the world;
On friends I deem most noble, wise and true,
  The plundering, murderous brigand's name was hurled.

"And I your idol, selfish, useless, blind,
  Whose casket symbolizes woe of heart;
Whose wasteful wealth that keeps one life enshrined
  Leaves shrinking pale one's passion's reeking mart,
Leaves famine to the mother and her brood,
  And to half-famished manhood, bitter thought
Of death's deep bed beneath the icy flood,
  Or wild revenge by torch or dagger wrought.

"Through tear-lens of keen sympathy I trace
  The matted wrongs that God with pity views;
The wrested heritage, the exiled race,
  The reckless havoc speculation strews.
But mortgage rests on each in human claim,
  No scheming magnates can remove its weight,
And swift foreclosure must result the same
  As in the *hosts'* and *chariot riders'* fate."

She paused, transfigured with o'erwhelming prayer,
  That swelled for wretchedness throughout the earth,
Her soul-throbs knocking on the door of care
  That shuts from mortals all that life is worth.
To him, as in the twinkling of an eye,
  Stern truth confronted ancient codes of fraud,
Of sanctioned wrongs, of crimes that underlie
  Man's dire transactions—blasphemies of God.

Then memory turns the "volume of the Book"
  That brands oppressors and defends the weak,
Whose *holy* inspirations never brook
  The base achievements wily graspers seek.
Greed's condemnation stamped on every verse,
  In vain the rich man scans the Sacred Word;
The plea, the mandate, prophecy and curse
  Once scarcely noticed, now like thunder heard.

Can *he* exclaim, "Who thwarts the Father's plan
  Defeats the answer to the Savior's prayer?"
The soul's Accuser cries, "Thou art the man,
  Though of thy sin uncounted thousands share."

It is for him to take with spirit bold,
　With patriotic fire, and potent zeal,
Christ's golden rule for Mammon's rule of gold,
　That henceforth he may work for human weal.

It is for her like Miriam by the sea
　To lift her voice not with triumphal strain,
But with a Marseillaise the land to free
　From hard Monopoly's imperial reign.

SYMPATHY.

NOT like the glaciers of the sea,
　　Cold and repellent stand,
But let the tide of sympathy,
　　Flow out from heart to hand.

Stern and forbidding natures start
　　By love's electric thrill,
The icy crags of thought depart
　　Where sunny beams distil.

One word hath power the heart to move,
　　If *love* its motive be,
And we by our experience prove,
　　The worth of sympathy.

Too many hearts are crushed by woe,
　　Too many minds despair,
Tho' dark may seem the earth below,
　　All heaven is bright and fair.

Then let not gloom nor sorrow chill
　　The rising pulse of life,
Let light and joy our spirits fill,
　　Whate'er may be our strife.

TRUE GOODNESS.

WHERE shall we find that wealth of soul,
   True goodness pure and deep,
That worketh by the golden rule
   Its recompense to reap?
Not in the soul whose lips would speak
   In loud and lengthy prayer,
Yet feeleth not for others' needs
   Their sorrow and their care.

It glows in smiles of tenderness,
   In every loving deed,
In thrilling tones of sympathy
   They prove a friend in need;
And in the heart, deep rooted there
   Is its true glory seen,
Shedding a Christ like radiance,
   As did the Nazarene.

O ever blessed power of good,
   Within my being shine!
And may thy graces lovingly
   Around my spirit twine;
For I would crave the pearls of truth,
   And purity of heart,
To deck my spirit now in youth,
   And joy to me impart.

That mine may be a life made blest
   By goodness e'er untold;
Thus weaving for my spirit form
   A robe more bright than gold,
That is not dimmed by length of years,
   Nor worn by moth nor rust,
But brighter grows by deeds well done
   While in this form, of dust.

"HOW SWIFT THE SHUTTLE FLIES THAT WEAVES THY SHROUD."—Young.

TIME with a swift momentum plies,
  As through life's web his shuttle flies,
Twining the fibres that fate has spun
All through the years since life begun;
Threading the woof of hours and days
Drawn through our devious winding ways;
Loosing the tangled ends of time,
Weaving them all in rythmic chime;
Binding the broken threads of thought
Each by his skillful fingers caught.

* * * * *

Soon shall the garment woven be,
Ere thou shalt enter eternity,
But, O thou mortal! be not proud,
Time with his shuttle weaves thy shroud.

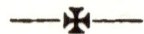

FORGIVENESS.

LET us forgive; we all sometime have erred,
  Have sometime brought the tears to smiling eyes,
Have sometime Mercy's gentle call deferred,
  Have failed to help the soul that strove to rise.

Not all through malice have these deeds been done,
  Not always have the blows been aimed by hate,
Nay, love hath often crushed a smitten one,
  Or waked to pity when it proved too late.

It is not new this little tale I tell,
  'Tis past invention of small art like mine,
But, if it cheer some struggling one, ah well,
  It proves that ancient jewels still may shine.

'Twas at the day's first dawning, gleaming rays
  Fell soft on lofty minaret and spire,
When Islam's prophet, filled with reverent praise
  Went to the mosque, as holy rites require.

The ashes on his forehead were of death,
  And accents trembled where they once were strong,
As there he taught with failing, feeble breath
  The greatest lesson of his life grown long.

"If there be one (so spoke the dusky saint)
  To whom I owe a debt, if there be one
Who honestly can offer a complaint,
  Speak now, and let great Allah's will be done.

"If I have wrongly judged a fellow man,
  Who have borne rule in Allah's wondrous name,
I pray you tell me now, the telling can
  Bring not a touch of censure or of blame."

No sound was made, save but a sob of woe,
  Till one—a woodman spoke in solemn way,
"My Prophet, one small sum to me you owe
  For needed fuel brought to you one day."

"Allah be praised!" Mahomet kindly said,
  "'Tis well with those who reckon ere too late;
Take home thy dues and be thou comforted,
  We will not fear to meet at Heaven's gate."

And so, his face serene with tranquil smile,
  And heart from toil and earthly burdens free,
He passed the gate of death, praying the while,
  "Allah forgive my sins, I come to Thee."

SILENCE.

BE quiet, soul, still as the distant stars
    That tread all noiselessly their way along,
  In circling orbits moving ever on
In perfect harmony; no earthly jars,
No warring tones their solemn grandeur mars;
    Then gaze into the silent depths where throng
    The starry multitudes; list the heavenly song,
The music of the spheres, beyond earth's bars.
Thus in thy depths, O thou unfathomed soul
    A power invisible holds sway supreme,
Awake to consciousness, own its control
    And keep thy inner life calm and serene.
Hark the voices, "deep calling unto deep,"
In soulful silence heaven's best gifts we keep.

RENEWAL.

WE seek communion blest through silent breathing
    prayer,
  With ministers of light who oft drew nigh,
And, as we turn from scenes of outward sense and
    care,
  We feel their inspiration from on high.

They quicken unto zeal, they come with conquering
    might,
  From thrall of error's chains to bring release;
Through strife of elements betwixt the wrong and
    right,
  They bear the prophecy of rich increase.

They bring a chastening power, repentance deep and
    true,
  A gift for Zion's children far and near,

To cleanse her courts from sin, and covenants renew,
  Her sacred laws and statues to revere.

They will revive the flames of holy altar fires,
  Where souls sincere to God their offerings bring,
And find the blessed power that wakens new desires
  To live for truth, and to its precepts cling.

Then Zion's broken walls rebuilt shall firmly be
  By those who willingly her principles maintain,
"One faith" and "one baptism," "one Lord" they all shall see,
  And heart to heart be linked in union's golden chain.

To Faith's clairvoyant eye the future seemeth bright,
  Though shadows now may Israel's glory dim;
More radiantly will glow true revelation's light,
  Than did Shekinah over Cherubim.

And all those sacred gifts will more than be restored,
  That once have rested on the Lord's household,
When over multitudes His spirit shall be poured,
  As prophecy declared in days of old.

Then old philosophies, and husks of earthly lore,
  No more the hungry mind will seek as food,
For "hid with Christ in God" is wisdom's boundless store,
  And those who there abide find every good.

Ideals grand in truth as pictures will adorn
  The chambers of the soul from sin made free,
No glittering dust of earth with raiment shall be worn,
  But gems whose light can never tarnished be.

God's temple then will stand restored and purified,
  And 'neath her threshold roll a living stream,

Whose currents deep and clear with broad outflowing
    tide
  Life's desert wastes to fruitage will redeem.

Pure inspiration's gift will light her glorious dome,
  Its oracles of truth spread far and wide,
That many souls may find in Christ a lasting home
  And know of holy joys that e'er abide.

PRESS ON!

PRESS on, true soul, with patient firm endeavor,
  Tho' life's to thee a heavy load of care;
Keeping thy heart in trust and hope forever,
  God helpeth those who bravely do and bear.
What tho' there dawns for thee no glad to-morrow,
  And life's made cold by harsh, embittering scorns;
What tho' thou wear'st the robe of grief and sorrow,
  And on thy brow a crown of many thorns.

Press on, true soul! e'en tho' the seed thou'st scattered
  On barren and unwatered ground was sown;
Think not in vain was all thy toil expended,
  Because no blessedness of fruit is shown.
There is no deed nor aspiration holy,
  But meets its recompense in realms above,
And loving ones descend to bless the lowly,
  Who daily make their life a work of love.

Press on, true soul! nor let thy footsteps falter,
  Tho' storms and shadows often intervene;
They win the prize, whose purpose does not alter,
  They reach the goal who brave each adverse scene.

All feet must pass the thorny road of trial,
    All hearts must suffer for the truth—the right;
And they who tread the way of self-denial
    Are precious in our heavenly Father's sight.

Press on, true soul! no night but hath its morning,
    And God's all radiant love shall shine at last;
Tho' ebon clouds eclipse the golden dawning,
    Faint not; the gloom of night will soon have passed.
Therefore, press on through weary scenes of sadness,
    Through summer's heat, and winter's stormy strife;
Thou soon shalt reach the vernal heights of gladness,
    Where blooms the summer of eternal life.

GETHSEMANE.

THERE was a garden where the Savior prayed,
    In agony of soul. Dark was the night,
  The stars refused to shine, the moon to light
The deep seclusion where the Master strayed.
Alone He suffered, while His soul was swayed
    With throes of pain endured for truth and right.
    Our minds retire, night hides from us the sight
Of God's blest Son by wicked man betrayed.

  And O, our Father! bend Thy listening ear
When we to our Gethsemane retire,
  We agonize, we bow in reverent fear,
O satisfy our longing and desire,
  And in these hours send angel helpers near,
To lift our stricken souls to regions higher.

THE LAST NIGHT OF JESUS ON EARTH.

HOPE with joyous, starry pinion
   Speeds into the coming day;
Love goes back through time's dominion
   On the pilgrim's rugged way,
Love goes back to him who sorrowed
   O'er the wicked and perverse,
Back to him who toiled and suffered,
   To destroy the Eden curse.

Love, like Mary, bows and listens
   When the multitudes are taught,
In her eyes emotion glistens
   When the miracles are wrought.
What, to her, is learning's station
   With its pompous iron sway?
Better far the soul's salvation
   Spoken of in simple way.

Parables, from nature taken
   Illustrate the law divine,
And the honest soul awaken
   To the truths that round it shine.
Still the world will kill the lowly,
   For it loveth but its own;
Hearts that would be pure and holy
   Still the press must tread alone.

Jesus gave His life for others,
   None could minister to Him,
Though He fain would make them brothers,
   Yet their spirit-life was dim.
All they knew He had imparted,
   Streams their source can not supply;
They were faithless and faint-hearted,
   When the darkened hour drew nigh.

THE LAST NIGHT OF JESUS ON EARTH.

When the last sad meal was ended,
   And the solemn hymn was o'er,
They the mountain slope ascended
   With a grief unknown before.
All their love *to Him* had centered,
   They had known Him *as a man;*
But their hearts had never entered
   Into God's deep, holy plan.

When the grief He could not smother
   Pressed on Him with heavy weight,
They were striving with each other,
   Who among them should be great.
They were children, and He led them;
   Their affections round Him grew;
Carefully he taught, and fed them
   In the life and spirit new.

Oft He gathered them together,
   To baptize their souls in flame,
They, like lonely, desert heather,
   Knew not whence the spirit came.
Theirs was fervent, human feeling,
   Tender sympathy and love;
God was to his soul revealing
   Elements they knew not of.

Every human love must perish;
   Fairest flowers fading part;
And the closest ties we cherish
   Break and wreck the trusting heart.
Let this lesson ever waken
   Strength within the struggling soul;
Principles are never shaken,
   God has kept them true and whole.

They will grow and brighten, ever,
   'Neath the angels' chast'ning rod;
They will form our home forever—
   "Stones" approved and blest of God.

O my spirit, thou art lifted
  With a burst of holy song,
And thy inmost sight is gifted
  With a vision, sought for long.

What to thee, is earthly trial?
  O, behold the heavenly state!
In the clouds of self-denial,
  Toil, and for fruition wait.
Numbered not with any nation
  Truthful hearts must strive alone,
Till a glory and salvation
  Shall throughout the earth be known.

PERFECT THROUGH SUFFERING.

A CLOUD o'erhangs my way; I can not see;
  A darkening trial fills my soul with dread,
And every doubting step my feet must tread,
Leads but to labyrinths—uncertainty,
Where weird-like shadows flit unceasingly.
  O faithless heart! O blinded sight that's led
  Where phantom shapes their ghostly presence shed,
Anoint thine eyes with faith and thou shalt see,
Shalt see the cloud fringed with hope's radiance
    bright;
  Shalt see thy woe an angel sanctified,
That gently leads thee on through sorrow's night,
  If thou but calmly trust in faith abide.
Ope wide thy soul, let in the holy light,
  And lo! thy inner life is glorified.

BE CALM.

BE calm, O thoughts, that flit like restless birds
    In ceaseless flight on light fantastic wing,
  As swallows circle in the air of spring,
Which know not of the wondrous power that girds
The universe, where God's deep thought hath stirred
    The impulse of creative life, which brings
    The growth and beauty of external things,
Blest gifts upon our mortal state conferred.
Thus in the depths of soulful silence wakes
    The consciousness of a celestial sense;
    Bright reflex of Supreme Omnipotence
Which on the inner life in glory breaks,
Of imperfection full cognizance takes,
    And gives for sacrifice a recompense.

SUNRISE AROUND THE WORLD.

GREAT symbol of the Universal Light!
    We marvel not that men have worshiped thee,
For in thy coming speeds the darkest night,
    Thy glory lumes with gladness land and sea.

First morning dawns o'er the Pacific isles,
    O'er palm grove, coral reef and the lagoon,
Where nature's grandeur in luxuriance smiles,
    And spicy breezes yield a rare perfume.

Westward its course, irradiating still
    Australia vast and beautiful Japan,
Where golden ores proud Britain's coffers fill,
    And kingly gardens sweetest zephyrs fan.

Next Java's seas and China's waters gleam
  With shimmering sunlight soft and warm,
One decked with spots where life and fragrance teem,
  And one with many ships of antique form.

O ancient land of prehistoric lore !
  Of idol gods and philosophic dreams ;
Though countless as the sands upon the shore—
  Thy children greet with joy Aurora's beams.

The Himalayas catch the early rays,
  Which brighter glow upon the lasting snow ;
And widely spreads on either hand the day,
  O'er Tartar land and ocean waves that flow.

Through jungle dense, and mountain's deep defile,
  The shining shafts of morning penetrate,
Adown the grim old temple's lonely aisle
  Where Hindoo Buddha is enshrined in state.

On, on to Afghanistan's plains and hills,
  And Persia, whose imperial race is run,
Where Parsee worshipers of fire kneel still,
  And bow before thy shrine, O morning sun !

Mount Ararat, with snow-capped summit bold,
  Now blushes with the halo o'er it spread,
Surrounding seas within their bosom fold
  The genial warmth upon the waters shed.

The desert sand cooled by the nightly air,
  Drinks in the heat as morning rises high,
The lone and patient camel resting there,
  Retreats beneath the palm-tree's shade to lie.

The mosque and minaret are now revealed,
  On Zion's hill, where vandals reared each wall,
When God His judgement unto Israel sealed
  And prophet-tongues proclaimed the temple's fall.

Still it advances on its ceaseless round,
    Illuming classic shores of Greece and Rome,
Then far away where Caffre hut is found,
    And where Laplanders dwell in snow-built home.

Zambesia and the valleys of the Nile,
    The Russian Steppes and Grecian Isles aglow,
The same rays feel that Eastern lands beguile,
    Or Alpine heights clad in eternal snow.

The shades of night now chased from valleys broad,
    Reveals the rolling Rhine and Fatherland;
The plains of France, where toil brings its reward,
    The slopes of Spain where vineyards fair expand.

The noble British group come next to view,
    The greensward of old England now is seen,
The Scottish hills and emerald vales anew
    Shine out in morning's clear and lovely sheen.

The old world, lighted by the orb on high,
    Still on it moves to meet the wider West,
Where hill-tops tower and broad savannas lie,
    Where God's bright crown of blessing seems to rest.

Now high the waves of the Atlantic roll,
    And kiss the shores whose wondrous bounds they keep;
With light all radiant from pole to pole,
    A thousand sails are mirrored in the deep.

A new world now the glory shines upon,
    From South America to Labrador,
The giant valley of the Amazon,
    And archipelagoes around its door.

The cities populous with throngs untold,
    The mighty streams that onward course their way,
The broadening fields and wooded mounts of old,
    Embrace the coming of the dawning day.

On marches morn where fertile mead outspreads,
  And dark primeval forests grimly frown;
O'er winding way the Mississippi threads,
  By rich plantation, busy mart and town.

The waters of the great north-western lakes
  Like broad white silvery sheets embosomed lie,
And all unruffled as the morning breaks
  Reflects cerulean blue of ambient sky.

The waving prairies stocked with golden grain,
  Shake off the nightly dew from waving plume,
And welcome sunlight unto earth again,
  That ripens up the seed within the glume.

O'er Andes heights and Rocky Mountains crag,
  Where the lone condor trims his plumage gray,
And at its base where feeds the harmless stag
  There cometh *too* Aurora's cheering ray.

Adown the rugged cliffs and pleasant slopes,
  It pours its tide on Chilian cities fair;
The golden gate of the Pacific opes,
  And mirrors all its pearly beauties there.

Again the march of day is o'er the deep,
  Where calm and tranquil tides flow out and in,
And soon amid the beauteous isles that sleep,
  The glorious course of sunrise will begin.

SPRING'S FROLIC.

WE augur Spring is coming
    Snow-jewels trembling melt,
Through sunlit ocean's drumming
  Her bounding pulse is felt.

SPRING'S FROLIC.

Afar on glistening mountain,
    She rings her castanets,
Till every living fountain
    Its frost-wrought basin frets.

A burst and than a trickle,
    From leaf impeded rills,
And gusts intensely fickle
    From hollows in the hills.

The fir and pine-trees' whistle,
    Beneath each long mustache,
Though last year's sapless thistle
    May think the action rash.

The storm-dismissing pibroch
    Old chieftain March shall ring,
And play till pool and wee brook
    Shall dance the highland fling.

O'er cliffs that look quite Scottish
    All jubilantly break ;
All turn to waltz and schottische
    For happy girlhoods' sake.

A pause from whirl of pleasure
    To smooth each flounce and frill,
Then glide through maze and measure
    Of stately lakes' quadrille.

Another pause, outflowing
    Some tears beneath the larch;
Anon all gladsome going
    To join the river's march;

To learn the step, the motion
    Of that triumphant force,
That journeys to the ocean
    With music in its course.

From crag-tears pearled or lighted,
　　To billows of the sea,
The earth and heaven are plighted
　　For the Springtime's Jubilee.

A SNOW STORM.

DENSELY fold the vapory clouds,
　'Rolling in white and misty shrouds;
The sun has hidden his smiling face,
And the hills are screened with a veil of lace;
For thick and fast the snowflakes fly
Down from the gray and sombre sky;
And what we thought was the breath of Spring
Has changed to a blast of the old Ice-King.
The merry laugh of the dashing stream
Is hushed—as the memory of a dream,—
Which but a few short days ago
Bubbled with joy in its overflow,
And the plants that burst with life aglow,
Hide 'neath the mounds of virgin snow;
Valley, meadow and hills—high capped—
Are in a spotless mantle wrapped.
O, the beautiful falling snow!
Every tree 'neath its weight bends low,
Crested and plumed in grand display,
Trimmed for a festive holiday.
Drifts mount up like the wave-swept sea,
Over the highway, over the lea,
Down the ravine, and through the wold
Spread the snow-sheets, fold on fold.
From the sunny south-land came too soon
The birds that warble spring-tide's tune;
Now they are flying round and round,
Lighting on paling, fence and ground,

Seeking shelter in barn and shed,
Where by kindly hands they're fed.
And as we stand from the storm aloof,
Off from the heavily ladened roof
Falls the snow like a white cascade,
Thundering down to the canyon's shade.
Surely, the storm-king has his way,
Turning this would-be April day
To a gala time for the Arctic sprites
Ere they speed their way to northern heights,
And the mellow breath of the rosy Spring
Shall warm and gladden every thing.
Her step is slow, but her silent wand
Waves in prophecy over the land,
And earth by magic of powers unseen
Will soon be decked in a robe of green.
Hasten, O Queen of the woodland bowers:
Scatter thy precious wealth of flowers,
Nature's voices shall welcome thee
Tuned to a gladsome minstrelsy.

HUMAN PROGRESS.

WAKE! pulseless muse, to throbbing life again,
    Till quickened currents course through every vein,
And inspiration thrills the heart and brain,
With glowing thoughts of fire.
Thy voice seems mute as winter's icy streams,
Thy wings lie folded in oblivious dreams;
Wake! and ascend amid the glittering beams,
And tune thy heavenly lyre.

Touch the deep chords that thrill the inner soul,
Swell the grand song that brings complete control,

Till symphonies in rapturous waves shall roll,
Uplifting hearts to heaven.
Lo! while time's lengthened shadows fall apace,
The history of past and present trace,
Behold how men of every clime and race
For life divine have striven!

Religion, latent in the human heart,
Has of its life forever been a part;
Not fashioned by the skilful hand of art,
Immortal germ so fair.
Like precious seed the husbandman hath sown,
Who patient waits until the harvest's grown,
So doth the Father all His planting own,
And nurtures it with care.

The good, sown broadcast by His bounteous hand,
From Asia's desert to Columbia's strand,
Hath borne abundant fruit in every land
Where cultured soil was found.
The swelling song of immortality
Hath rolled from mountain, vale and restless sea,
From hearts of bondmen, and from spirits free,
The circling globe around.

Old are the scenes that first gave life and birth
To seed that peoples now this glorious earth,
Seed that contained the growth of highest worth,
Grand possibilities!
In man's crude state and undeveloped sphere,
Strange thoughts of God, in stranger forms appear,
The mirrored objects of His awe and fear
He worshiped, but to please.

God works through laws for man's eternal good,
His laws are love when rightly understood,
They lead from idol forms of stone and wood
To worship that is real.

Up through progressive steps in every age,
Earth's perfect seed produced the seer and sage,
A war with cherished sins of times to wage
And teach truth's high ideal.

The opening mind by slow degrees is taught,
By forms objective to its senses brought,
And thus expands in loftier realms of thought,
By education's rule.
Experience gathered in the ages vast
Is through the mold of human progress passed,
And nobler types of manhood are recast
As teachers in life's school.

Thus darkened blots of superstition's blight,
The reign of ignorance and error's night,
Will by the glory of fair reason's light
Pass like a funeral pall.
And pure religion, struggling for its life,
Shall rise above dissension, feud and strife,
With blessed fruits of summer harvest rife,
Dispensing good to all.

O prophet martyrs! ye who lived of yore,
And gleamed as signals on time's rocky shore,
While tempest, storm and surge ye bravely bore,
Your light shone not in vain.
The truth has sped its way through currents strong,
By rocks and quicksands of opposing wrong,
And still pursues its glorious course along,
With sure and steady gain.

Material science to its place assigned,
Philosophy, the intellective sphere of mind,
With intuition's inner sense combined
Shall cease to be at strife;
These are to man the body, spirit, soul,
Which form in truth, the grand and perfect whole,—
The balance force—that keeps in full control
The varied powers of life.

And man by man in labor shall be blessed;
No man by title-deeds of hate oppressed;
But all his wrongs by love shall be redressed
In true equality,
For freedom rises in her sacred might
To break earth's shackles, and proclaim the right,
To rend the veil that screens the glorious light
Of heaven-born liberty.

Lo! words of peace are passed from shore to shore,
Beneath old ocean's waves and billows' roar;
Hushed be discordant sounds forevermore,
When nation's counsels meet.
And, as the years of swift revolving time
Bring to our land the gifts of every clime,
May all mankind blend in the hallowed chime
Of brotherhood complete.

THE SLAVES OF POVERTY.

O Heavenly Father, when the nights are cold,
    And bleak the dawning of the new-born day;
The thought of those who suffer young or old,
    Stifles the praise and we can only pray.

Hunger is hard to bear when there is bread,
    And cold is bitter, when the coal kings spurn
The cry of those whom hoarded wealth hath bled,
    And who must starve and freeze, their rights to earn.

Our hearts are pained, our eyes flash honest fire,
    Our souls grow sick at poverty's great needs.
Where are the authors of this system dire?
    Where are the monster-forgers of such deeds?

Is this the land of freedom and of grace,
   Where thousands eat at Charity's cold board?
Are these the legal masters of the race,
   Who steal the land to "use it for the Lord?"

"Use it for Satan," might be better said;
   "Use it to magnify the greed of pride,"
Instead of grain, the earth with blood is red;
   The feet of Cain tramp hard where Abel died.

Send us a man like Lincoln who will come
   To smite the shacklets, and unbind the chains,
The slaves are living yet, but O, they're dumb!
   And youth grows aged with its weight of pains.

Here at the block of trade the poor are sold,
   Or hounded where they walk in freedom's track;
O! are we blind that we can not behold
   The curse of slavery, be it white or black?

Nay we *can* see; the times are growing fierce;
   The falchions for the battle still are strong;
And there are ready hands that still can pierce
   The veil that screened the Holy Place so long.

The slaves to-day will be as giants yet,
   When trained endurance to the rope length runs;
And suffering manhood can not well forget,
   The fate that starved its helpless little ones.

O, is the life of pity all consumed?
   And are its brain and muscle worse than dead?
Nay, all the autocrats of wealth are doomed,
   And outraged nature soon will fight for bread.

THE FACTORY.

Down the dingy and cheerless street,
    Lo! the treading of weary feet
Sounds as if they were going to meet
    Some dread and final doom;
For, from the distant factory tower,
Rang the bell at an early hour,
Calling with tones of grasping power
    To loom! to spindle and loom!

So, with hands that are tired and worn,
Clad in garments dirty and torn,
Cherishing ever a hope forlorn,
    Buried in time and sense;
They plod their way with one lone thought,
How shall our scanty fare be bought?
Only as each day's work is wrought
    Cometh our recompense.

With faces wan and furrowed with care,
Follows the old, the young and fair,
Up the narrow and winding stair,
    Each to their place assigned;
Never a moment glad and free
Like birds of the air, or fish of the sea;
But one dull round of monotony,
    Dwarfs both body and mind.

Broad and lofty the grim walls rise,
Mocking the glory of earth and skies,
Prisons of human sacrifice
    Reared by monopoly;
Shut from beauties of mount and wold,
Slaves to masters who hoard their gold;
Strong in the greed of power they hold,
    Deaf to the poor man's plea.

There in the dim light doomed to toil,
Honest earnings the rich man's spoil;
Well may the feeling soul recoil
    From flagrant wrongs like these.
Threads from the myriad spindles twirled,
Then from the flying shuttles hurled,
Tell a tale to the thinking world,
    And set hearts ill at ease.

Coarse or fine be the fabric made,
Bartered, or sold by change of trade,
Never can value be on it paid,
    For none its worth shall know;
Ye who are wrapped in many a fold
Of costly raiment, priced with gold,
Think of the miseries yet untold
    Through which your comforts flow!

Capital, wielding its arm of might
Ruleth not with a love of right,
Nor with equity will it requite
    Labor and industry;
Stately palaces for its kings,
With scheming plans, and plotting rings,
Unto the toiler's hovel brings
    Woe and penury.

O there are waifs in mortal form,
Scarcely sheltered from rudest storm,
With little to keep the life-blood warm,
    The heirs of poverty;
Generations may come and go,
Never a better state to know,
Only to suffer while here below
    Where blessings flow so free.

But as the law of justice stands,
Air, and water, and fertile lands,
Should be given into the hands
    Of people in every clime;

Man, woman and child should be,
Raised into glorious liberty,
Borne to a knowledge full and free
    Of destinies sublime.

It is not noble work we spurn,
Nor from the marts of business turn,
Only for higher motives yearn
    Which prompt to impulse true;
And that a grander love of right
May turn life's sorrows into light,
May make the home and factory bright
    With aspects fresh and new.

Then shall the glad earth, joyous teem
With fruits of hope's elysian dream;
And all its wondrous wealth shall seem
    Like gifts from heaven above;
And the millennial star of peace
Shall usher in the truth's increase;
Then poverty and crime shall cease,
    For man shall rule by love.

AMERICA'S WORKING PEOPLE.

NOT Sparta's Helots, Labor's goaded host,
    The nation's builders, not a vassal race,
Their boon of freedom was Columbia's boast,
    Their dire oppression is her dark disgrace.

When will she rise and for her people speak?
    Yea, ring the welkin like a ponderous bell,
Proclaim a spirit neither loath nor weak
    Her laws to vindicate, her foes to quell.

Her laws distorted, fail in time of need,
    What are they by the simple rule of right?
They stand as walls around the realms of greed,
    They are as armor to the men of might.

A land of millionaires, a land of tramps ;
   A house divided that can never stand ;
A flashing gleam from Continental Camps
   Reveals a structure built upon the sand.

Would Pharaoh let the toiling people go?
   Concede to slaves what e'er for them was asked?
Their stern oppressor mitigate their woe
   Save by command, that they might more be tasked?

Ah well ! we read his folly and his fate ;
   That folly looming in the far away
Must not attract from hardness just as great,
   From mad perversity that reigns to-day.

How blind we are to unaccomplished work !
   How names and claims suffice for service true !
What giant wrongs all unmolested lurk
   Beneath the flaunted good that statesmen do.

They signed off *slavery* and our hopes were high,
   While Truth bent low, these humbling words to carve :
"It is not freedom ! 't is a burnished lie !
   Emancipation — liberty to starve !

"A liberation that absolves the care
   That selfish hands around their chattels threw ;
A legacy of tortures hard to bear,
   A broader tyranny than *bondage* knew."

This verdict graven round the altar stone
   Whereon the nation's sacrifice was laid;
That great burnt offering which could not atone
   For half the wrongs that slavery had made.

And years passed on, dark years of pain and blight,
   While daring traitors wrought despair and woe,
Yet, hear they not upon the mountain's height,
   A voice proclaiming "Let my people go."

Yea, let them go from poverty and fraud
   That have been meted out with burning scorn ;

Let them have place to share the gifts of God,
   For to His bounty all are equal born.

Who owns the earth, the air, the sea?
   They are the Father's, to His children willed;
And never, *never* can the land be free
   Till His behests are honestly fulfilled.

Then why should brothers fashion shackles strong,
   Or rob the weak with fierce barbaric force?
Arouse, Columbia! overthrow the wrong
   E'er retribution takes its vengeful course.

You were oblivious to one cruel sin —
   Monopoly and slavery are one —
Turn then, to justice, life anew begin,
   And reconstruct till servitude is done.

Are not the toilers many, and the wrath
   Of mad despair is like a wild cyclone
That trails the cloud-fire o'er its devious path,
   And hurls the avalanche as crag-dropped stone.

These wealth-producers starved and homeless are,
   Though toil's profusion glorifies the land;
Lest they should come to trust the battle star
   And hail destruction, lend a saving hand.

O give them place upon the broad domain,
   And help them to secure abiding home,
Then crowded industries no life will strain,
   And weary tramps no more need hopeless roam.

Athwart bright cities, towns and teeming fields
   Will be red sunrise, not red scenes of blood,
For all that freedom promises and yields
   Will bless the nation with undreamed of good.

Their plotting monarchies—the curse of time—
   Must helpless sink into their waiting graves,
When God's Republic rises up sublime
   And fells the system that produces slaves!

THE OHIO TEMPERANCE CRUSADE.

IT is a glorious work God has begun;
   Hold sacred in your hearts its trust of power,
And when some little victory you have won
   Let that but nerve you for the adverse hour.
O, put your faith in agencies divine
   That can inspire beyond all human strength;
And "greater works" than those of old, will shine
   Along your pathway's steep and rugged length.
'T is said a fearful river flows through hell,
   But can it match the alcoholic tide,
With rock, and whirlpool, and demoniac spell
   That scatter desolation far and wide?
We may conjecture that they are but one,
   Connected by a dismal open flume,
Where raging rapids unimpeded run
   To dash their victims through that gate of doom.
And as we trace the world's broad winding life,
   Our minds no darker, wilder flood can see;
Its miry banks with hideous reptiles rife
   Are shaded only by the gallows tree.
It is no myth; we know its burning streams
   That carry blight where'er their currents flow;
That bear away the heart's ennobling dreams,
   And sink the soul in passions base and low.
The waving harvests that the Father willed
   From year to year to show his mindful love,
Are first *usurped*, then wastefully distilled
   To make his blessing but an evil prove.
To bring to earth the waves of liquid flame
   Whose *touch* is madness, and whose *force* is death;
To exile man from that parental claim
   That fills the soul with inspiration's breath.
If but the horse-hoof pools along the road
   Miasma to the sunny air exhale,
Will not the river and its marshes broad
   With deadly venom laden every gale?

O woman, there is work that must be done,
    You have but *entered* on its weighty care ;
Its darkest sands the hour of sin hath run,
    The morning dawns with incense of sweet prayer.
The day shall brighten on your faithful toil ;
    The will of God within your hearts revealed
Will give to them the balsam and the oil
    By which the sad and wounded shall be healed.
God pleads through you, then let him freely speak,
    "Grieve not the Holy Spirit," give *free course*,
And you no more shall timid feel, nor weak ;
    He has prepared for you a strong resource.
For *never* in the history of Reform
    Has man attained a more illustrious plane
He nobly bears you through the conflict warm,
    His heart and hand your energies sustain.
O we the sisterhood who toil apart
    To bring redemption to the earth below,
Know how to prize each brave and manly heart
    That gives its might to evil's overthrow.
Life is so mingled on its every side,
    United efforts must its good achieve ;
The *father* may all liberally provide
    Yet must the *mother* tenderly relieve.
Go forth as angels on a mission sent,
    Clothed with the snowy robes of fervent prayer,
That all who see you may to God repent,
    And seek His law—His character to bear.
Your own true purpose, like electric wire
    Will flash conviction through the hardened heart ;
Your supplication like the altar's fire
    Will holy light to all around impart.
May angel choirs assist you when you sing,
    And may the Comforter your *words* impress,
Until the desert in its blossoming,
    Shall bring your hearts the blessing of success.

THE NINETEENTH CENTURY.

SHE stood upon the mountain's height,
    The morn of freedom round her shone;
Beneath her were the years of night,
    With blood-stained hands and eyes of stone.
They were not her ancestral train,
    Her lofty aims they never knew;
She came to bid the people reign,
    To form a system grand and new.
She was a stranger sent of God
    Through whom all nations should be blest;
She laid foundations strong and broad
    Provided for the earth's oppressed.
Priests, kings and conquerors were they,
    The Church and State their throne had been;
By law divine they claimed their sway
    And spurned the rights of toiling men.
The heritage that God reserved
    To be the refuge of the race,
By daring courage she preserved
    Nor gave to tyranny a place.
Where e'er his treacherous armies moved,
By sure defeat he was repaid;
    Triumphant still the century proved.
But in the beauty of her strength
    She turned to kinship with those years,
Along whose savage history's length
    The earth was drenched with blood and tears.
She turned her heart from patriot's dream,
    She quenched the glory with her born,
She kneels where politicians scheme,
    And where her sunrise flag is torn.
Beneath the golden-handled scourge
    Behold her at Britannia's feet;
O, will the blood of heroes surge—
    She for a loan doth there entreat.

*She asks for bondage. Through her greed
   She pawns her honor for a lie;*
She bargains for the serpent's seed,
   She flaunts her dotage. Let her die,
And dig for her an ample grave
   Wherein her sin and shame may hide,
And on its *warning-stone* engrave,
   "*Through her the hope of nations died.*"
But O, ye valiant, still be true,
   And freedom's cause will yet be won;
From failure, wisdom springs anew
   To teach the work that should be done.
Cast up the highway and prepare,
   Prepare the people to ascend
To learn in brotherhood to share
   And see in God an equal friend.
The murderous tactics of the beast.
   The demon strategies of war,
Will they have need to be increased
   When freedom stands beneath her star?
O ye, whose fathers left the hearth
   To meet the flame of battle smoke;
And ye brave exiles of the earth
   Who wrested off the tyrant's yoke;
And ye who on the hills of thought
   Still hear the angels' midnight strain,
Ye are empowered to bring to naught
   The systems of perpetual pain.
Let not corruption touch the plan
   Hid in the song of far away;
Teach justice first, good will to man,
   Then hail the grandest Century!

NEW LIFE.

BENEATH the long despotic reign
    Of Winter's icy hand,
How manifold the forms of life
    That sleep within the land,
His frigid fingers touch the trees,
    The grass, and flowers bright,
His chilling breath the waters close
    In slumbers of the night.

But ever on the earth revolves
    Around the orb of light,
And each gyration nearer brings
    The season of delight;
When, 'neath the genial quickening rays
    That fall to bless the land,
The germs of life in seed and bud
    In loveliness expand.

And sparkling waters burst the crust
    That hushed their murmurous flow,
The tender grasses pierce the sod
    To greet the sunbeam's glow.
In rainbow tints and perfume rare
    Spring forth the tender flowers,
By force unseen their beauties wrought
    From sunlight, dews and showers.

When selfishness and sin possess
    Dominion in the heart,
They sternly hold a frigid power
    That chills the spirit part.
But if we turn to seek the light
    That cometh from above,
We'll feel the warmth of angel life
    In sunny beams of love.

They will the icy coverings melt
    Of envy, hate and fear,
And joyously will spring's bright morn
    Within the soul appear.
The germs divine will then unfold,
    Life's fountain be unsealed,
And latent energies awake
    That long have been concealed.

Affection pure, like early flowers
    From wintry slumbers start,
'Mid verdancy of good desires
    Upspringing in the heart.
We see that this exterior sphere
    Is clothing for the soul,
Which is the vitalizing force
    That animates the whole.

The glorious sun that giveth life
    To all material things,
That from a dark chaotic state
    Such wondrous beauty brings,
Is but an emblem of the Truth
    And potency of Love,
The element in which all souls
    Have being, live and move.

TO THE MUSIC MAKER.

HAIL! Spring, thou rare composer
    Of symphonies and songs,
Though winter—croaking proser—
    His dismal stay prolongs.

Hie to the tablet glistening
    On mount and plain afar,
Haste to the brooklet listening
    For ice-gates to unbar.

TO THE MUSIC MAKER.

Write on the blue lines lying
   Where road-side streams are low,
And on brown furrows trying
   To rise above the snow.

Note music's magic lesson
   With flowers of prism hue,
And put a dulcet stress on
   The wee grace notes of dew.

The colt's-foot stars will twinkle
   In Nature's auburn hair,
And not a frown or wrinkle
   Betray her months of care.

The joyous birds that press on
   Through emerald-tinted haze,
Will learn that music lesson
   And render it in praise.

Æolian chords will wake in
   Gray grotto and green dell,
Wild cataracts will break in
   With base of richest swell.

Grove orchestra and chorus
   The forest's stately choir,
Light zephyrs chanting o'er us
   And waves with golden lyre,

Will claim as universal
   Thy heart's dictated score,
And give it grand rehearsal
   From mountain top to shore.

The reed will lift his baton
   To beat the perfect time,
Lest mocking echoes "Flat on"
   The rhythm and the rhyme.

The violin of rain-drops
  Let down from laughing cloud,
The interludes and main-stops
  With mellow strains will crowd.

What music so surprising
  As April's sunshine shower,
Whose bow of promise rising
  Predicts but half an hour.

When silence in glad heaven
  For that short space had birth,
Its harmonies were given
  As ecstacies to earth.

Then touch, beloved musician,
  Heart, soul and rapturous ear,
Thrill every intuition
  Thou minstrel of the year.

THE WOOD THRUSH.

WHEN the glad summer dons her robes of glory,
      Of green and gold,
And her interpreters reveal the story
      By Jesus told,

The story of the stately scarlet lilies,
      That do not spin,
Nor toil, like our own daffodilies
      That praise would win.

When from the sun-bathed fields of blooming clover
      The bee returns
To store with honey full and running over
      Its waxen urns,

Then from your dwelling's cool and leafy portal,
    Your plaintive lay
Comes to our hearts with music more than mortal,
    And cheers our way.

I have your secret yet, I have not told it,
    Nor will I tell,
To those who love, your own voice will unfold it
    I know full well.

O! Thrush, my bird of birds, my sweet-voiced psalmist,
    The tears will start,
Or smiles will come when your soft cadence calmest
    My troubled heart.

I never feel alone when you are near me,
    O, could you know
The kindness of my heart, you would not fear me
    And shun me so.

Ah, man has been your enemy to plunder
    Your precious life,
Nor seems to hear the notes that break in wonder
    Upon earth's strife.

I will not blame you for your trembling shyness,
    But wait and trust,
That all may reach the sympathy, the highness
    Of being just.

Then throstle dear, keep one enchanting chorus
    For souls like mine,
And from your church's topmost spire send o'er us
    A song divine.

THE WATERS.

I KNOW the streams that gush afar
    And foam o'er mountain's rocky side,
I know how deep the strand-waves are
    In ebbing or incoming tide.
Full oft with hand upon my heart
    I've watched the currents gliding by,
Whose ample floods made joyous start,
    But left their road-beds hard and dry.
I know sweet dreams of crystal sea
    Whose ripples bear the undertone,
Whose billows chant in every key
    Life's anthem as in Heaven known.
Yet, of the tears that sharply knock
    Against the eyelids closed in pain,
And crowding, break the fragile lock
    That sorrow fastens all in vain,
Divine I not, I can not tell
    The time for inward rains to fall,
For founts or streams of heart to swell
    Across affection's throbbing wall.
What laws of correspondence taught
    Through types translucent, symbols clear,
Sweet miracles of life are wrought
    Within the glistening of a tear.
Athwart the field like velvet shorn
    A diamond scarf all glittering lies,
Thence to the bosom of the morn
    I see it on the sunbeams rise.
God's blue enameled casket holds
    All nature's treasures, none are lost,
From rubies that the rose enfolds
    To pearl spray by the ocean tossed.
If such wee atoms hath His care
    Eternal as the ages roll,
Does He not hear the surging prayer
    And feel the deluge of the soul?

From memory's stubble wet with dew
    We count the harvest stored above,
Where heart-wrung drops that midnight knew
    Are fountains of ascended love.
Oft when we faint with desert thirst,
    Or fever pains in blinding strife,
Deep wells unlooked for bubbling, burst
    With waters of eternal life.

TO MY LITTLE SISTER.

I LOOK and see you standing by a stream,
    A thoughtful, happy, trusting little girl;
Half wrapped in mystery, half wrapped in dream,
    With wonder, watching every wavelet's whirl.

With nimble feet I see you press the grass,
    Or pluck with dimpled hands the violets blue,
Then listening to the song-birds as they pass,
    Repeat again the song they sang to you.

Through deep, dark forest, and through mossy glade,
    Where sun and shadow loiter hand in hand,
Where water-birds in gentle freedom wade,
    Again, I see your little figure stand.

What thought was that that bowed your sunny head?
    That made you pause and rest beside the stone?
Was it a sudden sense of fear or dread
    At being left beside the stream alone?

Ah, 'twas the music of an angel voice,
    Calling to you to cross the river wide;
I see you meditate as if in choice,
    And linger fondly by the rolling tide.

And time passed on, through weeks and months and
    years,
  Till youth matured where childhood smiled before;
Again the angel called, and bathed in tears
    Pointed the pathway to the farther shore:

The pathway o'er the blessed bridge of prayer,
    That crosses where the stream is rough and swift;
And gave to you a promise of God's care,
    And confidence to rest upon his gift.

In meek submission to the precious call,
    How glowed your soul with fervent love and trust,
How firm your covenant to give up all,
    And bow your haughty nature to the dust.

The vision deepens: Once again you stand
    Where wave on wave before your spirit rolls;
The angel comes and takes you by the hand,
    And leads you to the stream that cleanseth souls.

"Not yet, O nay, not yet," I hear you say,
    "Spare me the washing, O I fear the tide!"
The angel pleads, "There is no other way
    By which the spirit may be purified."

Down 'neath the limpid waves I see you go,
    You, and the angel that repentance brings,
And from the waters sparkling overflow,
    Comes the sweet echo of the song she sings.

And rising from the billows, pure and white,
    You felt new courage for the work of life,
New zeal to enter in the Christian fight,
    Against the sins that fill the earth with strife.

O, may you ever know where safety lies,
    Nor turn to Marah's dark and bitter streams,
But seek the cooling springs that have their rise
    Where rocks are smitten, and where sunlight
        gleams.

And when you stand beside Death's peaceful sea,
  Watching the coming of the tide that swells,
May life's last music to your memory be,
  Like wave-tones in the ocean's pearly shells.

WONDERMENT.

WHO hath not talked with Nature face to face?
  Who hath not felt her hand upon their brow?
If such there be, their thoughts I will not trace,
  I can but speak with kindred spirits now.

In this calm, quiet hour the heart must thrill
  With all the overflowings of pure thought,
And one must feel a peaceful influence, still
  Wafted on the air with incense fraught.

So now true souls, we'll sit an hour, and dream
  Of life's rare beauty lingering all around;
The splash of water from the mountain stream,
  The snow of flowers that whitens all the ground.

The plaintive music of the meadow thrush,
  The stirring of the wind among the trees,
The rosy glow of evening, and the brush
  Of all the busy honey-gathering bees.

These have we watched till darkness dimmed the scene;
  But O my friends, have we but watched in vain?
Can we not lift the veil that hangs between
  The World of Cause, and this our fair domain?

We love the outward scenes, yet thrill to know
  The underlying secrets of these things,
The mystic power that makes the flowers grow,
  That balances the birds on outspread wings.

That keeps the purposes of wind and tide;
  That lights the starry lamps that nightly burn;
That holds within its keeping vast and wide
  The volumes to whose glowing leaves we turn;

But turn in vain, for we can not discern
  The things revealed to Deity alone,
And though with homesick hearts we hope and yearn,
  We stand all ignorant of star or stone.

For science barely leads us to the brink,
  To the great ocean of unbounded laws,
And standing there she bids us pause and think
  What power created all, what unknown cause

Brought into being all that claims our sense,
  All that our minds aspire to and adore;
Then leaves us in the hands of Providence
  With this trite saying: "We can know no more."

We cannot tell from whence man drew his breath,
  Nor where obtained thought's jeweled diadem;
But this we know, he stands 'twixt life and death,
  Despising both, yet much desiring them.

A child of fancy, yet a friend to truth;
  A reed that every passing wind may sway;
A few mistakes must mark his transient youth,
  A little wisdom crown his closing day.

We cannot see one hour beyond, and yet
  Our lives are hampered with their unkept vows;
Like cloistered birds we struggle and we fret,
  And ask why God this ignorance allows.

And still no answer comes, no confidence
  To search yet deeper for the hidden thing,
Which still eludes our ever grasping sense,
  Or peeps in shyly like the birds in spring.

We are convinced that nothing is complete;
   That which we know with nothing can agree;
And though our lives with purpose are replete
   We cannot gain a perfect mastery.

But if our knowledge seems but nothingness;
   All vain the thought that prompts us to adore,
Still for the revelation we transgress,
   Where muffled footsteps never trod before.

For lack of sight we strain our eyes to see,
   Yet shake with fear still dreading to behold
The culmination of the mystery
   Which wise or foolish ones have never told.

We dare not speak, for language fails to reach
   The full expression of each trembling thought,
And weighted with the cumbrance of speech,
   It drops from fancy ere its form is caught.

And so we live, and ponder and explore,
   Yet fail where we had hoped new life to draw;
Still deaf to hear the wondrous mystic lore;
   Blind to discover God's divining law.

Death comes and finds us in the primer class,
   Reading the simple type with untrained lips;
Measures our sands of being in his glass;
   And leads us where the waiting boatman dips

The heavy oar that speeds our freighted boat
   Across the untried waters to the goal,
Where all the spirit force of man must float;
   The vast unknown dominion of the soul.

ACROSTIC.

"They shall spring up among the grass as willows by the water courses."

THESE lovely emblems of souls true and living,
    Hailing the breath of the glad sunny spring,
Eagerly ope the first buds of the banquet,
Yellow tipped censers of fragrance to swing.
Sweetly they thrive where the gentle stream murmurs,
Humbly they bend where the lily-cups drink,
And while the margin of lakelet adorning
Lo! their tall shadows reflect from the brink.
Light arrows darting from Sol's golden quiver
Speed through the finger-leaved boughs as they sway,
Poising like diamond points over the waters,
Rippling the song of the beautiful May.
In the lone dell where the violets cluster,
Near the thick copse where the nightingales sing,
Grow the sweet willow trees, fresh as the morning breeze
Up 'mong the grasses in beauty they spring.
Peerless amid the low shrubs of the woodland,
All in their emerald glory arrayed,
Mingling their manifold masses of foliage
Ornate in varying color and shade.
Nobly the oak on the hill-top may tower,
Grandly the elm its long branches may trail,
These in their majesty unlike the willow tree,
Heed not the bluebells that grow in the vale.
Eventide vapors ascending from everglade,
Gently bedew every leaflet and flower,
Rising in silver mist up through the wooded glen,
All the trees bathe in the soft dewy shower.
Stout limbs may break when the wild tempest rages,
Slender boughs bend to the fierce winds that blow,
And the green willows so yielding and pliant
Strike their roots deep in the soil where they grow.

Waving and free as when in the long ago,
Indian maidens with light fingers wove
Lithe branches clipped from the beautiful bower,
Low by the brook where the willows still grow.
Over the reedy marsh crowning the daisy beds
Wild birds on each flexile stem gaily toss,
Singing their matins sweet, morning and eve to greet,
Building their nest of the lichen and moss.
Youth of the year, what thy glory surpasses?
Thy freshness and odors infilling all space,
Heart of creation pulsates with life forces,
Evolving in forms of fair beauty and grace.
Who could choose better than did the good prophet
A symbol of humble contentment and peace?
"They shall grow up 'mong the grass as the willow"
Expanding in strength of a blesséd increase.
Right by the side of the still flowing waters
Children of Israel their virtues shall twine,
Open to heavenly sunshine and shower,
Under the care of a Father divine.
Richly He decks all the fields and the valleys,
Sheds His choice blessing o'er mountain and plain,
E'en so shall the soul robed in spiritual gladness
Shine ever brightly when earth's glories wane.

WHAT IS TRUE LIFE?

To eat, to drink and sleep, to tread the mill
   Of habit day by day with lack of thought
     We know is not true life, nor is it wrought
By the mere lapse of years, by selfish will,
Nor does the strife for gain life's ends fulfill.
   When earnestly faith's battles all are fought,
     When, in our strife another's good is sought
Then does sweet blessing on the soul distill.

The merry laugh that vibrates through the heart;
  The hopeful prayer that brings the future near,
The struggle, yea the tender tears that start;
  The cares that end in trust, the songs that cheer,
These bring to life its true diviner part,
  If thus we live, death brings no gloom or fear.

TO-DAY.

THERE'S a cloud on the restless earth to-day,
  It is a cloud of war,
For ages it has dimmed the ray
  Of sun, and moon and star.

There's a weight on our weary earth to-day,
  It is the weight of power;
Oppression hath a heavy sway,
  And slaves beneath it cower.

There's smoke on our darkened earth to-day,
  From the bottomless pit of lust,
Where human loves and hopes decay
  And human treasures rust.

There's a fog on our miry earth to-day,
  From her unchristian fen,
Where fraud keeps equity at bay
  And Christ is bound by men.

There's frost on the hardened earth to-day,
  It is the frost of pride,
The heart can not beneath it pray
  Nor seek the vital tide.

There's blight on our fruitless earth to-day,
  It is the blight of sin,
The buds of promise fade away
  And die as they begin.

There are mingled sounds on earth to-day,
   Of science and reform,
Like waves that fret their rocky way
   They herald in the storm.

Alone is Zion bright to-day,
   She gleams amid the gloom,
Her life that drank each holy ray
   Has brought the truth to bloom.

She sees amid the elements
   That curse the earth to-day,
That angels of repentance soon
   With help must make their way.

And cries, "O earth, new courage take,
   Let not thy voice be dumb ;
Though heavy lowering shadows crowd
   Before thy hope shall come."

WAR AND PEACE.

I LOOKED across the desert wastes of life,
  The world's great field of carnage, blood and strife,
And thought of all the treasure turned to dross,
The dire affliction brought through human loss,
The homes made desolate, the broken heart,
The bitter woe where ties were rent apart,
The mental wealth that all the world should bless,
Spent on the worst of crime and wickedness ;
The springs of love turned back unto their source,
And streams of hate pursuing in their course.
O tide of life, how dark thy currents flow,
Black as the stygian waves that roll below,
When nobler impulse yields her sweet control,
And war's stern passion overcomes the soul.
Fair history's page through all the years of time,
Was stained with darkened deeds of heinous crime,

The lusts of men engendered low desire
And filled their heart's with war's insatiate fire;
Thus love of power in vain ambition's van,
Ne'er heeds the sacred rights of fellowman;
But in her conquest overrules all right,
By force of strength, supremacy of might;
Thus kingdoms rise and hold the reins of power,
Thus empires glory but for one short hour,
Their prestige gone, they crumble into dust,
Because not based on laws exact and just.
O heroes vain! the laurels that *ye* wear,
The boasted name and honors that ye bear,
Came through the orphans' tears, the widows' pain,
The moans and cries of those in battle slain.
The time will come when only he who stands
With courage fortified, and outstretched hands
To fight all giant wrongs, and meet man's needs
With honest words and love's heroic deeds,
Will be the hero of immortal fame,
And in the nation's heart hold dear his name.
The right! the right! I see it grandly rise
Triumphant o'er the world's great sacrifice;
Sustained by justice, linked to truth's great cause,
It teaches men to frame diviner laws
Than those which now appeal to instincts base,
The laws that elevate and bless the race;
And peace angelic spreads her snowy wings,
Glad tidings to this blighted earth she brings,
Proclaiming in her heaven-commissioned flight,
"Forever fled is error's ebon night."
The day has dawned whose brightness has no bound,
Whose golden circle shall the earth surround;
Till every nation, kindred, tribe and clan,
Shall learn to love in truth, their brother man,
Then, navies with their whitened sails unfurled
Shall bear the commerce of a busy world;
And forts and arsenals be turned to marts
Where industry her peaceful life imparts.

For peace and labor clasp fraternal hands,
And justice in their council chamber stands;
No war to scourge, no poverty to blight,
Love rules by the eternal law of right.
No dream Utopian brings this vision grand,
Upon the mount of prospect now I stand
And see the world progressing to that end
Where all in unity and peace shall blend,
When governments shall seek each nation's good,
Thus form a universal brotherhood.

COLUMBIAN LIBERTY AND PEACE BELL.

THOU art the symbol of the inward bell
    That pleads and teaches with the still small voice,
But strikes the hour for action with a swell
    That wakes the spirit to heroic choice.

Ring out, O blessed bell, a tocsin sound
    To call brave warriors to the Cause of Peace,
To make all earth for once, a battle ground
    Through whose triumphant victories wrong shall cease.

Ring loud, O ring the very wrath of God,
    Omniscient zeal, that naught of evil brooks;
True as the plummet, sure as measuring rod,
    Devoid of fancies, free from schemes and crooks.

Bring love baptismal, bring the vital strength
    That Michael and his angels had of old,
Till clothed in her right mind the earth at length
    Shall know the fabled, dreamed of Age of Gold.

Ring fearless peals, to thunder far and wide
    With leveling force like horns of Jericho;
Ring out in earnest, Heaven is on thy side,
    Till bastile, fort and citadel are low.

Ring shame upon the navies of the deep,
   Those monsters for iniquity, those floating hells,
O'er which the pitying angels pause and weep
   While demon pride each rivaling nation swells.

Ring shame that carnage with its blood-red hand
   Presents the engines used in Christian might,
That would be spurned from darksome horror-land
   As far too evil for Plutonian night.

Ring till the Christian bells in steeple tower
   O'er legislative halls, and learning's fane,
O'er mart, and mine, and factory own thy power,
   And vibrate with the justice of thy strain.

Till heathen lands their passion-rousing din
   Shall silence for thy chimes so pure and blest;
When war retreats with legion hosts of sin,
   Thy music then, shall "charm the savage breast."

Ring soft and low sweet gratitude and prayer,
   Ring "Peace on Earth," so sadly long delayed;
God's joyful band again shall thrill the air
   Mid love-bought glory that shall never fade.

As human hearts their angel-hood disclose,
   The desert wastes in fruitfulness will sing;
The wildernesses blossom as the rose,
   And all the bells of Heaven with thee shall ring.

THE ANGEL CHOIR.

THE light of day had vanished,
   Its cares and toils were done;
The twilight gray departed
   And curtains dark were hung,

A silence brooded over,
   The night was hushed and still,
Save the moaning of the wind-harp
   Along the pine-clad hill.

I sought my couch at even
   To find from toil release,
But ere my weary eyelids
   Were wrapped in slumber's peace,
My thoughts flew back and forward
   Like a shuttle in a loom,
The fabric of my vision
   Was tinged with shade and gloom.

I thought of life's strange meaning,
   Its suffering, trial, pain ;
How many hearts to woe were tuned,
   Instead of hope's refrain.
When lo ! I heard above me
   As if in upper air,
Sweet angel voices chanting
   Divinest music there.

With ecstasy I listened,
   What heavenly harmony,
An anthem chorus swelling
   And then sweet melody.
I thought, "it is the ransomed
   Who in God's mansions shine,
The psalms of triumph singing,
   The Lamb's grand song divine."

It floated nearer, nearer,
   Until my inner sight
Perceived that choir immortal
   Arrayed in vestments white.
I reached my hands in trusting
   To touch their snowy hem,
That I might be made holy
   By coming near to them.

When lo! they spread their pinions
  And vanished from my sight;
And then I pondered deeply
  The vision of the night.
Not lofty ones descending
  From out the great unknown,
Who sing and play on golden harps
  Around the Jasper Throne,

But blessèd angel guardians,
  Who know our common needs,
Whose gentle God-like presence
  From sin's dark pathway leads.
O heaven-sent evangels!
  Descend the bright stair-way;
Come often, cheer and guide us,
  Direct us day by day.

O, those sweet strains of gladness
  Of love and joy and hope,
They tune my heart to noble themes
  And heavenly vista's ope,
Life's song has sweeter cadence,
  Earth seems more bright and fair
Since I heard that angel chorus
  The music in the air.

LOVE'S MINISTERY.

SHOULD golden lyres concordant chime
  In accents sweet and clear,
And pour their melodies sublime
  Into my listening ear;

Their rapture would my being thrill,
  Too soon to pass away,
For pleasures that the senses fill
  Are transient as the day.

I know of holier symphonies
    Born of the soul of love,
Whose ever present ministries
    A lasting blessing prove.

Her voice is soft as silver lute,
    Her power hath secret charm
To hold the tongue of passion mute,
    And keep the soul from harm.

Like fabled Orpheus of old,
    Her minstrelsy can sway
The beasts of nature strong and bold,
    Till gently they obey.

O love divinely pure! the crown
    Of our interior life,
For thee, the lower self laid down,
    No more shall rise in strife.

Angelic language is expressed
    In all thy words and ways,
The spring that rises in the breast
    Is everlasting praise.

Love tender, watchful, patient, kind,
    All clothed with charity,
Fair offspring of the Eternal Mind!
    Heaven's graces blend in thee.

Thou wreath'st the cross with roses bright,
    And lilies white and fair,
Till all its burden seemeth light,
    And easier to bear.

No heights so high, or depths so deep
    That thou wil't not explore,
And there with sleepless vision keep
    Thy blessed vigils o'er.

O who can sing thy canticle!
   From earth's attraction free,
Or picture of thy glory fill
   With truthful praise of thee.

Soul of existence brooding here,
   Spread thy celestial wings,
And intromit us to the sphere
   Of sacred heavenly things.

Where reign'st supreme thy queenly grace,
   In virtue's constant smile,
And in thy sun-illumined face
   Is seen no trace of guile.

'Tis carnal man that prostitutes
   Thy character and name,
And robes a baser substitute
   With mantle of thy fame.

High-born and God-like attribute!
   No sin can tarnish thee,
Thy ways all calumny refute,
   Thy heart is chaste and free.

'Tis lust conceived, that dearth brings forth,
   This human hearts may prove;
While all that's good in Heaven or earth
   Is fruit of perfect love.

———

LIFE WITHOUT LOVE.

LIFE without love is like a sunless sky,
    A night without its crown of glittering stars,
  An eventide without its golden bars.
A tree whereon fair blossoms wilt and die,
A stream whose pebbled bed is hard and dry.
    A vacant house where moldy wreckage mars,
    A broken harp, a soulless song with jars
Made harsh, a soundless ear, a sightless eye.
Life without love is like a bloomless spring,
    A fruitless autumn time, a breathless rose;
A chantless sea where wild waves rudely fling,
    A dreary desert where no fountain flows.
Life without love's divine, inspiring breath
Oh is not life, but hopeless, living death.

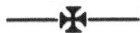

MY LITTLE BED.

WRITTEN FOR THE CHILDREN.

A LONG time since in the mossy turf
    Where the brooklet babbled by,
Grew a lovely tree from a seed as small
    As the pupil of your eye.

'Twas not the oak of the mountain top,
    For those from acorns grow,
But the emerald boughs of the forest pine
    In the valley just below.

Yea the lovely pine, where the little birds
    Attuned their rapturous praise,
And a covert found in the dewy night,
    And from noon-tide's scorching rays.

'Twas from this tree so fine and large
   That my bedstead small was made,
On which I rest when the stars shine out,
   In their silvery veils arrayed.

It was hewed apart from its native soil
   By the woodman's swinging tool;
Of branches shorn, and brought to the mill,
   And sawed by the sawyer's rule.

Then, grooved and planned by the carpenter
   Its frame was all complete,
And covered well by the painter's oil
   It was handsome, strong and neat.

A tick well filled with fresh sweet husks
   From the farmer's silky corn,
Makes soft and warm my nightly lodge
   From early eve till morn.

Two sheets as white as the driven snow,
   Or the blue sky's fleecy cloud,
Are spread all over my little bed,
   A sweet and dainty shroud.

They came from the land of golden fruit
   Where the grand Mississippi flows,
And the Gulf-Stream washes the shining sands
   And many a sweet flower grows.

For there on the broad plantation grounds
   Where the negroes toil and sing,
Grow the cotton shrub with their tassel bloom,
   And a harvest rich they bring.

The blossoms plucked by the tawny hand
   Are placed in a large machine,
Where the seeds are cast from the downy tuft
   Which makes them white and clean.

MY LITTLE BED.

Then drawn into threads of wond'rous length
    By spindles of glittering steel;
While the warp and woof with rattling loom
    The power of skill reveal.

And this is the way my sheets are made
    By many a busy hand,
And bought with a sum of golden coin
    From the vender's trading-stand.

My blankets come from the meadows green
    Where the blue-eyed grasses blow,
And daisies bloom, and hedges shade,
    And the dancing waters flow.

It may seem strange but 'tis even true,
    As the lambs might all declare,
They live on the verdant sod, and thrive
    By the shepherd's kindly care.

And the fleece of wool that covers them
    Protects when the sky is cold,
When the winds and snow of the frosty days,
    Blow over the shelt'ring fold.

But as soon as the ices melt away
    And the balmy June appears,
Mid fright and force it is taken off
    By the workman's clipping shears.

Then with spindles and loom, and warp and woof
    The blankets are quickly made,
What would we do but for sheep and lambs
    Through the chill of the nightly shade.

My pillow is made of the softest down,
    Though not from the icy shores
Where the eider duck builds her distant nest,
    But from flocks around our doors.

The feathers give rest to the aching head,
  Or when sleep the eyelids close:
And my coverlet is as fresh and clean
  As the whitest thing that grows.

What a goodly thing is my little bed,
  What a place for blessed dreams
Of the far away hills, and meadow lands,
  Where the sun in its brightness beams.

My mind is filled with the thought each day
  Of the many who have no bed,
Of how even the Saviour had naught on earth
  Where upon to lay His head.

And at even-tide when I go to rest,
  I will offer this humble prayer,
That a thankful heart may be ever mine
  For the blessings that I share.

POCKETS.

Could you think of a boy without a pocket?
  Never a moment could you!
For with books and traps and money perhaps
  What would a boy then do?
There are nails and screws that must find a place,
  With pieces of twine and hooks,
Big iron rings and numerous things
  That he thinks more of than books.
There are rolls of paper and finger cots,
  And matches we're sorry to say,
Such dangerous ware should be placed with care
  In a safety box away.
Do you know what fills his pockets out
  Appeasing hunger and thirst?
Those apples or pears he ever bears,
  All wearing to rends the worst.

And stranger things the pockets swell
    Some that we think not nice,
Potato bugs and slimy slugs,
    And even little mice.
Though the cat is fed and fishes too,
    By hand so kind and free,
There are other ways in which love displays
    Her deeds of charity.
Mysterious holes in the corners come,
    And many things slip through,
The lids are torn and the garment's worn,
    Too soon there is work to do.
There are suitable things to carry there,
    Handkerchief, knife and comb,
Perhaps a book, and a little nook
    Where the pencil may find room.
These pockets are handy we often hear;
    —Handy for idle hands,—
But in culture's school we find the rule
    Against this practice stands.
From pockets many in every robe,
    In jacket, coat and cape,
From pants and vest, surtout and breast,
    Bad things cannot escape.
Let boys now learn,—each in his turn—
    Some thought to well bestow;
To things they wear, give proper care,
    Good seed they thus will sow.

THE ROBIN.

SING, robin sing, from your cool sheltered nest,
    Your nest where the cherry buds blow,
Sing us the melody you love the best,
    The one that we love best you know.

The one that we followed when life's day was young,
    And mimicked with tin-horn and pipe,
Ah! these were the words we imagined you sung,
    "Sweet cherries, cherries, ripe, ripe, ripe!"

Sing, sing in the morning when first the glad light
    Like a telegram comes from on high,
And beautiful star-eyes that watched through the night,
    Close gently to sleep in the sky.
Sing when the dull orient bursts into flame,
    When crimson waves change into blue,
O child of the matin hours, gladly proclaim
    Your own cheerful message true, true!

Sing when the shadows cross woodland and wold,
    And the sun like a wise alchemist
Turns all the gray clouds into vessels of gold,
    On an ocean of pale amethyst.
O then when we offer the day's latest prayer,
    Ere sleep its fine drapery has spun,
Sing out merry chorister, thrill all the air,
    The day, that grand miracle's done!

And warbler, should you tarry here when I
    Have said to home and friends the last farewell,
Above my soundless ears in joyance fly,
    Your secrets to my silent heart to tell.
And when mayhap to sunny worlds above,
    Your loving notes will take an upward wing
To one who always listened from pure love,
    O happy robin, sing, sing, sing!

WELCOME TO JUNE.

BEAUTIFUL and happy June time!
    Wondrous days of cheer!
With your brightness and your sweetness,
With your fullness and completeness
    You are welcome here!

WELCOME TO JUNE.

Welcome! every opening blossom,
    Silver, gold and blue,
Matchless pearl and rosy dresses,
And the fragrance each possesses,
    Glad we are for you.

From beyond the sapphire arches
    Come the sun's warm rays,
And cold winter's crystal masses,
Metamorphosed into grasses,
    Make these lovely days.

And the merry birds of summer
    On their fluttering wings,
From the early morning blushes,
Till the gentle evening hushes,
    Each a glad song sings.

And the soft caressing zephyrs—
    Whence and whither they?
Laden without weight or measure
With the best of floral treasure
    Gathered on their way.

O, I hear the distant ripple
    Of the meadow rill,
Where the lamb its mother follows
Over hills and into hollows
    Where the world is still.

See the clouds with silver lining
    Watch the sun go down,
View the silent midnight glories,
Theme of new and olden stories,
    Earth's unfading crown.

All these things fair June has brought us,
    Scattering far and near;
Then farewell cold wintry brightness,
Diamond glitter, snowy whiteness
    And your merry cheer.

Every living passing beauty
    Speaks so well to me,
Tells me of our God in heaven,
By whose hand all gifts are given
    So abundantly.

He who guides the passing seasons
    Loveth human souls,
And his mercy he is sending,
Light and peace and joy unending,
    And each life controls.

Then let every grateful spirit
    Render ceaseless praise;
For the bliss of life that fills them
For the power of good that thrills them,
    Through these gladsome days.

A PICTURE.

THE time of flowers had come and passed away,
    While in the velvet fields of June
  Sat in the year's calm afternoon
October, in her daintiest array.

From orchards jubilant with song and shout,
    The merry children came, the glow
    Of health like ocean's undertow,
Just carried sportive spirits in and out.

We passed them on the roadway steep and wide,
    Their faces sobered, but the fun
    Was loth to hide, so first from one,
And then from all, burst forth the rippling tide.

Their manners bore the trace of Nature's school,
  No extra polish could we see;
  Their pants were shattered at the knee,
Their hats acknowledged ventilation's rule.

The nut-brown faces flushed in pink,
  The parted lips, the dancing eyes,
  Gave no strange feeling of surprise,
No evidence of new-found joy I think.

Nay, childhood's days are always much alike,
  The sweet abandon comes to all,
  Ere manhood's duties sternly fall,
Ere loyal hearts must feel and hands must strike.

I would not rob one youthful soul of joy,
  Nor mar its pleasure by an act,
  The days are near when sternest fact
Will curb the gushing life of girl and boy.

My soul said, "have your joy oh merry band,
  While hearts and spirits all are gay,
  The time is growing short for play,
The hours for work are very near at hand."

A TRIPLET OF SONNETS.

BLEST childhood, happy, innocent and free,
  Rose-lipped and blushing as the dawning day,
With eyes as brilliant and with hearts as gay
As the gazelle who loveth liberty.
Tho' glad the life, and full of mirth and glee,
  Yet all the questioning, through toil and play,
  Shows how unfolding thought and reason sway
And mold the face that speaks sincerity.

O joyful hours of early springtime dreams,
Which lead by rippling stream and flowery glade,
   When all the imagery of life but seems
Like some fair picture on a canvas laid,
   Whose beauteous shades are like the sunset gleams
That from the expanding vision quickly fade.

Bright ardent youth, life's kindled flames mount high
   As early day's transcendent oriflamme;
   Imagination leads to wealth and fame
And builds its airy castles in the sky.
The full-fledged bird its pinions oft may try,
   And none to freedom can deny its claim,
   Yet liberty shall prove an empty name
Lest thou of passions base, thyself deny.
   Be this thy motto, wrought by time's deft hand,
Health, virtue, truth, inwoven in thy life,
Blest principles to guide through toil and strife,
   That in integrity thy soul may stand,
   And long thy days may be within the land,
Full of good fruits, with peace and blessing rife.

I would not couple age with weary care,
   Or closely link it unto sorrow's load,
   Which lowly-bowed on time's long dreary road
Must walk alone in silence and despair.
Ah nay! 'tis day's decline all calm and fair,
   The genial rest that nature has bestowed;
   No heated strife life's waning powers to goad,
But tranquil peace diffusing everywhere.
   As is the morn, so proves the evening bright,
Yet, softened with the mellow-tinted rays
   That temper the full glare of glowing light,
And robe the mountains with a purple haze,
   Ere falls the curtain of the night,
And hides the traveler from mortal sight.

CARNATIONS.

WHAT beauty this my wondering eyes behold,
    Within the garden's border growing strong,
  Sweetly united in a happy throng?
Fresh buds are these, of red, and pink, and gold,
Most delicately fringed, while fold on fold
    They grace the slender stem, and all day long
    Wave gently to the tune of glad bird-song;
Their faces to the sun, their feet in mold.
Thus we may live and grow, and though of earth,
    Look upward with the faith that maketh glad,
May find the power that gives the angel birth,
    And gladden other hearts who're lone and sad.
Thus, like the flowers where grace and fragrance blend,
Sweet memories of our lives may cheer each friend.

AUTUMN.

SUMMER has passed with its long evening twilight,
    The birds with their chirping have gone from the eaves,
The beautiful flowers so full in their blooming
    Have dropped from the stems and left nothing but leaves.

Left nothing but leaves. Ah! how can we say so,
    Those rich tiny leaves with their various shades
That with delicate hands were tenderly gathered
    By brooklet and rill in the deep silent glades.

And now we behold them as memory's picture,
  The fern fronds, the daisy and buttercups gold,
We'll weave them together a wreath for the summer
  That bids us good-bye, for the year groweth old.

But autumn has joys, though faded the roses,
  And bare is the stem with its long amber thorn,
The high tasseled corn once rich in its plumage
  Is rustling a chant to the fields that are shorn.

The birds and the insects have sung their last chorus,
  The flowers and leaflets all trembled in tune,
And the last notes of joy to days that were passing
  We'll hear as an echo some fair afternoon.

Then listen and wait to catch the low whisper,
  For the song of the swan is sweetest at last,
The sound of the melody heard is the sighing
  Of trees that are bidding farewell to the past.

STARS THAT TWINKLE.

The following verses were written by a brother who was born, educated and reared in affluence in the West India Islands. His father was a highly cultured and wealthy nobleman. He employed a large number of natives of both sexes to work on his extensive plantations, and among the poor blacks, who were bought and sold like so many cattle, he chose him a wife. The result of this union was that a son was born to them, who, when in the strength of young manhood, gave his substance and dedicated his life to the gospel cause; he was an earnest advocate for the equality of the sexes and the abolishment of slavery. These lines were written by him a few years before the Proclamation of Emancipation was issued.

STARS that twinkle, twinkle down
  Like bright diamonds in a crown,
Wherefore are ye winking?

Look ye forth upon the earth
God hath filled with joy and mirth
   Of its sorrows thinking?

On the mountain capped with snow
Where the linches only grow,
   He hath placed no sorrow,
In its robes of purest white
Towering almost out of sight
   Looking for the morrow.

Midst the forest clad in green,
Where the humming-bird is seen
   Flitting hither, thither,
Trees are waving in the air,
Knowing not that weary care
   Blithest hearts can wither.

Where the streamlet glides along
   Purling forth its joyous song,
   Moving to the ocean,
Tiny fishes in the stream
Never in their sporting dream
   Aught of sad emotion.

On the sunny everglade
Where hath trod the Indian maid
   Wandering o'er the prairie,
There her joyous songs uprise
As with nimble feet she hies
   Like the eastern fairy.

In the placid lake is seen
By the moonlight's silvery sheen,
   O'er its bosom skimming,
Clouds reflected from the air,
Pictured from that mirror there
   On its waters swimming;

Landscape of the distant hills,
Echoes of the mountain rills,
  All indeed is gladness;
Why then mourns each glistening star,
As it looketh from afar
  Thinking of earth's sadness?

Look upon the boundless sea!
Hear its billows in their glee,
  Onward, onward sweeping,
Where 'tis said in ancient lore,
Mermaids dwelt in days of yore
  In its caverns sleeping.

See the brilliant sun at length,
Rising in Titanic strength
  Flooding earth with glory.
On yon distant mountain top,
Shining in each dewy drop,
  Speaks he sorrow's story?

As he wields his radiant wand
O'er the ocean and the land,
  From his chariot smiling,
Troops of fleecy clouds advance
Joining in a joyful dance
  O'er each other piling.

Joyous thunders rolling round,
From each hill and vale rebound
  Full of music crashing;
Earth is gladsome as she sees
Lightning gleam amidst the trees,
  O'er her bosom flashing.

Rainbow arched upon the sky,
Seem like pictures placed on high
  Promises of blessing;

Drops descending from above
Tell that God is full of love,
   Every good possessing.

Then ye stars of radiance bright,
Why does not your pretty light
   Steadily be shining?
Why as veiled by passing clouds,
Weeping, each his face enshrouds
   Constantly repining?
Is it all a golden dream,
As the earth indeed should seem,
   Yet but poets fiction?
Know ye ought that mars the scene,
Casts a darkening cloud between
   Telling of affliction?

Ye who have for ages wept
As the car of time hath swept
   In its ceaseless travel,
Keeping vigils all the night,
There is mystery in your light,
   Will you now unravel?

REPLY OF THE STARS.

WE looked on the earth as the daylight was gleam-
   ing,
And wept for her children, yea, wept for them all,
For while some reposed on their soft cushions dream-
   ing
In many a house was the funeral pall.

We saw that the earth was indeed made for gladness,
   And nature's rich blessings were freely poured down,
But man by his folly, his pride and his madness,
   Hath turned every smile to a sorrowing frown.

We looked on the ocean where sunbeams should smile,
And thought upon Erin the Emerald Isle,
The infants were weeping, their parents were dead,
The hope of their country had fallen or fled.
Their eyes were all sunken—how hollow the voice!
Their sports had all ceased, they could not rejoice;
Gaunt famine was stalking as though he had come
To gather them all to his last charnal home;
The tears were descending, like rain drops they fell,
And—hark! in the distance that deep tolling bell,
O, souls are now passing from this joyful earth,
Who never yet tasted of ought of its mirth.

We turned to Britannia, her flag was hung out,
As though she would fill the whole earth with her shout,
The sound of her drum we could hear o'er the sea
As it rolled thro' the valley's, o'er mountain and lea;
Her coffers were filled with the bright shining gold,
And brave were her warriors, all strong men and bold,
Her queen was enthroned in a palace of state,
And round her were gathered the wise ones and great,
High lords and grand ladies—a motely array—
Each trying to set forth his rank, for display;
In satins and silks they were flaunting around,
Wrung out from the poor they had crushed to the ground.
Rich bishops were strutting full pampered and fed,
Regardless of those who were crying for bread,

While round them the bayonet, cannon and sword
Were keeping in awe the poor famishing horde.
Aye! many a heart was down-trodden by care,
Whom God had created his blessing to share.
We saw as we looked o'er this island of pride,
How thousands were trying their suffering to hide;
The widow was selling her bridal ring worn,
The cries of her children her heart-strings had torn,
She wept not, for tears could not flow from her eyes,
But God surely heard the poor widow's deep sighs.
And is this the Albion of Poetry's song?
The home of so noble and gifted a throng?
The birthplace of Spencer, of Milton and Gay?
And others who shone with so dazzling a ray?
Of Howard, best known as the prisoner's friend?
Of Fry and of Bixton whose good deeds ascend?
O shame on thee, Britian! O blush for thy pride!
The rough shodden horse o'er thy children doth ride.
The pomp of thy glory is tinsel and show,
While from thee we hear the low wailings of woe.
O turn from thine errors! repent thee in time,
E'er storms of destruction thy death-knell shall chime!

We saw where the snow king on Muscovite land
Was wielding the sceptre of ice in his hand;
The storm clouds were gathering and howling around,
O'er the lakes and the rivers his cold hand had bound.
The cot of the peasant was humble and low,
His pathway was covered with deep drifting snow,
We marked as he entered his aspect of care,
He strove to conceal it—yet sorrow was there;
He rested a moment his hand on his face,
Then walked to and fro with a quick restless pace,
He looked at his daughter—he patted her head
The infant was sleeping on her little bed;
O never again will his eyes e'er behold
The dear ones he loved more than silver or gold.
The Czar had commanded, the conscript must go,

Where Danube's dark waters through Hungary flow.
The knout is hung o'er him, its dread lash in sight,
He dares not complain, but hastes on to the fight.
The sword of the Hussar may cleave through his brain,
And rid him of all of earth's sorrows and pain.

O weep for the land where the Austrian doth ride!
The Magyar is fallen and ravised his bride.
The tomb of his mother the rude shot has torn,
They could not let her rest in her last earthly bourne.
The church where his father had worshipped of yore
Is clotted and stained with the deep crimson gore.
O speak not of gladness!   O tell not of joy!
The hand of oppression is stretched to destroy;
The blood of the murdered is crying aloud,
And smoke from the cannon ascends like a cloud;
"How long, O thou righteous," the martyred ones
    cry,
"How long shall those shrieks be uprising on high?
Will thou not avenge us, O merciful God,
And take from the despot his scorpion rod?"

Italia, thou land of the jasmine and vine,
In vain did thy forces 'gainst Austria combine,
The city of islands must soon fall a prey,
And Hapsburgh will over her once more hold sway;
Where steered the light gondola swiftly along,
No more may be heard the gondolier's song.
The boom of the cannon, the bursting of shells
Are all the rude music thy minstrelsy swells.
No more, Adriatic, shall wedded to thee
Proud Venice be mistress again of thy sea;
And Rome the eternal, hath dug a wide grave,
For those who have fallen their country to save.
What then, if o'er Italy beams the bright sun
And green is the wreath which her artists have won?
What though the sweet music her minstrels have sung
A charm o'er the nations of earth may have flung,

REPLY OF THE STARS.

What, what are they in the grief of the heart
When those who have loved thee are called to depart?
When she who caressed thee in youth's early day
And hushed thee to sleep with some sweet plaintive lay,
Whose knees were thy pillow, whose heart was thine own
Is struggling to death in her last bitter groan.
The shot of the foeman is doing its work,
The Christian is worse than the heathenish Turk.
To the walls of the city she hasted at dawn,
Her heart with her children to battle had gone,
She thought that perchance they were weary and sad,
"At sight of their mother they'd surely be glad."
She flew through the streets, but she hasted in vain,
The thunder of cannon was heard once again.
O Mother! the day of thy sorrows are o'er;
She sinks to the ground, she is covered with gore,
Her features are mangled, and glazed are her eyes,
" O leave me to die! " the poor wounded one cries.
One quiver, one gasp and the spirit has fled,
And Visla is ranked with those who are dead.
O France! the heart's blood thy escutcheon has stained
Will tarnish the glory that thou hast e'er gained,
What are the proud victories thy Bonaparte won,
To comfort the heart of the poor orphan son?
And what count the trophies thou wavest on high,
To hush up the sound of the lone widow's cry?
La Belle France, La Belle France! thou art drunken with wine,
And dreamest that sunbeams of liberty shine;
Thy sins are like oceans whose waves never rest,
But vainly are moving from East unto West;
The bark on her bosom careering in joy,
She dashes in fury that she may destroy;
Although for a moment she seemeth to smile,
'Tis only that she may the seamen beguile;

No peace for her waters, but onward they roll,
Forever she moveth from pole unto pole.
These are the dark sins which have crimsoned thy soil,
They lead thee in darkness, thy beauty they spoil ;
No rest to thy people, no peace to thy land :
Ho! ho! they are driving thy bark to the strand.
Thou dreamest of freedom, but knowest not now,
The breakers before thee, right under thy bow,
Sleep! sleep out thy revel, then wake up indeed,
And mourn o'er the thousands thou madest to bleed,
Proclaim through thy borders, Jehovah is king,
And works of repentance as offerings bring.
It may be that God in his mercy may hear,
And wipe from the eye the sorrowing tear,
May open the store-house of gladness and love,
And pour out rich blessing from heaven above,
Cause peace and prosperity o'er thee to reign,
And happiness banish thy sorrow and pain.
Thou askest " why twinkle we, twinkle we down
Like diamonds set in a bright golden crown?
And why weep the stars as they look forth on earth
Which God has endowed with a fullness of mirth?"

We passed the Alhambra, o'er Castile we sped,
And saw where the proud Moorish noblemen bled.
O Spain! thou art cursed for that dark deed of thine
Which banished the Moor from his favorite shrine.
No more in Granada we hear his soft lute,
Nor listen at dawn to the sound of his flute;
The moonlight shines down where his footsteps have
    trod,
But yonder he resteth 'neath Africa's sod.
We looked where the Arab was hasting his steed
O'er sand of the desert with lightning-like speed.
He held in his hand the sharp glittering spear,
For the shout of the Frenchman sounds in his ear.
Alas! that the desert itself cannot hide,
But sorrows earth's children forever betide,

O Africa! who can e'er number thy woe,
Or measure the ocean of tear-drops that flow;
Involved in the darkness of midnight, no more
Are Esops and Hannibals found on thy shore,
But cruel white men thy children enchain,
And drag them across the rough billowy main.
Where Brazil's bright diamonds are glistening around,
'Tis there where the bones of thy children are found,
Or where on Havana's stout castle is seen
The banner hung out of Castilian green,
Unless 'neath the waters they gave them a bed,
And left them to slumber alone with the dead.
How bitterly, bitterly art thou repaid
Espagna, for the flesh thy myrmidons flayed!
Each colony planted and watered by thee
Is blighted and cursed, aye, polluted for thee.
And like as the dry leaves the wind shaketh off,
So have they done to thee, they curse thee and scoff.
The star-spangled banner will wave in the breeze,
The eagle will stoop down and from thee shall seize
The diamond thou prizest, the rich shining gem,
That long has adorned thy bright diadem.

But thou, O Columbia! the stars look to *thee*
For on thy bright standard our picture we see;
The eagle is fierce when he clutcheth his prey,
And soareth on high to his eyrie away.
But look up to heaven whence cometh the night?
And is not thy heart filled with sweetest delight?
The stars are all shining, how pretty their beams,
They seem to be wishing thee bright pleasant dreams.
Sweet peace they are breathing—O peace to the heart
That striveth in love this rich gift to impart.
No more let the sound of oppression arise,
Nor slavery fill thee with horrible cries;
No more let the lash of the driver be known,
But hushed be the voice of thy black brother's moan.

O let him go free, free as thou art thyself
And grieve not his spirit for perishing pelf.
Then, when the stars twinkle and weep for the earth
Thy coasts shall be filled with thanksgiving and mirth;
And God will watch o'er thee, and bless thee that here
Oppression no longer can call forth a tear.
Then when the stars twinkle like gems in a crown
On happy Columbia their love will pour down.

PEACE OFFERINGS AT THE WORLD'S EXPOSITION.

EARTH brings her tributes to her gods,
    And piles her splendid altars high,
Exultant queries, where the odds
    That from the earth to heaven lie?

Amid the splendor here achieved
    What thinks she of the other side?
The wrongs that never were retrieved,
    The war-made wrongs half deified?

She heaps her gains and great they are;
    Flung up like waves that oceans toss,
A bulwark that doth vision bar,
    And screens her penury and loss.

For war and famine;—fiends of death,
    Sent forth by the oppressor's hand,
Have breathed destructive sulphurous breath,
    And fever-blight on every land.

If from their wreckage grim and drear
    Such wondrous beauty, skill hath wrought,
How would earth's opulence appear
    Had Peace and Freedom aided thought.

Had they with gentle mother-heart,
  Instructed in the life sublime,
What wealth of Genius, Toil and Art
  Would teem to-day in every clime.

Long ages ere the midnight choir
  That sweet momentous message bore;
Isaiah said with tongue of fire,
  That nations should learn war no more.

Their weapons beaten out and changed
  To implements for bough and sod;
Then man no longer strife estranged
  Might walk within the light of God.

Yet after crimson lapse of years,
  Fringed by the so-called Christian reign;
With smoke, flame, flood and quenchless tears
  All unfulfilled the words remain.

To-day there is no nation ripe;
  Yet, there are workers tried and true
Who strive with zeal of every type
  The vast millennial work to do.

Yea, they who in the name of Peace
  Bring pruning-hooks, and plough and bell,
Would see the Bethlehem light increase
  O'er fields of snow-white asphodel.

For needy sufferers that abide .
  Would bid rich ambient harvests wave,
And thus remember side by side
  The home of life and soldier's grave.

Oh, who of all the motely line
  That thither crowd, shall know or feel
The import of the Day-Dawn Shrine
  Whose incense would the nations heal?

Or who will prize the wedge of worth,
  The ploughshare fashioned from the swords,
That shall upturn the glad new earth,
  When Christians own, it is the Lord's?

The pruning-hooks must thought prepare,
  Strong as the cedars of the hill,
Till growth of wisdom all can share,
  In fruitage of parental will.

Yea, they must cut the deadly bane,
  The branches of the strange wild vine,
Till earth can bear on every plane
  Fair clusters, dropping heavenly wine.

When Christians turn from compromise
  To their own law with peace agleam,
This war-cursed earth will realize,
  The angel's song, and prophets' dream.

"AT LAST."

TO JOHN G. WHITTIER, FRIEND AND POET.

ENTERED at last "the humble door" and mansions blest,
"The sheltering shade" and calm retreat from earth's unrest.

And found beside the silvery tide where strivings cease,
The "green expansions," of eternal love and peace.
In strains seraphic heard "the new and holy song,"
And "'neath the healing trees," oh, may thy rest be long.

The soulful lays of by-gone years remain to bless;
Sweet benediction of thy life of righteousness.

O poet-heart! through eons past thy mould was cast,
In full perfection's glory wrought to shine at last.

The star of heavenly poesy, the peerless gem,
That glistens in the world's immortal diadem.

BRYANT.

LONG hushed the voice that tuned the hymns of praise;
  Folded the hands that touched the lyre of song;
  The heart that burned with inspiration strong
Beats now to rhythm of immortal lays.
His was the giant's strength of earlier days,
  He shared the joys and sorrows of life's throng,
  And, battling bravely 'gainst the tide of wrong
He strove to lead mankind in perfect ways.
Across his sunset gleamed the bars of gold,
  And purple fringed was every changing cloud
  That wove for him the royal, kindly shroud,
That wrapped his noble form within its fold.
  A garland fair all nature for him weaves
  While tribute true his memory receives.

HAZEL BLOSSOMS.

IT was but yesterday, on woodlands wild
    The sweet brier twined its strong and thorny stem
    With leaves of green, and set its blushing gem
Of pink, where fell the shades that day beguiled
And early sunbursts where the morning smiled.
    But now, when brown leaves skirt the forest's hem,
    The hazel wears its tawny diadem,
And follows on, a lonely pilgrim child.
Again its time to bloom will come and go,
    We may not see it in the lonely way,
But, in that love which bade its gold to blow
    Along the flowerless paths in autumn gray;
We can, like it, though late, a chaplet bring,
And lay upon life's shrine, an offering.

THE DAISIES.

WHEN the sun is bright and warmest,
    When the sky is richest blue,
When the rain-drops come the clearest,
    And the gentlest falls the dew,

Come the lovely little daisies,
    Treasures of the flower god,
Living beauties of the meadow,
    Scattered freely o'er the sod.

See them! fairy queens of nature,
    Wearing crowns of pearl and gold,
Nodding to the balmy zephyr—
    Who their casting would remould?

THE DAISIES.

One might wonder which reflected,
  Earth beneath, or vaulted sky,
Whether daisy-land was mirrored
  Or the star-realm far and high.

But be that all true or fancy,
  We do love the little things,
Everywhere the earth rejoices,
  Every heart with gladness rings.

Little insects kiss their petals,
  Bees hum out their welcome tune,
Bobolinks and birds full many
  Sing the praise of daisy June.

Oft these happy birds so deftly
  Steal their locks of jeweled hair
With which they build, and thatch an awning
  For the wee ones of their care.

O ye graceful little blossoms
  Mid the ripe, red berry vines,
With your faces turned to heaven,
  Where the sun so brightly shines,

Teach us to be free and lowly,
  Teach us how to live and grow,
Tell us by your silent motion,
  Every good thing that you know.

Tell us of the light and shadow,
  Tell us of your hiding place,
Nor forget for one bright summer
  To reveal your wondrous grace.

WHEAT.

SOFT golden billows on the sunny plain,
    Now ebbing, and now flowing like a tide,
Or resting on the sloping mountain side.
Now singing to the patter of the rain,
Now whispering of heaven's fair domain,
    Where dwelleth rarest beauty far and wide;
Riches far more than gold within thee hide.
Thou swaying, whispering, singing golden grain;
For thee our hearts are filled with gratitude,
    And thou art found in all the haunts of men,
        Making the circle of the earth complete.
We look on thee as God's beatitude,
    The universal manna come again;
        The Father sends His blessing on the wheat.

A HAPPY MOOD.

I WOULD laugh with the rippling rivulet,
    I would join in the bird's glad tune,
Like dews distill doth joy upfill
    These sunny airs of June.

O, bliss of unbounded loveliness!
    What charms hath nature wrought,
My fancies fly with the clouds on high,
    Freighted with joyous thought.

The flowerets wave in rhythmic time
    And song fills the balmy air;
E'en the forest trees whisper matinees,
    As soft as an angel's prayer.

I fancy I hear the grasses rise
    On the wing of the solar ray;
While the budlets ope to a wider scope,
    In the fresh, free light of day.

My heart is glad in this vernal time,
   For music and joy are here;
New gifts arise like sweet surprise
   As if from a fairy sphere.

And another thought wells up within,
   As my eyes new beauties see,
With wisdom fraught, are all things wrought
   O Infinite Deity.

THE MEADOW-LARK.

OUT in the fields where like billows of gold,
   The harvests now swells and ebbs like the sea,
Where the bright brook in its merriest glee
Laughingly plays with the pebbles that hold
The mysteries told to the muses of old
   Lights the glad lark on the grasses so free,
   While swinging and singing so cheerily
Its musical notes that can not be told.
Oft, happy bird, have we heard thy glad tune
   So charmingly sung, while breezes at play
Kept time to thy song each fair day at noon,
   While through the windharp the branches would say
"All nature is joyous while yet it is June,
   But soon 'twill depart with its sweet roundelay."

GOD IS EVERYWHERE.

IN breast of earth what wondrous treasures lie!
   What affluence of beauty and delight!
   And how man seeks them with his mind and might.
Deep beds of gems, entrancing to the eye;
Diamonds whose brilliance no glitter can outvie,
   And rubies glowing with a crimson light,
   Emeralds dipped in spring's new verdure bright,
And sapphires holding azure of the sky.

The topaz blazoned with the golden gleam,
And like the blushes of the morning beam
  Behold the purple amethyst so fair.
Who tinged below this crystal dust? who wrought
These lucid drops? 'Twas *God.* His power and thought
  Are truly manifested everywhere.

PHYSICAL RESURRECTION.

IS this temple—painful prison—
  With its throbbing bolts and bars,
All the dwelling of the spirit,
  When redeemed from earth-made scars?
Shall the body be triumphant?
  Shall this accident of sin
Make or shape the life eternal,
  Clog, or give us power to win?
Shall the humpback, and the cripple,
  And the dwarf, diseased and lame,
Take their bodies, somewhat bettered,
  But essentially the same?
Shall the soul that hid its evil
  In a beauteous form of clay,
Still unchanged and undiscovered,
  Dwell in heaven's unclouded day?
Shall the face that screened, and shaded
  Feelings tender, deep and true,
Mask the soul that toiled and suffered
  For a life and spirit new?
All things in the Lord are perfect;
  Accidents are not of Him;
They belong to earth's confusion,
  To our own preceptions, dim.

If we seek the heavenly portion
  Of the meek in heart, and pure,
God will mark our earnest travel,
  Bless, and make our treasure sure.
Then the soul shall dwell in victory,
  Far above the body's fate,
And be seen undimmed, unshadowed,
  In its true and perfect state.
If we feel the resurrection
  Of the spirit day by day—
Feel the power of God, that bears us
  From earth's elements away—
Shall our thoughts to graveyards center,
  When our loved ones are set free?
Shall we give our loathsome body
  All our wealth of sympathy?
We are called to know the spirit,
  And let dust to dust be given;
While our hearts, with love unfailing,
  Find their kindred hearts in heaven.
O how pure and how exalted,
  Is the faith by which we're taught!
Through the door of Revelation,
  We can "see what God hath wrought."
From the earth he made the mortal;
  But he never marked the place:
Why should we of death's dark portal
  Seek or leave the slightest trace?
Lay my frame in earth's cold bosom,
  When my spirit takes its flight
To that land, where fruit and blossom
  Never suffer frost nor blight;
Not on stone, or sculptured marble,
  Be my memory ever traced;
But from hearts that hold and love me,
  May it *never* be erased.

TEACH ME TO TRUST.

TIME'S golden sands are flowing, one by one,
    Our life its course below will soon have run.
Then whither wilt thou go O soul divine?
Where are the realms of day, in which thou'lt shine?
What subtle power controls thy destiny?
Why wrap thy future life in mystery?
"Enough to know is given," a voice replies,
"Prepare thy soul for heaven," the spirit cries!
Then trusting, I will wait, and hopeful be,
For I know the angel's love rests over me.
And though my path may lead up mountains steep,
The hand that guards all life, will guide my feet.
And I shall learn through faith, that hand is just;
O blessed light of heaven, teach me to trust!

THE MOUNTAIN LAKE.

HOW calm and still this dear lake seems,
    Shut mirror-like from all things rude,
As we are sometimes clasped in dreams,
    Within God's great beatitude.

How rise the towering mountain peaks,
    And on its silvery face look down;
How kindly nature's language speaks
    From lips that crimson flushes crown.

No sound is here to mar the peace,
    Save insect's hum and sweet bird note,
And may these melodies increase;
    God's message comes from every throat.

O would that human hearts might learn,
   The fullsome lessons of His love,
Nor in this world of beauty spurn
   The things we hope to have above.

Behold we make our happy sphere
   Our under-world as well create,
The true elect are now, and here,
   There is no partial hand in fate.

So as we leave this peaceful lake
   Where sun and stars and clouds look in,
We feel a prayer within us wake
   That man may find the way from sin.

That he may find the bridge that spans
   The lake 'twixt God's and human wills,
And trust as calmly in His plans
   As these blue waters trust the hills.

LORD, INCREASE MY FAITH.

LORD, increase my faith,
   That its power may be
A light to shine 'mid darkness,
   A guiding star to me.
Though ebon clouds hang o'er me,
   All lesser lights grow pale,
Yet faith's unfailing glory
   No storm-clouds can assail.

Lord, increase my faith,
   My heavenly guide 'twill be
To lead o'er trackless waters
   Life's foaming, wave-tossed sea.
Oh! what am I without it?
   A wreck upon the strand:
My faith, my sure deliverer,
   Guides with unfaltering hand.

Lord, increase my faith,
  May it gleam a beacon ray,
Pierce through the midnight shadows
  And cheer life's stormy way.
When fierce the tempest rages,
  And high the billows roll,
This fadeless light from heaven
  Reveals the shining goal.

Lord, increase my faith,
  Its power is strong to save,
It fills my heart with courage
  To walk upon the wave.
My star, my guide, my comfort
  I'll follow evermore;
Through it I'll brave all danger
  And reach the heavenly shore.

THE CIRCLE OF THE YEAR.

WITH magic key he comes to ope
  Another realm for us to tread,
He bears a shining lamp of hope;
  A crown of stars is on his head.
All silently the crystal gate
  Swings forward on the field of snow;
We enter as by power of fate
  And list its closing, soft and low.

The bridge of ice that spanned the moat
  Is drawn up on the other side;
For us there is no ferrying boat,
  No backward wave on which to glide;
But footprints even now are seen,
  Time waits not for the tardy feet,
But onward speeds to valleys green,
  To bloom of spring, and summer's heat.

Then to the rainbow of the land,
   The season born of sun and frost,
Whose half-bewildering glories stand
   Like sunset clouds on nature tossed.
But naught alluring can prevail,
   Though flaming leaves his pathway strew,
He presses for the snowy vale
   Where once again his life is new.
And as we contemplate his round,
   And view the miracles that rise,
What lessons for our lives abound!
   What wisdom that should make us wise!

It is for all to work with zeal
   Against the curse that bringeth death;
It is for all to gain and feel
   The power of the Almighty's breath.
That power that made a living soul
   Of him who was a mass of clay,
Is needed like the winds, to roll
   Over humanity to-day.

By revelation's light we read,
   The grand old myths and draw their worth;
See God has spread the Spirit seed
   Through all the nations of the earth.
The deathless seed of love's own vine
   That shall in brotherhood appear,
With clustered branches that entwine
   To give the earth its *new* New Year.

JANUARY.

OLD Time moves on, nor once forgets to bring
    The pearly days, the brightest of the year;
Starred crystals, diamond lights and glowing cheer.
The silent hills, where in the leafy spring
Amid the trees, the birds so sweetly sing,
    Are clad in whiteness which could not appear
    Imperfect in the holy angel sphere;
Resplendent beauty gladdens everything;
The wanton ways of wind and freakish frost
    Perhaps make havoc where the clear sun shone,
But there is pleasure in the flake-cloud tossed,
    And music echoes in the wild wind tone;
And like bright chandeliers from heaven lost
    Seem all the pendant ice in sunlight grown.

FEBRUARY.

THE sun begins to shed a warmer glow,
    Yet piercing winds sweep down with wailing cries,
    Each northern blast the southern breeze defies,
A virgin whiteness wraps the plains below,
The pine-clad hills are drifted high with snow,
    The frozen meadows and the frosty skies,
    The chilling mists which in the valley lies,
Still tells that winter holds its grasp below;
The days begin to lengthen, cheering thought!
    Ah! did I hear a whisper 'neath the snow?
    The stir of seed-buds in their beds below?
The merry tinkle of the stream I caught.
Despite the rimy airs the north winds bring,
We wait the wondrous miracle of Spring.

MARCH.

NOW are the days that winds blow fierce and high,
    Now are the days that quick revolving snows
  Give merry chase to winter as he goes.
Behold the sun's long glowing in the sky,
It heralds beauties coming bye and bye;
  Fair May-times silvery bloom and June's red rose,
  When every brook shall ripple as it flows,
And verdant meadows gladden every eye.
But now Æolus rules the upper air,
  He tosses up the storms, with clouds he plays.
When *his* reign passes, bright Aurora fair
  Will usher in the lovely golden days.
But hasten not away light frisky gales,
The pleasure that you give us never fails.

APRIL.

WITH dripping locks and face with tears bedewed,
    Sweet April comes with calm and passive will,
  To soften earth and gentle dews distil,
Till germs upspring with inner life renewed.
Loud caws the crow, its welcome a prelude
  The mellow notes, that soon o'er vale and hill
  The choristers of nature's choir shall trill
To burst the bonds of wintry solitude.
Anon she smiles, and rends the veil of mist
  That formed in shadows dark around her brow;
Light shades with emerald and amethyst
  The garland earth is weaving for her now;
Bespeaking joy the heart can not resist,
    She rests in beauty 'neath her early vow.

MAY.

THE diamond snow-wreaths from the hills she takes,
    And carpets all the fields with soft green plush,
  With rich embroidery of blossom-blush.
She calls, and hark! the matin choir awakes,
The pearl-shades melt and golden glory breaks.
    She laughs, and happy crystal fountains gush
    Like silvery ribbons through the valley's hush,
And fair her face when mirrored in the lakes.
Upon her warm air-ripples soft flecks play
    As do the mermaids on the ocean's crest;
She swings her censer through the whole glad day—
    Her fragrance-gift is sweetest and the best.
Her sunset smiles, star-fringe and moon-lit gray
    Make her the queen whom all the gods have blest.

JUNE.

FAIR June is here, she has not overslept,
    Or dreamed too long 'neath the magnolia's shade,
  But tripping through the southland everglade,
To northern clime with blithesome spirit stepped.
With cheek of ruddy bloom her youth hath kept,
    Her lips are wreathed in smiles like pearls inlaid,
    She wears a garland of sweet rose-buds made,
And in her path by odorous breezes swept
    The wild flowers nod, and o'er the waving grass
    A welcome murmur seems to gently pass.
The wood-nymphs all in leafy bowers convene,
    A happy chant the songsters swell enmasse,
The hills and vales in gala robes are seen,
    Glad festival for summer's beauteous queen.

JULY.

JUNE roses languish 'neath the summer's flush,
   Red berries shrivel for the lack of rain;
   Yet taller grow the ripening fields of grain
Where rhythmic breezes break the noonday hush.
The sun-kissed cherries deepen now their blush,
   And robin red-breast counts it all his gain,
   Nor boy, nor bird, their appetites restrain,
But share their spoils with mirth and music's gush.
Now clicks the mower through the daisied mead,
   And lowly lies the plumed and seeded grass;
The grazing herds in quiet pastures feed,
And from the flowing brook supply their need;
   Soft shadows o'er the landscape quickly pass,
For clouds, rain-freighted, on their mission speed.

AUGUST.

CALMLY we wait while evening's gate unbars,
   And watch the Virgin beautiful and fair
   Climb noiselessly her temple's mystic stair.
Trained knights guard her around, their scimitars
Are diamond-set, and bear no battle scars,
   No crimson stains, no emblems of despair.
   But hark! her messenger is in the air,
Bearing to earth the edict of the stars;
Kind Nature welcomes the auspicious guest.
   She decks the land with emerald and gold,
   And brings out all her gems to grace the scene,
And while the music floats from east to west,
   She gathers all her treasures manifold
   And sends her compliments to summer's queen.

SEPTEMBER.

GAY-hearted harvester, we know thy worth.
　　The loaded cornucopia of time
　　Lets fall its bounteous blessings on our clime;
When thou in splendor walkest through the earth,
The happy huskers with their songs of mirth,
　　The boys who pluck the fruit to cheerful chime,
　　With wayward notes and merry-making rhyme
Feel life anew.　There is no sign of dearth,
While high in heaven's etheral vault, behold
　　Justice, thy sister, with her starry scales
　　　Weighing with steady hand earth's harvest yield;
And from her mints kind nature brings her gold,
　　Stamped with the true inscription that prevails,
　　　And sends her creditors through wood and field.

OCTOBER.

MOST royal season of the rich, round year!
　　We greet thee with a heart filled full of praise,
　　Nor cease to love thee through thy course of days.
High in the sunlit ether, sweet and clear
The glowing maples' flaming flags appear,
　　And O, the glory of the golden blaze
　　In myriad forms that meets our tireless gaze;
The crown of all things beautiful is here.
O, bright October! fresh with generous zeal,
　　Thy gifts like willing showers fall at our feet,
We take them, but to Him who hears appeal
　　And prayer, we lift our thanks and love most sweet.
They to whose lives, these joys may not reveal
　　Have lost a good that makes true life complete.

NOVEMBER.

NOVEMBER comes upon us unawares,
   His seeming frown has cast the hills in doubt,
  And all the gay lights of the woods are out.
O, not for him the hand the scepter bears,
A jeweled cross is on his breast, he wears
   The crystal rosary, a monk devout,
  With glittering cowl of snow drawn close about;
He offers for the year its dying prayers.
'Tis not with cruel smile he mocks the flowers,
   His is a blessed mandate manifold;
'Tis his to stay their bloom for summer hours
   And bring us blossoms from the winter's cold;
Garlands of frost-work hang above his head,
And diamonds scintillate where he doth tread.

DECEMBER.

LAST but not least dear month, why call thee sad?
   Is it because the blue-winged days are o'er,
  And snow-paved ways have led us to thy door?
The temple of thy grace makes my heart glad.
I love thy long white aisles all crystalled through,
   The holly-room where holy blessings flow,
  And marble altars draped with mistletoe,
All with divinest service rendered new.
I love thy zephyr-harps so low and sweet,
   The fullness of thy organ's richest blast,
Thy "peace, good will to man" in soul replete,
That as thy offering angel choirs repeat.
   And as a friend when all the rest are past,
     I love thee, dearest month, though thou art last.

YEAR OF LIFE.

SHADOWS short'ning by the way,
    Shadows length'ning out again,
And we say 'tis early day,
    And we say the night is then.

Dewy violets in the grass,
    Flowing sands are moving slow,
By the measured hour-glass,
    All the flowers of childhood blow.

Greenness climbing on the wall,
    Hanging scarlet clusters out,
Summer brooding over all
    Flings her jewels round about.

Spotless lily-cups with tears,
    Through the summer days are wrought,
Joy drops for the early years,
    Tears for those with sorrow frought.

Changed the flush of summer sky,
    Golden light and silvery mist,
Now the distant mountains lie
    In a haze of amethyst.

Golden-rod upon the hill,
    Aster buds to purple blown,
Gentian glories now distill,
    Hazels waiting sad and lone.

Changing woods 'neath autumn's touch,
    Russett green and amber-massed,
Age glows in the wealth of such,
    And life's sands are flowing fast.

Frost-work 'neath the cold moonbeams,
   Flakes, and pearls, and clear starlight,
Purified the winter seems
   In its robe of changeless white.

Crimson roses in their bloom,
   Climbing over childhood's door,
Snowy roses on the tomb,
   And we say time is no more.

THE CROWS' LECTURE.

FOR THE CHILDREN.

THE day was oppressive the noontime was passed,
   And silence that spell-bound the leaves of the trees
Slipped down to the glen where blue shadows were cast
   And closed with her fingers the lips of the breeze.
Just then in the Northwoods a clamor I heard,
   'Twas from a convention of crows,
That seemed to be talking of something absurd,
   Or largely dilating on woes.
They all spoke at once, " 'tis the natural way
   For birds and for mortals " I thought;
"Till each one's importance has had some display
   No order or peace can be wrought."
And yet of their jargon I nothing could know,
   Though each shouted loudly her *caws*,
Till one with the famous "sweet voice of a crow"
   Came forth to elicit applause.
She spoke of the hardships they had to pass through,
   Of strings, traps and guns out of sight,
And then such a picture of *Scare-Crows* she drew
   That they all screamed aloud with affright.

She spoke of the frail, trembling Dove with the leaf
    When waves sought in vain for a shore,
And declared that the Raven had found the first reef
    And "returned to the ark nevermore."
She went on still further for ancestral good,
    And pleasantly over she told
How the Lord sent the Raven to carry out food
    To Elijah the Prophet of old.
She said, "It is written, He heareth the cries,
And the needs of the hungry young Raven supplies;"
Then scornfully added, "It is my opinion
That must have occurred before man had dominion.
E'er Adam in Eden departed from law,
His soul had a knowledge of all that he saw;
And when for renewal each bird and beast came,
Divining its nature, he gave it a name.
But man the usurper, remorseless, severe,
What black sins havè filled up his lengthened career;
God's most gentle creatures now timid and wild
Instinctively shrink from the steps of a child.
Each brave, noble beast is ferocious and shy,
Yet man with his cruelty these can outvie.
But now to return to our own special state,
Some items of interest I'll strive to relate.
Our spotless complexion is subject of talk,
And prejudice spurns it in every walk,
The foot too, whose beauty we know nothing lacks
Has man's hideous scrawling compared to its tracks.
Though we are not strong, we're ingenious we know;
Just think of the tale of the Pitcher and Crow,
The Pitcher had water, the Crow could not get it,
In vain were her efforts to turn or upset it.
She filled it with pebbles and soon at the brink
The cool bubbling waters afforded her drink,
We find her condemned for the wonderful skill
That picks out the worm from the corn-planted hill.
For she, unlike humming-bird, squirrel or bee,
Must not gather food from the field or the tree.

To illustrate poverty man does not know
A more fitting maxim than 'Poor as a crow.'
And yet I have thought that in some kind of weathers,
He might have been richer in garments of feathers.
But he is no judge of how pleasant they are,
He so seldom wears them except over tar.
Unprincipled foxes have stolen our cheese
And left us to chant the unmusical keys.
When we shall have sustenance earth shall resound
With our unceasing melody all the year round,
And e'er we accomplish this one wished for thing
'Tis moved in Convention that each one shall sing.
And when we obtain all the 'Rights' that we know
'Twill be demonstrated a Crow is a Crow."
The speaker concluded; the burst of applause
Exceeded in volume man's shouts and hurrahs.
And while they dispersed o'er the brow of the hill,
Their voices continued most vigorously shrill.
Two things they accomplish at once it appears,
They both shock the "glottis" and my hapless ears.
As in the far distance died out every sound,
I woke from my revery long and profound.
'Twas Fancy interpreted all that I heard
And put into form the wild speech of the bird,
But my heart felt within a deep pity arise
For the black speck that oft pierced the cold leaden skies;
When I've sat in peace at a bountiful meal
I've seen the poor Crow through the wild tempest reel,
And thought when with mankind we live in true peace,
The terror of us will in wild creatures cease.
And they'll come in their need to the grain-barn and mill,
Confidingly seek e'en the dwelling door-sill;
And from our abundance we nothing shall miss,
But we'll find in our spirits a new source of bliss;
For God's love will be, as an unfailing fountain,
When none shall bring fear into His holy mountain.

CONTENTMENT.

HERDS in the full rich pasture lying
   'Neath the oak tree's shade;
Flocks of white doves homeward hieing
   Where their nests are made.

Lambs on the verdant hillside bleating,
   When the sheep are shorn;
Bees in the ruddy clover meeting,
   In the dewy morn.

Birds when the springtime work's completed,
   In the old elm tree,
Happy songs so oft repeated,
   Thrill with melody.

Squirrels out on a nut excursion,
   Winter's store to fill;
Swallows out for a day's diversion
   Over vale and hill.

Buzz of insects ceaseless winging,
   Crickets on the hearth;
Harvest locusts gaily singing,
   Old-time songs of mirth.

Meadows trimmed with bright eyed daisies
   Tossing white wreathed heads;
Full plumed fields of wheaten mazes
   Bound in golden threads.

Ripening ears in tall corn hiding,
   Wrapped in silken fold;
Silvery streams by waysides gliding
   Gladdening wood and wold.

Earth with life and beauty teeming,
   Joy and peace combine,
Pulsing warm, in day-tide dreaming,
   Sweet content enshrine.

Man alone through turmoil pressing
   Never seems at rest,
And though placed in midst of blessing
   Always seems unblest.

THE BIRD LEGISLATOR.

I LOVE the dear birds O, ever so well
   Indeed I could never begin to tell
The feeling of pleasure upfilling me
Whenever I think of them, hear or see.

I never had thought that birds could do wrong,
I thought their lives were lives of sweet song,
That flitting about 'mid beauty and light,
Of course they couldn't do else but right.

But I changed my mind one bright May day,
Was filled with astonishment I must say,
To see what seemed like a selfish thought
In a tiny bird brain well outwrought.

The air was clear and the breezes warm,
And I sat in the midst of the happy calm
Watching a bird on the telephone pole
Making best friends with an oriole.

He was just the shade of a bit of blue sky,
The color that always so pleases my eye,
I thought that a bird so daintily dressed
Was as pretty a thing as the earth possessed.

But he sat in his wonted place too *long*,
And herein consisted his notable *wrong*,
While the wee lady strove with all her might
To make a home for the oncoming night.

I thought of the men, the "conference" men,
Who sat in converse from now till then;

How the women could toil in the self-same hall
Hanging new paper all over the wall,

They could stretch, pull and strain the live long day,
"Such work was easy," the men, said they,
"But the women are far too weak and fair
To *sit* and *speak* in conference *there*."

Just so this bird sat perched, proud and prim,
The trouble of labor came not to him,
Chatting as ever all men love to do
With never a sign of once getting through,

At the same time watching with calm content
The frail lady bird as she came and went
Carrying straws three times her length—
But the stronger bird *conserved his strength*.

Perhaps he was wise as most wise men are,
But he gave to the woman her rights too far,
Her rights as designer and work the whole,
But the *funds* he kept under his own control.

Although much engaged in the "suffrage cause"
He still thought it better to make up the laws,
To call in all parties, the martin and crow,
Robin and sparrow—all men folks you know,

And handle life's subjects in various ways;
Equality, justice, and length of work days;
Such things are too rough for the feminine brain,
So they do this hard work lest the women complain.

He knew he was kind and generous too,
I knew what he thought, I could see him right through,
But I wished that lady would turn her about
And turn *him within* and *she rest without*.

I wished all the weak sex would rise in a mass,
And all politicians were sent out to grass,
Until they could work with honest good wills,
More with their *claws* and *less* with their *bills*.

GUEST-ANGEL.

MAKE Truth the pure guest-angel of thy heart,
   Nor walk from her in all life's ways apart,
Thy chamber halls she will adorn with grace,
And give each ornament a fitting place.

Choose well thy words from out her volume rare,
Whose shining pages no dark symbols bear,
Chaste and refined, clear as a crystal sea
From gross exaggeration wholly free.

If all thy motives to her court appeal,
Then shall each act be stamped with heaven's seal,
And no deep blot life's record e'er shall mar,
Or from angelic peace thy soul debar.

Vain imagery of every worldly charm,
That's framed to please, yet poison holds to harm,
Flees from the glorious presence of her face,
The good and true alone win her embrace.

Where'er thy footsteps tend, be this thy prayer,
"O Guardian Spirit! take me 'neath thy care,
And let no shadow intercept thy light,
That leadeth ever in the path of right."

If mirth rise high on pleasure's airy wing,
Or in thy heart should pain and sorrow spring,
Keep by thy side the safeguard of thy youth,
This bright *guest-angel,* beauteous heaven-born *Truth.*

TRUTH.

I'LL wear the shield of truth and self-control,
   That careless words that fall like arrow's dart,
     May never harm my soul.
Then sweetly I can render good for ill,
And love shall reach and soothe the erring heart,
     And echo peace—good will.

REVERENCE.

I DEEM myself but some poor lifeless clod
   Without a sense of homage for the good;
   'Twere better e'en to bow to stone or wood
Than have no inner consciousness of God.
As breath of spring upon earth's frozen sod
   Wakes and quickens from her somber mood,
   And gladdens e'en the dreariest solitude,
Where grasses wave and beauteous flowers nod;
So stir the living forces of the soul,
   And dormant powers to active service rise,
When love infinite holds supreme control
   And all unfolding life intensifies;
   Then we behold with truth and glad surprise
That reverence *deep* all goodness underlies.

SOLEMN THOUGHTS.

HOW lengthened seems each passing year
   As memory spreads her pictures clear,
And brings again our loved ones near
   From the celestial shore.
We would not wish them to remain
To undergo earth's grief and pain,
Yet joy to know they come again
   To greet us as before.

Our mortal life is fleeting fast,
Time's pilgrimage will soon be past,
Will we regret to leave at last
   This tenement of clay?
Yet some at thought of death have fear,
They dread its presence drawing near,
Terrestrial joys to them seem dear,
   No future hope have they.

Those who have comforts shared below,
And felt not pangs of want and woe,
Care not another state to know,
    Nor seek for purer bliss.
Yet when the final change they meet,
They find their heaven is incomplete,
For barren paths await their feet,
    As they have walked amiss.

The poor, the lowly and despised,
Who selfish loves have sacrificed,
Rejoice in bowers emparadised
    And virtue's ways pursue.
Adorned with flowers that bloom through prayer,
The fruits of blessing grown by care,
These shall the upright ever share,
    Whose souls are pure and true.

The Master, by love's impulse led,
The naked clothed, the hungry fed,
Yet had not where to lay his head
    In Palestine's fair land.
The mount he sought to pray and fast,
Till, trials and temptations past,
Truth's golden heights he gained at last,
    The home where victors stand.

Though low is brought our nature proud,
And deepest griefs our way enshroud,
A silver lining hath the cloud
    That ofttimes veils the goal.
We shrink because of little faith,
The change to life we think is death,
Yet, know the grave no triumph hath,
    O'er the immortal soul.

IMMORTALITY.

IS future life a shadowy dream,
  A myth that puzzles still the brain?
Or, closely folded as a ream
  Of unwrit leaves, without a stain?
Closed volume to material sense,
  That governs with imperial rod,
And brings the meager recompense
  A final home beneath the sod?
* * * The soul recoils; a secret spark
  Flames with the light of endless day;
No longer veiled in dungeon dark,
  Or screened by perishable clay,
It rises up on Hope's bright wing
Of immortality to sing.

UNBORN POETRY.

"There is a river that makes glad the city of our God."

PASSING over the river is not to die
  With outstretched limbs in state to lie,
For as a man thinketh, so is he,
In time or in eternity.

To die is a change that none forego,
The peasant, the king, the friend and foe,
Go hastening on in weal and woe,
To the land of ghosts which none may know.

Know as we know the things of earth,
In manhood, youth, and back to birth.
Mystery of mysteries from the beginning!
Why do we live? love? Why keep on sinning?
Where did we come from? Whither go we,
Men, women, and children, bond and free?

To die is not to pass over the river,
For still we live, live on forever,
But there is a river that's never dry
That none may pass over until they die,
Die to the life that reproduces
The race of man without abuses.

The end has come, the summer has ended,
The harvester death, with life is blended,
Life—eternal life, from the throne of God,
The Lamb was the first, the first who trod
The banks of that river—the river of God.

LOOK UPWARD.

LOOK upward, e'en tho' trials compass thee
    And clouds hang o'er the path thy feet must tread,
  And doubts and fears disturb thy heart with dread,
O, ever trust, and watchful, humble be,
And from temptation thou wilt yet be free ;
    By waters calm and sweet thou wilt be led,
    Thou wilt have living joy in sorrow's stead,
And hope will gladden thee continually.
All hearts must know vexation, pain and grief,
    All feet must walk the valley dark and drear,
But thro' God's mercy cometh sweet relief,
    His love hath power to banish every fear ;
Look upward then, and thou wilt yet behold,
The fadeless, golden light of heaven unfold.

BEAUTIFUL DAY.

NIGHT'S silvery stars melt in morning's soft blushes,
    Her dark spectral shadows glide noiseless away,
While nature, enwrapped in her deep silent hushes,
    Awakes to the call of the beautiful day.

The light-hearted songsters mount upward in gladness,
  And trill their sweet music all blithesome and gay;
What heart could respond with a feeling of sadness?
  For joy crowns the beautiful, beautiful day!

The sun gilds the crest of the forest-clad mountain,
  And brightens the vale where the early mist lay,
From woodland and meadow, from streamlet and fountain,
  Come voices of welcome to beautiful day!

From flowers, the honey-dew fragrance ascending
  Is wafted along by the breezes at play;
Creations of beauty around us are blending
  In praise of the glory of beautiful day!

We gratefully share of life's bounties external,
  Which come like a day-dream, nor yet come to stay;
But still look beyond to that region supernal,
  Where beameth forever a beautiful day!

The forms we are wearing, the scenes we're beholding,
  Are subject to change and the blight of decay;
But germs of the spirit, God's light is unfolding,
  To bloom in eternity's beautiful day.

SUNRISE.

THE night hath furled its shadows, from on high
  The sun pours gladness over plain and hill;
  The trembling mists that distant valleys fill
Are luminous with light, across the sky
Like phantom ships, white-winged they onward fly.
  A breath of fragrance, glint of dew, a trill
  From yonder tree; a burst of joy, a thrill,
Her garment's hem we touch as Morn goes by.

O fair, sweet Morn that sunrise always brings !
   Thy gleaming mantle holds a hope impearled ;
Though sorrow spreads her dark and hovering wings,
   We wait to see thy curtains bright unfurled.
For out of night the laughing morning springs,
   And there is sunrise somewhere round the world.

DAY DAWN.

IN the still hour of the morning
   E're the light began to shine,
When the blush-rose of the dawning
   Fluttered to the silvery line ;
When the silvery line expanded
   Changing to a fan of gold,
And the rising mists were stranded
   As the glory upward rolled ;
Woke I then from peaceful slumber
   To review a darkened earth,
With its burdens that encumber,
   With its ignorance and dearth.
Custom, creed and superstition
   Form the veil of every land,
Usurpation's Inquisition
   Works below to starve and brand.
There the countless, toiling masses
   Never see with normal sight,
Life, the nightmare, as it passes
   Brings them only pain and blight.
To support the torturing errors
   That their hearts are forced to know,
War, with all its blackening terrors
   Fill them with appalling woe.
There are noble souls contending
   With the monsters of the world,
Scaling high, and low descending,
   Wheresoe'er the serpent's curled.

But, I said, O vain devotion,
   What will all the effort do?
Will the reeds beside the ocean
   Change its rolling or its hue?
'Twas a thought of earthly reason
   Unillumined by the light;
'Twas a doubt, and doubt is treason
   To the sacred cause of right.
Quick reproof my heart was taking,
   When a vision o'er it came,
Faith, that like the day when breaking
   Flushed it with a holy flame.
And I saw, not trembling grasses,
   But the angel world of thought
Bending down to reach the masses
   Through the minds that it had taught.
They will tear the veil asunder,
   They will rend it thread by thread,
Show the tangled warp of plunder
   On which scenes of blood are spread.
They commissioned, strong, indignant,
   That false covering will destroy,
And declare that God benignant
   Made this world for peace and joy.
God's estate, in fair division
   To his children doth belong,
Might has cancelled His decision,
   Brutal might that fights for wrong.
But an angel power is coming
   Like the billows of the sea,
Hark! the waves are softly humming
   Snatches of a symphony;
When the broken strains are blended,
   And the music is complete,
War and darkness shall be ended,
   Light and harmony shall meet.
When the lands of every nation
   To the people are secure,

Earth shall know a new salvation,
   And her peace will then be sure.
To this end O let us labor;
   Every one can take a part,
Love to God and to our neighbor
   Forms the bond of every heart.
O, a mighty day is breaking;
   We must hail its light, and grow,
Earth and heaven alike are shaking,
   Only truth can safety know.
Light alone the truth will cherish,
   And expand its latent bloom,
But the rankling wrong shall perish,
   Day dawn ushers in its doom.

NIGHT FALLETH.

NIGHT falleth, gently falleth,
   And another precious day
Swiftly as on wings in silence
   From my life is borne away.

Night falleth, gently falleth,
   And my spirit bendeth low,
'Mid pulsating light and shadow,
   'Neath the stars' mysterious glow.

Day with tent-like curtain covers
   From our gaze the starry dome,
While her joyous light discovers
   Beauty in our earthly home.

But the night writes wondrous stories
   On the clear scroll of the sky,
Yet but half reveals the glories
   That beyond our fancies lie.

Like a child beside the ocean
    Watching waves that gently flow,
With a tender, deep emotion
    My stilled spirit bendeth low.

IN THE MOONLIGHT.

SWEET time! pure inspiration fills the soul
    When tender hushes still the noisy land,
    And silent blessings come from God's own hand.
O, happy then if free from sin's control
We lift our hearts, and hear as onward roll
    The love-songs of the spheres so full and grand
    And well their sacred meaning understand,
All, all may hear, e'en to the icy pole.
O happy moonlight time! when God reveals
    His light, and listens to our pleading thought,
When holiness of life our own life feels,
    And gains the great help it has often sought.
Each silvery beam with magic power unseals
    A hidden truth; who wills to learn, is taught.

LAND OF OUR DREAMS.

ACROSS the gulf of terrors thou didst leap
    Fawn like, and safely gained the better side,
    And found more genial life beyond the tide
Where sylvan vales lie sweetly calm and deep,
And wood-clad hills eternal silence keep;
    Where gentle streams with rippling music glide
    And fragrant flowers bloom ever at their side,
While odorous gales from spicy islands sweep.
Such is the land of all our earthly dreams,
    When restless passions sleep to wake no more,
And though at times heaven's radiance o'er us gleams
    Yet patient wait we till the race is o'er,
And well we've wrought the task that easier seems,
    While faith and hope light up the distant shore.

WAKING THOUGHTS.

THE rosy light of morning broke
   From a cerulean sky;
And nature from her dreams awoke
   To tell the dawn was nigh.
And I awoke, as if from dreams,
   Thus did my heart aspire,
To fill the day with sunny gleams
   Of noble, true desire.

And with an earnest soul and will
   I rose to meet the day,
Its many duties to fulfill
   That cumber us alway,
But ere a few short hours were spent,
   My plans — forgotten, all, —
On other missions too intent,
   My lips let harsh words fall.

O life's wasted, wasted power
   Of aspirations vast,
That thrilled my soul at morning's hour
   To bless ere day was past.
O lofty thoughts! resolves that burned
   Within a living flame;
Those vital fires to ashes turned
   From whence no brightness came.

O thoughtless words! O idle thought!
   Yea, weak and erring will;
Life's misspent hours that should be fraught
   With good instead of ill.
And as I viewed by sunset light,
   My failure and defeat
I rose with more encouraged might
   Life's many foes to meet.

New experience to us opes,
 Suffering brings us joy,
And on the ashes of our hopes
 We build to God's employ.
But hark! I hear a soft voice speak,
 Which bids me bravely bear,
And while my erring heart is weak,
 I'll seek the strength of prayer.

---✠---

THE WAR IN EGYPT.

1884.

O CHRISTIAN lands, where is your creed,
 And where your Guide "without a stain?"
Down thro' the ages wars of greed,
 Huge fiery serpents form a chain.

E'en now they hiss their sulphurous smoke
 On ancient Egypt's withered face,
She bowed beneath the iron yoke,
 Wrought at the forge of your disgrace.

The blood is streaming from her breast,
 And o'er her tattered garments spread,
But ah! its sluggish tide is pressed
 On the invaders pallid dead.

Is there no *nation* in the world
 That can redeem the Christian name
And come with banner white unfurled
 And fearless left the cry "shame!"

In social life they ostracize
 The brigand with his murderous trade;
But *nations* among nations rise,
 The more their slaughtering hosts invade.

And still they say, "Thy will be done,"
  With pious cant and soulless care;
E'en while the ponderous mocking gun,
  Is belching hell above that prayer.

O England! with thy royal church,
  In purple clad and drunk with gore;
What crimes upon thy altar perch,
  What sorrows cluster round thy shore!

Yet thou unblushingly, canst plot
  Thy hideous schemes in Freedom's name,
Without a mar, a shade, or blot
  Upon thy honor, faith or fame.

Yea, loud thy Parliamentary Halls
  Resound with sophistries for wrong,
While proud Westminster's hoary walls,
  Repeat their counterpart in song.

Earth has not one whole Christian land
  Whose scathing voice might censure thee;
But here and there, a heart or band
  Abhors thy inhumanity,

And scorns thy pagan rites, that bless
  The fiend work of "victorious arms,"
That make the maelstrom of distress
  The torturing depths of all that harms.

And shall that scattered few not speak,
  As witnesses and council brave?
Who dare defend the poor and weak,
  Who can proclaim the powers that save?

The breath of God is in the Spring,
  It stills the storm, it melts the snow,
It makes the woods with gladness ring,
  The blossoms breathe, the sunshine glow.

God give us energy and zeal,
  The brave self-sacrifice and hope;
The ardor that the warriors feel,
  And we with every wrong can cope.

SHAKER HOMES.

O, happy homes like Eden-gardens fair,
  Whose inmates are contented,
Whose lives are free from worldly strife and care,
  By love's pure bond cemented.
The lust of power, and sordid greed of gain
  Rule not with sway of might,
They seek not pleasures that are false and vain,
  But follow truth and right.

While direful woes encompass land and sea,
  And trouble fills life's measure,
A restful heaven in these homes I see
  When souls seek heavenly treasure.
From whence come bitter wail and sad unrest,
  The war of words and strike of hands?
From sway of human passions all unblest,
  And sin's enthralling bands.

This changeless law can never be repealed,
  " Men reap just what they sow,"
From tares and thistles sown, life's field
  Will tares and thistles grow.
Crime stalks abroad, though churches raise
  Their steeples to the sky,
And well paid preachers thank and praise
  The God who rules on high.

They call Him "Master," yet they follow not
  The steps of Him who came
"To seek and save," nor yet the poor forgot
  Who called upon His name.

His work was wrought through noble sacrifice,
    For love of truth and good,
And on the basis of His life shall rise
    The human brotherhood.

O, sweet communion of the pure and just,
    Who equal blessings share,
Where love returns confiding love and trust,
    And all life's burdens bear.
Where those who occupy the highest place,
    God's precious gifts dispense,
And gladly minister His saving grace,
    Nor seek a recompense.

Such are my people, and their dwelling place
    Is an elysium blest,
Where all who from their spirits sin efface
    Shall find sweet peace and rest.
Ye witnesses of truth who wrong condemn
    And righteous laws obey,
As prophets of the New Jerusalem
    Proclaim the living way.

CHRISTMAS DAY, 1886.

WORDS SPOKEN BY OUR BELOVED MOTHER, ANTOINETTE DOOLITTLE.

THE angels sweetly called unto our spirits,
    And gratefully we sought the house of prayer,
In union with our loving gospel kindred,
    And longed to feel a heavenly solace there.

Before the holy shrine of true devotion,
    On bended knees, with reverent hearts, we poured
Strong supplication, through our soul's deep yearnings,
    And humbly sought the blessing of the Lord.

The day indeed seemed sacred in appointment,
  The name and blessed life of Christ are dear,
Appearing in their grand and glorious meaning
  In lives of all true Christians through the year.

And while assembled in that hour of worship,
  The doors of heaven seemed to stand ajar,
The flood-gates of the sea of life were opened,
  And tide waves flowed without a check or bar.

But best of all that met our *outward* vision,
  Our loved and tender shepherdess was there,
To comfort those whom she long years had cherished—
  Encourage those who but lately felt her care.

Though all unable for the great exertion,
  She rose up calmly in her place, and said:
"I bless the word of God, when truly spoken,
  It is unto my soul as drink and bread.

"You, who have climbed the rugged mountain bravely,
  And forded manfully the river's tide,
Give thanks to God, still trusting in that power,
  That oft has been your shield, your stay, your guide.

"Continue in the blessed work assigned you,
  And kindly help the youthful and the weak;
Hold out the loving hand to those who falter,
  Give nourishment and aid to those who seek.

"You, who have just begun the upward journey,
  Take love, and hope and courage by the way,
And every step you take will be more easy,
  The cross and yoke will lighten every day.

"We'll make this day a season of rejoicing,
  Nor idly spend it as a feasting time,
But fill its hours with prayer and soulful feelings,
  With loving deeds and union gifts divine.

" 'Twere better if the world would teach their children
  The story of the true anointing Christ,
The Holy One of Israel, the Redeemer,
  Than fill their minds with joys by folly priced.

"Then let us all rejoice as one together,
  And be as humble children in the Lord;
Sincere in heart, and true in our aspirings,
  The chosen ones, who have their full reward."

"WE RISE TO CALL HER BLESSED."

In the memory of Eldress Antoinette Doolittle of the North Family of Shakers, who passed to spirit life December 31, 1886. Over sixty years of her earth life she spent in the Order, nearly fifty of which she bore a heavy burden both in temporal and spiritual things. She was widely known as a speaker and writer, and was universally respected by the public, and beloved by all who personally knew her. For three years she was editress of the first dual paper ever published, called "The Shaker and Shakeress," and in 1880, by request, wrote her autobiography, giving an interesting account of her early life previous to her becoming a member of the Society, also an outline of her life and experience among the Shakers.

———✠———

A MOTHER'S LOVE.

WHILE sitting in communion blest
    With kindred friends and parents dear,
Upon my spirit was impressed
    A gift to cherish and revere.

A Heavenly Mother's tender love;
    The life and center of our home,
That shelters as with wings of dove,
    All hearts who 'neath her influence come.

Each child this love so constant shares,
    Though oft it changes form and guise;
The needed gift our Mother bears
    With patient heart and purpose wise.

It is the power that causeth grief,
    Repentance deep and true for sin;
That brings the spirit sweet relief,
    And lights the lamp of hope within.

It is the two-edged sword that wounds,
    And then the balm that soothes and heals;
It is the fire that sin consumes,
    And light that endless life reveals.

It is the hand that smites with death
    Those elements which are of earth;
And then becomes the living breath
    To souls who find angelic birth.

It sometimes comes like thunder peals,
    To waken slumbering souls to life,
And oft like angel music steals,
    To calm the troubled waves of strife.

And when we pass through battle heat,
    Through surging tides or valleys dark,
This gift will stay and guide our feet,
    And point us to the shining mark.

O, boundless is its power for good,
    United with a Father's grace,
This precious love of Motherhood
    Will prove a saviour of the race.

BLESS AND CURSE NOT.

A FLOWING streamlet gushed from rocky bed
    And spread its crystal treasures far and wide ;
Each plant and floweret on its mossy side
Grew bright and vernal, for each blessing shed
A purer fragrance, and in their sweet way said,
    O heart of man, in life's glad ways abide
    And let not selfishness thy jewels hide,
But give and in love's peaceful paths be led.
The barren tree, it cumbereth the ground,
    The heart unfruitful, void of precious gifts
That blesses not, but scatters hate around
    Is dead to all the inner soul uplifts.
O, let us all in love and grace abound,
    And walk in light that every dark cloud rifts.

GIFT OF FRIENDSHIP.

SNOWY chalice filled with nectar sweetness,
    Fragrant leaves its spotless heart unfold,
Spicy bloom that circles in completeness
    The rare and delicate bouquet I hold.

Gift of friendship, lovely as the giver,
    Clustered emblems in full beauty wrought,
Unexpressed, the joy of the receiver
    Flows to thee from purest springs of thought.

Pure as lily-cup our hearts be ever,
    Fresh as leaves in union intertwined,
Rich as purple bloom that fadeth never,
    These in harmony our souls shall bind.

Thanks for love exhaled from each fair token,
  Thanks for blessings strewn along my way ;
To keep the bond of unity unbroken,
  Be this my care and effort every day.

──✠──

GO FIND-THY FRIENDS.

COMPLAIN not that thy life is void of friends,
  Be but a friend thyself, and thou wilt find
The amplest means toward the longed for ends,
  Which thine to every other heart will bind.

The master sculptor, Michael Angelo,
  Could see the finished statue in a block
Of roughest marble, and the slow
  And patient hand the portal could unlock

Which hid the vision from all other eyes.
  The poet sees in words the perfect form
That fills his soul with throbbing and surprise,
  And rouses him as thunder wakes the storm

To bring his angel out in finished verse.
  The wrapt musician, all his soul aglow
With melody, longs only to rehearse
  The harmonies that saints and seraphs know,

And shows his soul's bright angel unto men.
  A friend is more than statue, verse or song,
Is more than any joy within our ken,
  Or rapture which to mortals may belong.

Despair not then, but through the cold and heat
  Of wild adversity seek thine ideal
Within the hearts of men, and thou wilt meet
  In shining form the angel of the real.

Wilt find thy friends as genuine and pure,
    Yea, truer than a fancy of the mind
Worked into perfect mold from miniature,
    According as the Master Will designed.

Thy true friends found, make then thyself as one
    Who consecrates all service willingly,
And greater fame hath never master won
    Than that which waits to place a crown on thee.

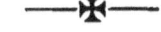

LANGUAGE.

O POWER of speech! thou wondrous gift to man,
    Thou potent messenger of good or ill,
    With joy or sorrow thou the heart dost fill,
Bring'st peace or discord to the social clan.
The mind may fields of knowledge amply scan,
    But were it not for thy inventive skill
    That stirs with eloquence the listless will,
How vain and futile were each mental plan.
    Ah, may this lesson, wisdom to us teach,
Through his creation, man excels the brute;
    This glorious gift, this lofty power of speech,
Lifts him above God's creatures strangely mute;
    Destines to lofty heights he yet shall reach,
Where language bears its richest, sweetest fruit.

FUNERAL DAY.

A TRIBUTE TO THE MEMORY OF PRESIDENT GARFIELD.

RING myriad bells your requiem chimes to-day
  Ere unto dust our martyred dead we lay,
Tell all the world before the sun departs
A nation's love, that flows from saddened hearts.

Through air and sky send forth the solemn peal,
A universal mourning to reveal,
While all the people with united voice
Speak praise of him who was their willing choice.

The hum of busy marts is hushed and still,
A hallowed spirit steals o'er vale and hill;
Earth yields in rarest gifts her latest bloom
To wreathe the bier and lift the gathered gloom.

Our great souled chief! Ah! many tongues will tell
How by the bold assassin's stroke he fell
With mortal wound, that care and skill defied,
Which sapped the strength of manhood's flowing tide.

His wondrous fortitude and will, sustained
Through months of agony that waxed and waned,
The frame more feeble grew, till that brave soul
The powers of life no longer could control.

The ocean moaned, the fair sun hid his face,
A sable shadow veiled his resting place,
O'er trembling wires the last sad message sped
Around the world; "Our president is dead."

And quick response came like a throb of woe
From kingly courts and e'en from stations low,
One feeling reigned, one impulse deeply thrilled,
And kindly sorrow every nation filled.

Bright omen of the blessed bye and bye,
When love shall form the happy gordian tie
That none can break, when o'er the whole wide world
The star-gemmed flag of peace shall be unfurled.

* Did not the silvery belt that gleamed on high,
And spanned from west to east the evening sky,
Portend a meaning deeper than we drew,
A bond 'twixt Continents both old and new?

The thronging millions of our own free land
With heads uncovered by their altars stand
And seal their countless prayers with unfeigned praise,
And bow in trust to "God's mysterious ways."

No North, no South, but one true family,
Blend in one common flow of sympathy.
Be this a link these sacred hours shall weld
So firm that hate forever shall be quelled.

Who knows his virtues best can on them dwell,
His grandly rounded life shall history tell,
For lofty aims inspired him from his youth,
His guiding motive was unsullied truth.

The press and pulpit, with each other vie
In eulogies that place our martyr high,
In all that gives to man a lasting name,
A niche of grandeur crowning mortal fame.

Bear gently to the tomb the last remains
Of him whose broad career wears no dark stains;
Whose private honors rest in hearts of grief,
Where precious memories bring sweet relief.

Our prayers, our wishes, are not vainly lost
Through all the trial, sacrifice and cost,
The rod that chastens blooms with life anew;
A nation stricken shall be strong and true.

---

* A phenomenon in the sky.

God of our fathers! look on this our land,
For its salvation now stretch forth thy hand,
Bless him who steers the mighty ship of State
With sight to shun the sands and shoals of fate.

May congresses of noble souls gone forth,
Send power and inspiration down to earth,
That men may feel where sacred duty lies
And give our country counsels good and wise.

Purge fraud and selfishness from human laws,
Help justice plead her rights in every cause,
Hasten the day when full equality
Shall make all nations from oppression free.

AMERICA IN SHAME.

SHE was the earth's great refuge land,
    Designed to be a home indeed,
Where noble souls erect might stand,
    Beyond the reach of throne or creed.
Does she maintain the world-wide cause
    For which her fathers struggled long?
Or only mid her pleasures pause
    To give to liberty a song?
There is no time to sing nor dream,
    No moments for the banquet hall,
Behold the cloud whose lightning's beam
    Is like the writing on the wall!

With childish pride, elate and warm,
    She sees the past with ruddy sky,
Unconscious of the brewing storm,
    That darkly, wildly gathers nigh.

Her laborers, in their need for bread
   Implore her for the right to toil;
She drops her hands, she drops her head,
   And *whispers*, this is freedom's soil!
Above her breath she dare not speak;
   Her tyrants awe her with their might;
She scarcely knows that she is weak,
   Or that the *right is right*.

Whence is this power, this conquest sore
   At which her lips may not demur?
Has the invader gained her shore,
   Or foreign despots conquered her?
Ah! many masters calls she lord,
   And many kings she must obey;
Monopolists, a soulless horde,
   Degrade America to-day.
From valleys to the mountains' tops,
   Her heavy golden harvests stand;
Her soil is teeming with its crops,
   But want is seen on every hand.

The factory and the foundry still—
   Or, only making broken sound—
The workshops long untrodden, will
   With rankest weeds and grass abound,
And idlers, idlers, everywhere,
   And tramps that no one could employ,
Till satan takes them in his care,
   And makes their reckless hands destroy.
The crimson flame is in the sky;
   The crimson blood is on the ground;
But crimson of a deeper dye
   Might on the nation's face be found;
For she who saw not the distress,
   Nor heard the pleadings of her throngs,
Could call her armies to suppress
   The rage that swelled against these wrongs.

O had she heard them when they cried,
  And waked to effort for their good,
Prosperity would now be wide
  Where dissolution's terrors brood.
But wealth above, and mines below,
  And commerce on the open sea,
One clutching, grasping system know,
  One law, and that *monopoly!*

Can God o'erlook a crime so great,
  And human fiends his projects foil?
A few usurpers seal the fate
  That gives his children want and toil?
He made all nations of one blood,
  And views them with parental eye;
He sends his blessing like a flood
  To all who dwell beneath the sky.

The *Golden Rule* that Jesus gave,
  To each would make a portion sure.
The *Declaration* of the brave,
  Would human rights secure.
But hath the nation power to say,
  "Ye shall not in my name oppress?"
Or can the Church in Truth's array,
  Demand the work of righteousness?

O, fair Columbia, captive now!
  By thine own household foes betrayed;
Lift up thy voice, lift up thy brow,
  And let thy standard be displayed.
The craft of Church and State is there,
  Wherever poverty is found,
Then be it first thy urgent care,
  To know that conscience is unbound.
Hear thou the prophecy that thrills
  Through every heart that loves the right:

> *"God is not dead, his spirit wills*
>   *A work of overwhelming might!*
> *And thou shalt not in bondage groan*
>   *Nor be to tyrannies a prey;*
> *For he has claimed thee as his own*
>   *To consecrate to Liberty."*

INWARD PEACE.

AN aged pilgrim by the open door
    Sat leaning on his staff to greet the sun,
    The gleaming sands of time were almost run,
And long experience he pondered o'er.
His life seemed like a smooth extended shore,
    Outreaching far from where the line begun,
    Till *past* and *present* merging into one
Lay like the sunshine on his path before.
    He lifted up his head in calm content,
And sang, with heart attuned to inward peace,
    "Glory to God on high, for days well spent,
For blessings given and for truth's increase:"
    A new light glowed upon his face intent,
    Like some sweet dream where heaven and earth were blent.

A FINANCIAL PANIC.

O YE that prize the Nation's life,
    Her honor and her noble call,
Awake, arise, and join the strife
    To gain equality for *all*.
Financial systems based on fraud,
    Like empires, cover all the earth,
Distorting sacred laws of God
    And giving countless horrors birth.

Look on the scene that but of late
    Was re-enacted far and near;
'Tis but the index of the fate
    That swept through every lowly sphere.
They stood around with faces paled,
    And eyes aglow with fires of dread;
Their heavy hearts within them quailed
    As if all hope of life had fled.

'Twas not the battle's sanguine heat,
    Nor vessels' lonely wreck at sea;
'Twas not the hour when tempests meet,
    And earth convulses mightily;
But there was wildness in the air;
    Men struggled as with forms unseen,
While some close pinioned with despair
    Gazed motionless upon the scene.

The tumult of that human tide,
    The darkness of that mental sky,
All earthly terrors far out-vied;
    For there was *heartfelt agony!*
The crush of hopes, the loss of place,
    The homes that in their grandeur fleet,
The pain of every household face,
    The rugged paths for tender feet;

The plans that were but idly wrought,
    The schemes for boundless wealth and power,
The long life efforts brought to naught,
    All crowded through that fearful hour.
And ever and anon there came
    New messages that seemed like death;
The failure of each trusted name
    Was listened to with bated breath.

Some felt their quivering reason fall,
    Some wept as if to break the spell,
Some hazarded their little all
    In hope that it might yet be well.

But there were some, O hearts of steel !
   Where were your human pulses warm,
That like the wreckers, could but feel
   Exultant through that rending storm ;

That like the wreckers fiercely grasp
   The treasures of that sinking crew ;
That callously the hand unclasped,
   That nerved itself for life anew?
Yet you and they were of *one kin ;*
   Had fortune but reversed her wheel,
Like yours, their hands would joyful win ;
   Their hearts be dead to all appeal.

Now from your splendid ruins turn
   To watch the waves that carry woe,
To where the flickering tapers burn
   In garrets high and cellars low.
Think of the children starved for food,
   The strong men humbled in their pride,
The women robbed of womanhood,
   The crimes to wretchedness allied ;

And pledge, against this weight of sin,
   The time that to you yet remains ;
You have ability to win
   The country from commercial chains.
Change, from the *word to very deed*,
   "*The Declaration*" that was given ;
Let Christ-like action meet the need ;
   There is no poverty in heaven.

COMPARISON.

MY soul has visions, and I turn to where
    The great sea lies spread out, a boundless field
    That in the regal moonlight blossoms yield ;
The happy songs of sunlit hours are there
With anthems full, in music rich and rare.
    The diamonds gleam upon its steel blue shield,
    Upon its mail-clad breast the tempests wield
The maddening forces that the wild winds bear.
And, in my life I find all these to be,
    The shield of faith to gird my breast about,
I sing such songs as ripple on the sea,
    I feel the sterner elements of doubt,
While truth's bright sun illumes my shaded hours,
And in my spirit blooms the night-born flowers.

MONOPOLY.

GROSS superfluity is fruit of sin ;
    The palace rests upon a thousand huts ;
The hand that seeks unbounded wealth to win,
    By each success, some door of blessing shuts.
By each success some misery is sown,
    Some sorrow for the future day to reap ;
Some guilt is kindled, that when years have flown
    Shall through the heart like streams of lava sweep.
Monopoly is but the larger theft,
    The robbery that swells beyond the Law ;
A subtle power which hath the earth bereft
    Of that sweet good which its Creator saw.
It is a blight upon the human race ;
    It fills the cities with their dens of shame ;
It sits a threatening fiend in every place
    That honest industry might rightly claim.

The angels see it, and their eyes are stern,
    Yet full of pity for the poor and weak ;
Before their tribunal how shall conscience burn !
    And who will for the grasper dare to speak?
Ah, who could plead the cause of him who made
    By usurpation, want's appalling pains?
When shall his crimes from his own vision fade?
    And what forgiveness could remove his stains?
Not till the dwarfed and smitten, thrive and bloom,
    Not till the crushed and thwarted rise to life,
Not till his spirit toils revoke the doom
    With which his earthly deeds were ever rife.
Not till all marks of penury depart
    From souls whose mortal destiny he made,
Not till the depths of his own sordid heart
    Break forth in sympathy — in loving aid.
O, not till then can he the past forget !
    This is atonement that will never fail ;
For, by this law shall sin's dark train be met,
    And through this law shall deathless truth prevail.
The angels say to every heart : "Do right,"
    Though man-made systems may sustain the wrong ;
Guilt still be guilt, in God's impartial sight,
    And not less heavy carried by a throng.
Before the angels, pomps are types of woe ;
    The gorgeous fruitage of a pois'nous tree,
Whose cruel roots luxuriantly grow
    From hearts long buried in fell misery.
With deep compassion, over earth we trace
    The ills that through Monopoly have come ;
One spot is radiant — *it* has no place
    Within the borders of *our sacred home.*

THE HOME THAT WE HAVE FOUND.

NATURE'S myriads wake to greet us
    At the dawning of the day;
Blossoms, birds, and fragrant breezes,
    All "Good-morning" seem to say.
And the dreams that filled our slumbers
    Whether sorrowful or bright,
Melt away like mists of morning
    In the affluence of light.
Then we meet and bless each other,
    With a feeling deep and true,
Mingled with our thanks to Heaven,
    For a life so sweet and new.
Then, I think of hearts that suffer
    In the world's distracted state;
How the morning breaks upon them
    But to show their bitter fate.
Quickly from that dismal picture
    Turns my spirit in deep pain,
Praying that the powers immortal,
    Will not ever strive in vain.
For, amid earth's boundless beauty
    Nations dwell beneath a pall,
Having with a grim precision,
    Things adapted to the Fall.
Who shall rend the veil of darkness?
    Who shall break the clouds of sin?
God must shake the old Creation,
    That His truth *its* place may win.
So the burden of my spirit
    I consign unto the Lord,
And in gathering to His children,
    Feel His blessing and reward.
Thus the day with all its labor
    Rolls so swiftly to its close,
And its shadows long and quiet
    Bring the heart a deep repose.

When the royal robe of evening
  Is exchanged for mantled gray;
When the silver stars like spirits
  Come so softly o'er our way;
When the wind that rocks the maple
  Sings the robin to its sleep,
And unnumbered sounds are blended
  In a concert grand and deep;
Then our thoughts, like lambs are gathered
  To our hearts, as to a fold,
And we try to count the treasures,
  That can never all be told.
There are words of precious counsel,
  Acts of kindness, love and care;
Thoughtful eyes that looked a blessing,
  Smiles of joy and peace are there.
And perhaps, "Good-night" was spoken,
  And its gentle tones we hear
Like an angel voice above us,
  As the realm of sleep we near.
For in silence, or in music,
  In the shadow, or the light,
Nothing but the hearts that love us
  Ever truly say, "Good-night."
Scenes transcendent may surround us,
  Heaven and earth with gifts abound,
Yet the faithful hearts that love us
  Form the home that we have found.

ADIEU.

TO A SISTER, ON CHANGING HER HOME.

OUT from a heart whose throbbing pulse another's
    heart-beat feels,
Out from a fount whose sympathy the soul's clear
  depth reveals

Flows forth a tide of feeling deep, by kindred currents met,
Whose mutual streams of blessing can never backward set.

True love and chaste affection, like the gentle dew and rain,
Our chalices with sweetness fill, allay our grief and pain,
And a tender tie of union binds us closely heart to heart,
Which makes us one in spirit though we may be far apart.

Amid the strange vicissitudes that vary life's dull way—
The somber night of sorrow, or the gladsome light of day—
We're learning some new lesson from the open book of life,
We're gathering strength and courage to endure the ceaseless strife.

I ask not that inertia's rest shall come to *you* or *me*,
I ask not that a dead'ning calm shall settle o'er life's sea,
But that our soul's activities may find a fitting place,
And all our labors be imbued with love and Christian grace.

Where'er the Spirit's voice may call, we'll lay our selfhood down,
Though cragged rocks our feet may pierce or thorns may be our crown;
'Tis better far to suffer, than enjoy the things that please;
No soul can reach perfection's height through flowery beds of ease.

Our faith has led to sacrifice of kindred ties of earth,
The germs of the immortal life have struggled to the birth,
Its joys and pure relations promised greater love and gain—
A recompense commensurate for agony and pain.

We cherish that communion founded on eternal right,
And we would share its fullest peace redeemed from sin and blight;
With love magnanimous and free, Christ's mission was replete,
The children of the Orient learned sweet lessons at His feet.

Shall we recluse-like gather, each within our little cell
Abjuring e'en the name of love, yet count our prayers full well?
Depending on salvation by each selfish penance given,
While counting on the glories of some future unknown heaven?

Give me the power of loving here, no greater bliss I'd know,
The mant'ling cloak of charity on other's faults to throw,
No bitter judgment would I mete the spirit's growth to blight,
Nor like the stern inquisitor, give torture day and night.

Each soul a jewel-casket hides within its chamber fair,
Each gem therein a luster holds, made bright by toil and care,
And though unseen by mortals now, good angels *charge* shall hold,
Till all unveiled, their glory yet shall many eyes behold.

O leave not to the great beyond our hope of things to be,
The time draws near when we more clearly, eye to eye will see,
When the inharmonies that now our tensioned harp-chords thrill
Shall give the place to notes as gay as spring-time warbler's trill.

Now kindly we will bid adieu, with naught but love for thee,
If faith our light, and truth our staff, our journey safe will be;
With firm reliance on the gift that makes our home secure,
Let us find a closer union in a life that's good and pure.

COURAGE.

THE earth hath always need of heroes brave;
   Not such as fame with withered wreath hath crowned,
   Not souls who glory seek on battle ground;
Not they who proudly civic honors crave
And find applause where flaunting banners wave;
   But such as speak with no uncertain sound
     'Gainst giant wrongs where darkening crimes abound;
This is the courage that a world will save.
O strong white souls! touched with God's altar flame,
   Engird our hearts with fearless love of right;
We too must work in God's most holy name,
   And storm the citadel of error's might.
We turn our gaze where faith's high watch-towers lume,
And courage take 'mid life's encircling gloom.

MATERNAL SPIRIT.

O, Mother! hear our earnest prayer;
We look to thee for strength and care.
Thou art our fortress and our stay,
Thou art the Light, the Truth, the Way.
Thou art the Bride arrayed in white;
And revelation's perfect light
Reveals to us that thou art She
Who *was*, who *is*, and *is to be*.

Who *was*, when light from chaos sprang,
And morning stars together sang;
Who *is* the second Christ divine,
The lily fair and blooming vine;
The Heavenly Comforter in need,
From whence all goodness doth proceed;
And rich are we who share her love
'Tis pure as nectar from above.

And thou art She who *is to be*
Soul-center of humanity;
Above all other hills shall stand
The scepter planted by thy hand,
Where eagles thither shall be led
To waters pure and living bread;
For where the body pitch their tent,
Exalted spirits oft are sent.

Such find just what their souls desire,
The cleansing fount and furnace fire;
These will refine from earthly dross,
Make holy by a daily cross.
O blessed Spirit! brood o'er earth,
And teach man of the second birth,
How he must die if life would win
And heaven's kingdom enter in.

How all must suffer ere they reign
Triumphant over sin and pain,
And willing sacrifices make
Ere they pure heavenly joys partake.
Maternal Soul! to us most dear,
Embrace thy children far and near;
"Our feet as pillars fast shall be,"
Our hearts, made glad, rejoice in thee.

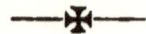

A MOTHER'S LOVE.

LONG time ago when e'en the years were young,
    When this dear earth was beautiful and new,
  When light first dawned, when dropped the first sweet dew,
An Angel came from Heaven, sweet praise she sung,
As fairest things entranced she walked among.
  Filled with delight she sought the best they knew,
  A child's sweet smile, fair flowers of tender hue,
And mother's love—to these she closely clung.
When Heaven's pearl-gates she reached, the smile had gone,
  The fragrant flowers had withered in her hand;
But oh! the mother's love by flight unworn
  Was pure as streams that wash the golden strand.
"There's naught so *good*, amid earth's treasures born,"
  Said all the angels of the heavenly land.

OUR BELOVED MOTHER IN ISRAEL
ELIZA ANN TAYLOR.

ADOWN the vista of thy fourscore years
    Thy children look and lovingly behold
Thy Godlike life, which, free from sin appears
    Bright as the diamond, pure as well-tried gold,

A soul well moulded to the Master's will,
A voice which bids all baser thoughts be still.

The true nobility, the constant zeal,
   The patient fortitude which firmly stood
And bore and suffered for a people's weal,
   Preserved the covenant which brought us good;
These are the virtues which will live and shine,
And mark thee as a hero-soul divine.

Behold the woman on whose brow is sealed
   The impress of the living Christ on earth;
The Motherhood in God, to those revealed
   Whose souls have found the new and second birth;
Transfigured on the mount of truth they stand,
And catch far glimpses of the heavenly land.

We see thee as a lily snowy white,
   Sweet emblem of a pure and chastened soul,
Whose pearly chalice holds the sunbeams bright,
   Waving in all the zephyrs as they roll.
And deeply planted in the parent sod
It grows, and blooms, and breathes its soul to God.

We see thee as a palm-tree tall and fair,
   Whose spreading branches make a sheltering shade
Where weary ones may come, and resting there
   Find comfort, yea with none to make afraid.
No harmful influence finds a place in thee,
Thy healing leaves are love and charity.

We see thee as a rock 'mid ocean's waves,
   Unmoved when storm and tempests surge around,
Firm as the rockbed of that faith which saves
   All those who build on its foundation sound.
So true art thou to God, so true to souls,
True as the magnet to the electric poles.

We see thee as a Shepherdess, so calm and strong,
   Gathering thy little lambs within the fold
Safe from the outer world, where they so long
   Had wandered, shivering in the storm and cold.

O tender Shepherdess! thrice blest the name,
Dearer to us than queens with all their fame.

We see thee as a Priestess of the Lord,
    Standing within the Temple's Holy Place;
From whose pure lips oft came the living word,
    Clothed with the mantle of thy truth and grace.
In knowledge wise, in innocence complete;
Thy heart a shrine where angels love to meet.

From out that inner sanctuary pure,
    We've often felt thy testimony swift
As lightning's flash, then answering thunder sure
    Bespoke the power abiding in the gift—
The gift that comes to us in God's good way,
A guiding star by night, a sun by day.

And we have felt thy tender mother-love,
    That broadened in our souls as they grew more,
Just as when pebbles strike the waves above,
    The widening circles kiss the outer shore;
Embracing all within thy watchful care,
The least one in the fold thy love might share.

And now at last life's race is nobly run,
    Life's jeweled crown is resting on thy brow,
Toward the west thy golden setting sun
    Appears but brighter as we see it now;
Life's beating waves have anchored into calm,
Life's undertones have blended in a psalm.

OUR ROLL CALL.

LET us finish the work we have nobly begun,
    Let us cling to our faith till the victory is won,
O Christian Believers! our work is not done,
    We must gather more into the fold.

Lead forth in the march, raise our voices in song,
Remember the order to which we belong,
Let us show the right path to the one in the wrong,
   And gather more souls in the fold.

'Gainst caste and monopoly conscience must fight,
For in heart and hand labor we know we are right,
Our leaders are trusty, they walk in the light,
   And will gather more into the fold.

We own all our dwellings, we are not oppressed,
We labor with pleasure, and so earn our rest,
From the north and the south, from the east and the west,
   We are gathering them into the fold.

THE INCREASE.

IF but the Polar regions we had known,
   How could we paint the tropics rich and rare?
Or of a strange seed sparsely round us thrown,
   E'en guess the harvest that it yet might bear?
The lightning, drawn upon a single string,
   Seemed but like child's play in the years gone by,
And now it forms for earth a magic ring,
   On which her thoughts and interests safely fly.
We know fair Spring and sunny Summer hours,
   We know rich Autumn and old Winter cold;
But there are round us and within us powers
   We can not know till they their life unfold.
We may not tamper with the lightning's flame,
   Nor gather fruit in misty blossom time,
Nor from green summer, autumn's treasures claim;
   But we must wait the viewless laws sublime.
The earth revolving on her aerial course,
   Or turning to the star-space, or the sun,
Receives momentum from a hidden force,
   And thus secure, her dangerous path can run.

But out among the midnights of our life,
   We grope in darkness, or we stand in tears;
Contend with shadows, wage an aimless strife,
   Or cowering, shrink before our gathered fears.
And what we lack is *Faith that can confide*,
   And never count the measure of its trust;
A deep reliance spreading far and wide,
   Till doubt and disobedience are as dust.
And then the heavenly, hidden law can take
   Our willing souls to govern and recast;
No lingering weakness, and no gloom can break
   Our growing prospects in the future vast.

THE VICTOR.

LIKE a brave knight in panoply of war,
   He laid his armor by with kingly grace;
   Life's battles he has fought, and run the race,
And nobly won the garter and the star.
Bring laurels fair, ye sons from near and far!
   Bring blossoms rare, O daughters to this place!
   Ye see no more the patriarch's sainted face,
With shining ones his soul has crossed the bar.
   Oh long, and tried, and true his life has been,
With justice he has wielded trusted power,
With righteousness has meted out his dower;
   And, guided by the perfect light within
     Has conquered self and vanquished every sin,
Has wrought for good each passing day and hour.

SELF-DENIAL.

MAN has failed of true progression,
   Crippled by the serpent's bruise,
Though he holds in his possession
   Strength that he has but to use.
'Tis the power of self-denial,
   Scholars, statesmen, know its worth;
All unquestioned is its trial,
   In the *outward* things of earth.
He who seeks for star or planet,
   Will not join the midnight dance;
He who studies plant or granite,
   Does not leave his thoughts to chance.
There is system, there is order,
   In the wondrous realm of mind,
Science's far extended border
   Vanguards forward press to find.
From the ruby tide, thought-freighted,
   Flowing through each throbbing frame,
To the spirit chained and grated
   By the griefs without a name;
From the mosses on the mountain,
   To the sky's bright fleece of snow;
From the bubbles on the fountain,
   To the gems the oceans know;
From the wealth that heaven discloses,
   To the riches earth conceals;
All proud Intellect encloses
   In the circle of his seals.
But the *Soul* has been neglected
   In this royal, mental reign,
Crushed, unknown, or misdirected;
   Hers, the years of cloud and pain.
Let her have emancipation,
   Give her sunshine, pure and warm;
As she rises, all creation
   Will assume its highest form.

Let us meet in council holy,
  To discuss the laws of heaven,
Bravely, yet with spirits lowly,
  To receive the truth that's given.
Is there *one* who would awaken,
  One with aspirations true?
Know, the heavens and earth are shaken,
  To convey this call to you.
Come! O come! ere yet within you
  Turns to darkness every gleam,
Come! the angel bands would win you
  To the Life of which you dream.

RESIGNATION.

O LIVE by faith, yea, calmly trust and wait,
  Nor fret for that which time may yet reveal,
  An earnest hope, 'tis life and joy to feel,
But harsh impatience brings no happy state.
'Tis best to work, be efforts small or great,
  Self sacrificing for another's weal;
  Then God who feels desire may soon unseal
Some fount of bliss and open heaven's gate.
When frost abounds, we wish for summer air;
  When storms becloud, we long for sunny light,
When blossoms come, we want the fruitage fair,
  But wait we must, God's way is ever right.
Yea, calm content with patient toil and prayer,
  Will give more peace, and happier thoughts invite.

THE NEW YEAR.

HE comes to us in regal vesture white,
    Laurelled by praise and song. Already now
  He bears aloft the palm, and on his brow
He wears the stars that crown this royal night.
The moon has spread her carpet of soft light,
    And holly boughs are trembling overhead,
    While he advances in the old year's stead,
Which like a king subdued retires from sight.
His jeweled hand holds out a pearly book,
Offering each day a page whereon each look,
    Each thought and action may be clearly traced,
    Or virtue's golden flowers there be placed;
Then from life's blossoms let us choose the best,
And leave them on these snowy pages pressed.

LENGTHENING DAYS.

I LOOK abroad, no signs of summer fall
    Upon my sight, but the glad happy sun
    Shows its bright face, as if a cheering one
Bound close in the strong power of winter's thrall
Peered through the fingers of his ermine shawl.
  The day grows longer, night, the black draped nun
  Is slow to lower her veil, the light to shun,
And lifts it sooner to the morning's call.
And so to us, as life's long year wheels round,
    May the bright, happy hours of joy increase,
And hope with trust in every heart be found,
    Till we are blest with lengthened days of peace,
When with the love of God our hearts abound,
    The wrongs that pain us will forever cease.

THE DEAD YEAR.

THE year is gone, its griefs and sorrows fled,
    Upon a marble couch in royal pride,
    It yields the crown and sceptre undenied.
The funeral star-lights burn above its head,
The rosary is told, the prayers are said.
    Take down the purple drapery, the scarlet hide,
    And on the unstained door let crape be tied,
For o'er the world the pall of death is spread.
We saw its last day sinking in the west,
Crimson and gold were lying on its breast,
    No trailing wreath of rainbow tints we bring,
    Vain relic of the long departed spring,
Subdued it rests in simple robes of white
And pearly flowers have wove themselves of light.

THE FROST ON THE PANE.

AWAY in the past, though I'm not so old,
    Are fantasies strange that memories hold;
But the dearest of all that my mind retains
Is the frosty work on the window panes.
For hours I've stood in an old arm-chair
When a wee, happy girl, and wondered where
Was the artist who drew such quaint designs,
Such airy castles and delicate lines,
And how did he work when the night time came
Without pencil, or chalk, or candle flame.
But the old folks said, when I older grew
I'd study the science of frost and dew,
'Twould then be revealed both clear and plain
The wonderful work on the window pane.
But I shook my head and said to myself,
    "I think it is some good fairy elf

Who lives mid the stars or over the sea,
Perhaps he sleeps in an old hollow tree,
I'm sure he is brother to good Saint Nick,
Who at Christmas is up to some funny trick;
His name, where he lives, in what street or lane
He never has signed on the frosty pane."
And now for the scenes of the long ago,
If fancy can paint, you shall surely know
Of wonderful things, of flowers and trees,
Birdies and insects, swift-flying bees. .
Turbulent oceans and rivers serene,
Whose waters were sparkling with silvery sheen.
Mountains and valleys and prairie lands,
Steep rocky summits and glittering strands.
There were gems that flashed in the sunbeam's glare,
Jewels and diamonds, tinted so rare;
Pearls that to me were of priceless worth,
Stars in the firmament, stars on the earth,
And pillars of marble pedestaled high,
Churches with steeples that pierced the blue sky.
And like King Solomon's temple of old,
The half, yea the half could never be told.
But 'tis strange to say, the older I grew,
Least so I thought, more wonders I knew,
And knowledge piled into a school-girl's brain,
Was often rehearsed on the frosty pane.
Latitude, longitude, changeable zones,
The science of light, of minerals and stones;
And tropical fields with their blossoms gay,
Monkeys and parrots that climb and sway,
And fishes that live in the stormy main
All real as life on the frosty pane.
Astronomy too, comes in for a share,
I know there was Caseopia's chair.
The Pleiades sisters of charming grace,
And Saturn's rings I could easily trace,
Bright silvery Venus, the virgin star,
And the war-god Mars flaming afar.

Botany too, I had almost forgot,
With pistils and stamens and names a lot ;
Indigenous plants, too common to tell,
Like buttercups, daisies I loved so well.
Exotics whose home was a warmer clime
Where palm trees wave through a long summer time.
Mosses and lichens of beauteous forms
That thrive mid the snow and the polar storms ;
And youthful visions of future years,
Those cloudless days without sorrow or tears ;
And hopes that were bathed in a rainbow dye,
All to be known in the far bye and bye.
If any moral in this you discern,
O, lay it to heart and a lesson learn,
For like all transient things the sunbeams came
And melted my bliss from the frosty pane.

STEAM AND WATER-WORKS — WHAT THEY COST.

FIRST they cost a pile of thought and dreams out side of sleep,
Then consultations with the wise that were both long and deep ;
And there were journeys up the hills and likewise down the hollows,
For if we take an upward path descent most surely follows.
It seemed to uninstructed minds that brethren must be playing
With instruments of various kinds, but lo ! they were surveying.
Well then they figured, scored and planned on horse-block and on gate-post,
And always brought their board in hand when they to meals came, late most.

At length we heard one signal night that it was done—
on paper,
And didn't we at once behold the horn of plenty's
taper?
We knew that e'er we reached the fount its outlines
would be swelling,
And we were all demurely mute when thinking of our
dwelling.
But here's a problem in this theme, the Deacons might
unlock it,
In digging drains, do men begin in earth or in the
pocket?
We think they cut the pocket first, at least they cut the
stitching
That smooths and sharpens up the tools and makes
them fit for ditching.
The brethren's wills we know had scope for when their
stakes were driven
To pull them up there was no hope till earth and rocks
were riven.
They said with Grant, "We'll take this line," and not
employ a plumber,
But we will lay the pipes ourselves if it should take all
summer.
Well, when the apple crop was ripe and gleaning had
diminished,
We sisters took a pleasant ride to see the project
finished.
'Twas said in olden time indeed that faith would move
a mountain,
But here it took both faith and works to even reach its
fountain.
We found it nearly to the brook that blithesomely was
humming,
Not even dreaming of the trap that to its brink was
coming.
Yea, it was finished just so far, yet it was uncompleted,
Like life, some all important parts were not yet made
to meet it.

The reservoir was quite a scrape, they never had a greater,
They dug and scooped as if to make a huge volcanic crater;
They piled the stones, they heaped the clay, but e'er from toil they rested,
We sisters went one sunny day and sang to them and blessed it.
The grove was fairly cleft in two, the road was also parted,
But when the dooryard you came to, your eyeballs must have started;
You might have thought of York Town's plight before it was vacated,
With heavy earth-works left and right in which Mac-Clellan waited.
Of course the house was undermined, and in some places entered,
Where'er these zigzags seemed to wind 'twas to the house they centered.
If man was made of dust, as said, we judge he must have floated,
But his descendents firmly tread when they with mud are coated.
The cellar was a forging place, although no rogues were in it,
It counterfeited every sound from anvil jar to linnet.
And all the intermediate clang of racket and of screaking
Made new confusion night and day; now this is mildly speaking.
For many a night the still small hours were small without the stillness,
While croaking prophecy was heard predicting lengthened illness.
The coils were down the chimney put while bitter winds were blowing,
The brethren then were dressed in soot from which red lead was glowing.

We had to guess, we were not told, that they the flues descended,
They were so curious to behold as round about they wended.
The explanations which they made, oblivion has recorded,
But patience which will never fade was to their souls awarded.
And if the dooryard was cut up with tunnels and with trenches,
The hills were heaped with loads of boards, pipes, tools and workmen's benches.
And what we saw was but a tithe of what they knew who did it,
But when they were the most perplexed they smiled and kindly hid it.
Ah well, we can not *count the cost*, though for that end we started,
There's but a rough sketched estimate in all we have imparted.
In days of drugs and pounds of cure there was a wise invention
To give the ounce a preference sure when taken as prevention.
The bath we know will henceforth keep the vital tide in motion,
Its home significance is deep as level waves of ocean
Thus in the value of the works for comfort, health and blessing,
A most confusing problem lurks that baffles all our guessing.
We can not count the labor done, we can not count the wages,
Then it a debt of Peace must run with interest through the ages,
Which we will pay in gold of love, the coin of consecration,
And our own loyalty will prove in every walk and station.

THANKSGIVING.

PRIDE spurns thanksgiving, but the humble mind
    Rich cause of gratitude can ever find;
God's mercies fall like blessings day by day,
And manna-strewn is life's once barren way.
No carping thought, nor yet imagined ill
The thankful soul with murmuring can fill,
For good within, attracts the good without,
And faith uplifting soars beyond all doubt.
Though darkling clouds o'erspread the arching skies,
God's goodness every shadow underlies,
And shines above our nature's changeful mood,
Illumes with peace the dreariest solitude.
The proud heart like the shallow pool is found,
The rains of heaven but stir its muddy ground,
The purest drops commingle with the tide
Where basest dregs of sinfulness abide;
No hallowed light reflects upon its face
The tender mercies of redeeming grace.
Give me the grateful heart, in which the good
Is perfume of exhaling gratitude,
Which cherishes the smallest blessings given,
And sees in lowliest things the gifts of Heaven.

WHAT HATH THE STRUGGLE AVAILED?

MY heart was weary with sadness,
    My hands were tired with their toil,
My eyes saw no sunshine of gladness,
    My feet trod on rough, sandy soil.
I sat alone in my chamber,
    While thoughts dark and lonely assailed,
And I asked of myself this close question,
    What good hath the struggle availed?

What bliss hath it brought to my spirit?
   What clouds hath it chased far away?
What reward do my toilings all merit?
   What gifts will my labors repay?
As I sat alone in my chamber
   This answer o'er others prevailed,
If any wise lesson's been taught you,
   Thus far hath the struggle availed.

The gayest of hearts oft need sorrow,
   And tears that are holy must flow,
But joy waits the glad coming morrow,
   And sunshine resplendent will glow.
The hands that are weary with toiling,
   Though oft to the cross they are nailed,
Will accomplish some righteous deeds for you,
   Some good that your works have availed.

The darkness that rests on your vision
   Comes only from shadows within;
Lift up the thin veil, and the sunlight
   With the glory of peace will shine in.
The eye is the light of your being,
   Keep its sight to God's blessing unveiled,
And then you will see that your struggles
   Have many rich conquests availed.

Did you say that your feet walked the lonely
   And rough rugged pathway of woe?
There was never a road where grew only
   The sweet thornless roses, you know.
If the goal of the blest is worth gaining,
   Why murmur at trifles you meet?
Why don the dark grave clothes of mourning
   Because the rough thorns pierce your feet?

There is no royal road to progression,
   There is no starlit pathway to bliss,
There are many rewards for true labor;
   But the sweetest are only in this;

Work *nobly* and *truly* for others,
   Though oft you have tried and have failed,
Then each diligent earnest endeavor
   Will *prove* what the strife hath availed.

THY WILL BE DONE.

O LORD, unto Thine altar pure I bring
   Each cherished idol for an offering,
That through Thy love my soul may chastened be
And though the sacrifice be hard for me
            Pray that Thy will be done.

If bitterness my cup of life should fill,
With trusting heart I will accept it still,
Endure the cross and trial, for at length
I know will come the love, the power and strength
            To say Thy will be done.

And whatsoever I must feel and do
I know Thy holy power will help me through,
Make light my burdens and relieve my care
And give the gifts that I should ever wear,
            But let Thy will be done.

Though roses crushed lie withering at my feet
There yet remains a perfume pure and sweet,
And though life's joys sometimes may clouded be
A sincere prayer ascends O Lord to Thee
            To let Thy will be done.

O push aside the curtains dark and grey,
Throw back the blinds of doubt that dim the way,
Let in the rosy hues of fadeless light,
Seek to unfold the real the inner sight
            And pray Thy will be done.

O may I gain that holiness of life
That sanctifies the soul and saves from strife,
And in the spirit of pure love divine
On bended knee at truth's most sacred shrine
     Know that Thy will is done.

THE CHURCHES OF OUR LAND.

LOUD ring their bells, and loud their organ tones
 Pour the grand anthems that by Art were given.
Wealth, learning, eloquence, their proud dominion owns,
 But what of God, of Life, of Love, of Heaven?
A seeming fitness blends all outward things,
 Concordant sounds and softly mellowed light;
We almost list the rush of angels' wings,
 And watch for saints in radiant robes of white.

Can heaped-up shams the Infinite allure,
 Or flattery charm the all-embracing mind?
Can systems that oppress and spurn the poor
 Be brought to God, and His acceptance find?
Is he deceived by fashion, pomp, and show?
 Can grandeur hide disease, deceit and sin?
May every wickedness the heart can know
 Come to these temples and gain entrance in?

If stern, misguided hearts go forth no more
 The Martyr's unrelenting fire to light;
If ruthless persecution cease to pour
 Its venomed darts with wild inhuman might,
Does there abound that precious gift of God—
 Faith in the good that is, and that which yet may be?
Is Christlike charity their basis broad?
 And is their focus —*Truth*— unmarred and free?

When youthful manhood, full of noble zeal
 An offering makes of his unfolding life,
Is there an inspiration he can feel
 To meet his ardor and award his strife?

And does the soul of woman bear no fruit,
  Nor spread its branches like the olive tree?
Beneath the ban that bade her to be mute,
  Must her expanding powers forever be?

Ah, is the altar's sacred fire dead?
  Can souls no longer meet the Spirit there?
Doth Pride with mockery give stones for bread,
  And scorpion answer to the cry for care?
Our prayer ascends, O be it thus no more;
  Come, sweet refreshing from the Source Divine,
And spread true Brotherhood "the wide world o'er,"
  Which poet-prophets saw in "auld lang syne."

Let Truth reveal to science Nature's laws,
  Let faith not die 'mid superstitions dim;
For truth and science both shall seek the cause
  That gave all souls one universal hymn.
Write God, write Goodness on the nation's heart,
  Not with a legal pen by man's decree,
But let iniquity the land depart,
  And make the young Republic *pure and free*.

SPEAK, LORD, TO ME.

SPEAK, Lord, to me, and show
    Thy law divine;
My inner soul would know
    Thy will, not mine.
The carnal mind may shun
    The cross, the light,
Again to Thee I come,
    Lead me aright.

O, send Thy chastening grace
    And holy fire,
Consume each darkened trace
    Of sin's desire.

Serenely I will stand
   In armor bright,
With sword of truth in hand
   Defend the right.

Speak Lord, Thy words repeat,
   Give life to-day;
Thy whispering voice so sweet
   I will obey.
Though lingering shadows fall
   Across time's vale,
If Christ is all in all
   Strength will prevail.

O, when I walk in hope
   And heaven's light,
In doubt I need not grope,
   In error's night;
Perfect Thy grace in me,
   Thy power and life,
And make me one in Thee,
   Through holy strife.

THE NEW FLAG.

NO flag of peace the earth hath ever known,
   E'en Freedom's voice was in the martial key;
And revolutions, death and havoc strown
   Flung up the paths for nations to be free.

But History's pages tell us o'er and o'er
   That war-won liberty, the sword must shield,
That freedom sown in dew of human gore
   Brings forth the harvest of the battle-field.

When carnage ceases from his work of spoil
   'Tis but to fashion deadly weapons new;
To teach his hellish arts to sons of toil,
   Then with their blood the earth again imbue.

He counts on labor for his rank and file,
  The landless wealth producers are his prey ;
But they who bask in fortune's crafty smile
  Bear off the laurels of each sanguine day.

A few ambitious monsters of the world
  Who personate the fiendish crime of greed,
Conspire to have the battle-flag unfurled
  And draw their victims from the realms of need.

All governments on force and fraud are built,
  On theft and violence they tottering stand ;
What drives the sword of conquest to the hilt?
  The lust for *land*, monopoly of land.

O if the nations e'er learn war no more
  And pruning-hooks and ploughshares are of worth,
All despots, all usurpers must restore
  Man's rightful heritage, the earth, the earth.

On that foundation, soon for peace will gleam
  A temple worthy, prominent and grand ;
A temple with foundations, not a dream —
  A structure built upon the solid land.

But ere that day, will come a wondrous light
  That will not be of either sun or moon,
The presence of the Lord, His power and might,
  The peace of God, His soul-exalting boon.

We will take courage even in our tears,
  We will take courage in our yearning toil ;
We will unite and through the coming years
  No powers of darkness shall our efforts foil.

Though clouds of death along our course are furled
  Our consecrated labors must not cease,
Until above this war-distracted world
  Shall flash the snowy ensign of sweet peace.

THE MILLENNIAL TIME.

THE ancient races versed in mystic lore,
    The great souled ones on whom God's glory shone,
Have left to us who tread time's present shore
    Their wisdom traced on brass or moldering stone.

The forms of life, the motions of the stars,
    The open secrets of the earth and sea,
Were but the outer and dividing bars
    O'er which to climb and learn each mystery.

With patient zeal to fathom every thought,
    And bring their treasures upward to the light;
To magnify the truth by Nature taught,
    And stamp it with the holy seal of right.

In Aryan forests by the cooling streams,
    'Neath shady branches of the sacred trees,
The learned Hindoos searched their mystic dreams,
    And demonstrated life's realities.

Or in the temple, safe from vulgar eyes,
    Discoursed the sacred office of the soul;
And caused the spirit to materialize,
    Thus made its secrets but an open scroll.

And through the gift of prophecy, foretold
    A perfect time when righteousness would reign;
When each his human brother would enfold
    In loving arms, dispelling every pain.

When unto earth the Saving One would come,
    And bring to them the sought-for law of good,
When doubting lips would all be stricken dumb,
    Before the glory of its magnitude.

The Moslem dreamed of Gardens where the blest
   Found for their senses every rare delight.
And Egypt's trusting children longed for rest
   In God's Great Spirit where there is no night.

And Chaldean shepherds watching on the hill
   Divined the ages' culminating plan,
When sun and stars should all their orbits fill,
   Then saving power would come to erring man.

'Tis native to the heart to have some goal;
   Some brighter hope beyond the dull to-day;
Some higher aspiration of the soul
   To keep it climbing up the unknown way.

The light of faith can not be dulled with years,
   And love must bear and suffer for the right;
God's truth will shine a beacon o'er man's fears,
   His promised blessing ne'er will leave our sight.

'Tis still before us like the guiding star,
   That led the ancient ones to seek the Child
In Bethlehem's quiet village, where from far
   It dropped its radiance over wold and wild.

The same glad impulse stirs our wondering lives;
   The same heart-throbs give courage to our feet;
The same dear lesson time's swift years survives;
   The same fair promise is our solace sweet.

We see with undimmed eyes the time to be,
   With the prophetic vision of the past,
And prophets will arise to further see
   The progress, which though good, will never last,

For every age must have its meed of strife,
   Its brave enlightened souls, its priests and seers,
Must have its aspirations for new life,
   Must have its time of sun, its time of tears.

Then let us labor for the weal of each,
  And seek the truth from Heaven's height sublime;
Thus shall our lives the grandest lesson teach,
  And help to bring the glad Millennial Time.

TRUE WEALTH.

BE my mind a sacred treasury
    Stored with gems and diamonds bright,
Where no dross shall ever gather
    That would dim their lustrous light.

Garnered there the wealth of knowledge,
    Truth and Wisdom's golden sheaves,
Richest fruits and fragrant flowers,
    Not alone life's fading leaves.

Walls of sapphire form the chambers
    By eternal Goodness made,
I will fill this heavenly structure
    With the sunshine, not the shade.

I will hang it round with pictures
    That shall give me joy to see,
Not the imagery of demons
    That would haunt and follow me.

Like the ghosts in ancient story,
    Protean forms of passions base,
Sordid loves and gross desires,
    These the temple would deface.

Innocence and pure affection,
    Deeds in consecration wrought,
Holy thoughts and aspirations,
    To this temple shall be brought.

Germs of good my soul shall cherish,
  Spurn the false and prize the true,
Look beyond the things that perish
  Where bright glories rise to view.

Brighter now appears the prospect,
  And the angel life is mine;
Growth and progress are eternal,
  In the spheres of truth divine.

RELIANCE.

As lifts the lily's snowy cup
  To drink the dews of heaven,
So turns the chalice of my heart
  For love as freely given.

Let fall into my soul, O Lord,
  Refining grace and power,
That every motive be to Thee
  A holy fragrant flower.

And every thought be at Thy feet
  Like pearly petals shed,
And every impulse of my heart
  To holiness be wed.

And when the harvest time of life
  Brings its reward, the best
I'll lay upon Thine altar Lord,
  O be my offering blessed.

WORDS OF CHEER.

THERE are brilliant eyes that are wet
   With tears that are hard to dry,
And many a glad hope has set
   Like a star in the midnight sky.

There is many a heart made void
   Of the freshness that life demands;
There is many a soul destroyed
   By cruel adversity's hands.

But those who are true to the test
   That tries them as heat tries the gold,
Will find the severe way the best,
   The narrow path leads to God's fold.

All tear-drops are sacredly kept
   In sympathy's deep golden urn,
Lost stars over which we have wept
   In beauty again will return.

Calamity prove but a tent
   Where angels may dwell in disguise,
Awaiting with messages sent
   From Him whose chastisings are wise.

Cheer up then whatever betide,
   Nor mind when the shadows are given,
The clouds that are dark the earth side
   Are gold on the side toward heaven.

The flowers that grow in the shade
   Are modest, and fairer than those
That flaunt for an hour and fade,
   The violet rivals the rose.

> Then bear up and master your fear.
>   And trust to the Lord who will bless,
> For while the warm sunlight is here,
>   Your sorrow must surely grow less.

POET AND PROPHET.

> OH mighty prophet—soul of love and song;
>   Thou rapt interpreter of truth divine,
> What other heart could echo songs like thine?
> Thy words struck vengeance, for their might was strong
> Against oppression in its court of wrong.
>   Like wintry starlight o'er the groves of pine,
>   Thine eyes beheld the light of freedom shine
> O'er ranks of slavery's sin-beclouded throng;
> And when thy magic fingers touched the keys
>   Of time's great organ, lo, the concert chord
> Struck the true note to life's grand symphonies
>   And rolled the finished anthem to the Lord.
> And, with thy knees upon faith's altar stair
> Thy gentle soul communed with God through prayer.

COMMUNION.

> AROUND my soul is gently drawn a veil that screens
>   From outward things which claim the heart and will;
> My ear and vision ope to heavenly sounds and scenes,
>   While earthly din and tumult all are still.
>
> O gentle calm, serene and holy stillness blest!
>   What sweet communion now my spirit holds
> With one who hovers near, an ever welcome guest,
>   Who tenderly in love my heart enfolds.

My blessed angel guide, and watcher ever near,
  My constant friend and helper through each strife;
To thee my inmost thoughts and motives all are clear—
  Those hidden springs that move the wheels of life.

Thou knowest all my faults; how oft my feet have strayed,
  Or slipped when steep and rugged seemed the way;
And how my soul hath wept, the struggles I have made
  To mend the past and truer live each day.

Through darkness and through light, thy presence I have felt,
  In joy or grief, as right or wrong I've turned;
And known that thou wast near, when secretly I've knelt
  To seek the conquering power for which I yearned.

And when with searching eye, I've turned those pages o'er,
  Whereon life's changeless records all appear,
Thy gift hath helped me learn the lessons which they bore,
  When in the light of truth they were made clear.

And with me thou hast gone beneath that river's tide,
  Which cleanseth e'en the memory from sin;
And on its sunlit banks where blessed ones abide,
  Hath helped me gain those gifts the purified may win.

Most grateful for thine aid, but needing still thy care,
  I ask anew the strength which thou canst give
To fortify my soul, God's searching truth to bear,
  That ever to His honor I may live.

"NOTHING NEW."

THE universal circle marks
    Creation's perfect whole,
From worlds ensphered in belted zones
    To life that crowns the soul.

A wise man of the centuries past
    In taking life's review,
Proclaimed that all earth's history
    Presented nothing new.

And so we ask, is there a thought
    Or word still unexpressed?
A fountain sealed that has not gushed
    Within some human breast?

Is there a light or depth untouched,
    Some secret hidden plan,
To yet unfold within the grasp
    Of ever reaching man?

The mines of knowledge still unsprung,
    Would seem but buried lore,
When brought to view the thing that's new
    Lo! it was known before.

The life we live is but one grand
    Rehearsal of the past,
The very motives of our souls
    In ancient mold were cast.

For human nature is the same
    To-day as yesterday;
The treadmill of old time moves to
    The same dull roundelay.

The mighty forces of the soul
   Well up and overflow,
In streams whose currents, swiftly on
   Through deepening channels go.

The fevered tide of human life
   Bears not upon its waves
The power that lifts immortal souls,
   The strength that heals and saves.

The savage though untutored still,
   With gifts of nature blest,
In his sublime simplicity,
   Bears truth within his breast.

While he who claims a fairer face
   And broader cultured mind,
Will prostitute the noblest gifts
   That Heaven for good designed.

And thus it seems, that all the dreams
   Of progress we have made,
When pressed to stern reality,
   Like fitful fancies fade.

For misery and crime increase,
   In ratio with the light,
Where good is found doth sin abound,
   The wrong pursues the right.

Thus quickened mind inventive plies
   Its skill in many ways;
Devising schemes in which to win
   The prize that *self* repays.

How vain ambition crushes out
   The equal rights of man;
How bitter discord mars the peace
   Of nation, home and clan.

And what we gain through toil and pain
  But trembles 'neath the power
Usurped by those who sceptres wield
  To triumph but an hour.

Religion, sovereign in the race,
  Still seeks expression free;
But cramped and bound with fetters strong
  Holds not its liberty.

And the experience of the past,
  Though changed the form it wears,
Is but the cry of burdened toil
  Through life's increasing cares.

Here generations come and go,
  Whose life seems but a day,
Vast empires from the dust arise
  To perish and decay.

Why boast of prestige, wealth or power?
  Why glory in a name?
For all of earth to earth returns,
  Man goes from whence he came.

And round and round the ages roll,
  The seasons onward flow,
Yet " vanity of vanities "
  Are all things here below.

" 'Tis hope eternal " that illumes
  And gladdens all our strife,
And righteousness alone can give
  The bliss of higher life.

HEAVENLY LIGHT.

The shafts of the morning—bright sunbeams of day—
Too soon from the sky fade like visions away,
And fair sunset glories melt in the twilight
While softly drops o'er us the curtains of night.

The star-lighted heaven's expanse we behold
Like a vast scene in grandeur and beauty unrolled,
Thus are we surrounded by day and by night
With blessings unfolding, to gladden our sight.

And while thus enveloped in sunshine and shade,
With glory reflecting from hill-top and glade,
We'll look to the fountain whence light has its birth,
And gather the rays that illume the *new* earth.

Our souls shall rejoice in a heavenly light,
And stand in its brightness redeemed from all blight,
No longer enshrouded by darkness within,
We'll rest in the joy of a life free from sin.

A PRAYER FOR RAIN.

The earth is famished, Father send Thy rain!
   In guise of prayer Thy children come to Thee,
Before Thy presence suppliants we remain,
   Prone to the earth with bended brow and knee.

Stretch forth Thy hand, the glorious works of Thine
   Are fainting in the land Thou gavest them;
And from the sun-tipped spires of oak and pine
   Sounds forth creation's solemn requiem.

Beneath, the withering forms of grass and grain
   Fall as though smitten by the yellow breath
That blows across Arabia's fair domain,
   And carries in its travel blight and death.

Smite once again the heavens! send forth the flash
   Of liquid fire across the slumbering clouds;
Send down the thunder with awakening crash,
   And after that the rain-spun winding shrouds.

Like Jacob we will wrestle with Thee still,
   E'en to the breaking of the tearful day,
Until to us in concord with Thy will,
   The blessing comes for which we toil and pray.

O Lord, increase our faith! we truly need
   The faith that taught the prophets long ago;
Strike from our hearts the bitter, baneful weed,
   And in its place Thy holier virtues sow.

Weak, erring, conscious of our human sin,
   Thy helping power of wondrous love we feel,
And with a sense of unearned grace within,
   Our very weakness strengthens our appeal.

We stand in ignorance before the law
   That made the sunbeams and the cooling drops,
That made the heavens without fault or flaw,
   That made the earth to yield her golden crops.

But this we know by intuition's light,
   That not a sparrow falls without Thy care,
That not an earth-born soul escapes Thy sight,
   That answer comes to every trustful prayer.

And as the path of duty grows more clear,
   Incline our hearts to search Thy mystic ways,
To come to Thee in harmony, not fear,
   To bring life's discords into tuneful praise.

Then shall we know the law that rules the stars,
   That rules the earth, and by Thy grace shall win
The God-like power that will uplift the bars,
   That every good we need may enter in.

Then hear our humble prayer, the gift is Thine,
   To give or take, to judge or to atone;
We are but units in the plan divine,
   The power and glory Lord, are Thine alone.

AFTER THE RAIN.

RHYTHMIC sounds of dripping, dropping
   From a million quivering leaves,
Diamond points each grass-blade topping,
   Rustling of the ripening sheaves.

Lily-cups with nectar bending,
   Violets low with glistening eyes, .
Sunny smiles with tear-drops blending
   Wreathing earth, and air, and skies.

Sunshine quivering through the rifting
   And the scattering of the clouds;
Through the valley light mists drifting,
   Looking just like fairy shrouds.

Down the hillsides full and gushing,
   Laughing streams in gladness flow,
Bright-eyed daisies lightly brushing
   Tall grass in the meads below.

Now the woods seem grander, greener,
   Fresher in their somber mood,
Nature's face with look serener
   Wears a smile of gratitude.

Hark! the sound of gladsome voices
  From the leafy grove and bower;
All creation's heart rejoices
  In the sweet refreshing shower.

LILIES OF THE VALLEY.

FOLD up the sable robes that grief has worn,
  And with them hide the mourner's veil away,
  For these white lilies blossomed in that day
When from our midst the loving one was borne.
With them we fringed the pall and wound the bier,
  And decked the pillow where the dear head lay,
  Within their sacred presence knelt to pray,
And mingle with their sweets the bitter tear.
And now we seek to gain the goal of life
  Within the merits these pure flowers possess,
With love and innocence we find them rife,
  Their fullest gift, return of happiness.
Joy fills our hearts, there is no fear of strife,
  For they are here again to cheer and bless.

THE TUBE ROSE.

O SWEET Tube Rose, of alabaster whiteness!
  Beauty and scent enshrined in petals fair
  Are more than gifts of earth and ambient air,
Are more than comes of day's exalted brightness.
We see upon thy stem of flexile lightness
  A crown of opening buds beyond compare,
    The clustering gems of God's pure thoughts placed there
To symbolize the bloom of chaste uprightness.

Rare pearls of hope! to fettered souls ye speak,
Whose powers for good in germ enfolded lie,
  Whose every struggle toward the light is weak,
And who to live, must first to nature die.
For life's most perfect blossom long we sigh,
Slow growth unfolds the flower of destiny.

TO THE FIVE-FINGER.

(*Potentilla Canadensis.*)

UNSOUGHT, unloved, with few to note thy ways,
    And yet we deem a mead of merit thine,
  Since bitter drops are mingled with life's wine.
For, like sweet charity that hideth dearth
Of soul, thou coverest the stony earth
  With thy five-fingered leaves, thou holdest up
  To heaven a chalice pure, a golden cup,
As if to render God both prayer and praise.
    Thy lowly heart in modesty retires,
    But, with thy little flower to heaven aspires.
  As in sincerity all souls are meek
  Who in humility Christ's goodness seek,
    May I like thee true virtue upward bear
    Refined as incense-odors, sweet and rare.

THE CALLA LILY.

LIKE some ethereal form in robe of white
    We watched it slowly climb the emerald stair,
  Until at last, unfolded sweet and fair
It crowned the stem, a coronet of light.
The ample leaf with surface burnished bright
    Drank in the moisture and the balmy air,
    While root and stem gave strength the bloom to bear,
Then beauty and perfection met our sight.

Thou chaste exotic, lily of the Nile,
  The jewel cup of Flora's fragrant bowers,
In thy deep center gleams a bar of gold,
Rare pearls and dew-glint diamonds dost thou hold;
  We call thee queen among thy sister flowers.

THE PURPLE PANSY.

FROM out the early morn, a tinted light
  Fell where the pearl white rose adorned its place,
  And on its spotless bosom left its trace.
The spirit of the sinking sunset bright
Vied with its shadows deep'ning with the night,
  And o'er the pansy's pale uplifted face
  She threw a robe of purple velvet grace;
That gift of beauty golden eyes requite.
But what the lesson this sweet flower brings?
  Does its rich life but teach us to be glad?
And, as the swan its latest hour sings,
  Should joy not reach us when our hearts are sad?
Its fragrant influence drawn from worlds above,
With floral tongue proclaims my "God is love."

THE SNOW FLOWER.

IT is a wonder in the world of flowers,
  That grows by glittering streams that never run,
  In sparkling regions of the midnight sun.
Out from the shelter of flake-woven bowers,
Its still retreat mid heartless boreal showers,
  It greets the hour the New Year is begun.
  Three days it rises and the third bright one
It blooms, then dies within the circling hours.

Made perfect in the image of a star
   Its petals shine, its pearly triplet leaves
All diamond-tipped, send happy light afar,
   And happy light from heaven's deep blue receives.
Fairy-like it comes, goes as fairies go,
   Where it fades, seed-jewels glitter on the snow.

BLIGHTED.

JUST in a night they withered,
   Touched by a blighting frost,
Their delicate nerves were shivered
   And their glory all was lost.

Those beautiful flowers that bloomed
   Through spring and summer hours,
And the balmy air perfumed,
   At the call of dews and showers.

They are gone, our bright hopes perished,
   And close to the earth they lie,
The sweet things that we cherished
   So quickly doomed to die.

O, thus on our spirits' flowers
   May come some chilling blight,
Though the germs by heavenly powers
   Were nurtured and brought to light.

Sometime when the sun's fair shining
   Promises setting clear,
And the clouds with golden lining
   Above life's hills appear,

There may lurk in the coming darkness
   Some cold and icy breath,
That swift in the sable blackness
   May hurl the shafts of death.

It may be the frost of sorrow
    Will fall on the nightly air,
To bring us a sad to-morrow
    And rob us of treasures rare.

Or a sudden chill of feeling
    May pass over hearts once warm,
A sadder wreck revealing
    Than comes of the passing storm.

Of the coming days we speak not,
    Of the future who can know,
Over our greenest earth spot
    Falleth the drifting snow.

Where our choicest hopes are blasted,
    May some new life take wing,
And the souls of flowers wasted
    Bloom in perennial spring.

FALLEN.

SHE stood amid a brilliant throng,
    Her face was fair, her eyes were bright,
Faint blushes stole her brow along
    Like crimson flushed in clouds of white.

Her robe was soft as jeweled snow
    That scintillates in morning's beams;
Her diamond chain gave glint and glow
    Like stars that follow twilight dreams.

Rare lilies and a glistening crown
    Secured the mist-wrought flowing veil;
With music floating up and down
    Came perfume rich as Eastern gale.

For blossoms surged along the aisle,
   Hung festooned o'er her shining head,
And drifted to an alter pile
   Where she to statued wealth was wed.

A fallen woman! What, the child
   Of culture, wealth and christian grace?
Who e'er? what e'er her heart beguiled?
   Whence came the brand of black disgrace?

A fallen woman! She would shrink
   From tattered sin-stained sister's form,
Her guarded spirit scarce could think
   Of outcasts mired in passion's storm.

She did not know why wind or sea
   Should rise and sweep life's good away;
Why hearts could not untempted be
   As regulated fountain's play.

That fall, before the angels' eyes
   Though piteous, ranked not as her own;
'Twas of the grasping worldly-wise
   Who human sympathies dethrone.

Though gaunt starvation walked the street,
   Or lay neglected, cold and bare,
While suicide with maddened feet
   Plunged o'er the chasm of despair,

'Tis doubtful if one joy would flit
   At sight of what that grandeur cost,
For deeper than its christian pit
   The world of affluence is lost.

Woe! woe is earth! that noble souls
   By boundless wealth abnormal grow;
Warped where blind selfishness controls,
   Life's amplitude can never know.

Ah! not alone to alleys grim
  Where sin's wild, hideous rites are kept,
Have gone the heavenly seraphim
  And o'er earth's erring children wept.

But they have bowed in princely halls
  And mourned 'mid pleasures' gorgeous train,
Where golden are the serpents' thralls,
  And holy pleadings prove but vain.

To them transgression wears no mask,
  Its heaviest weight, its darkest hue,
In vile prosperity may bask,
  But truth perceives it through and through.

And liberty in grief bemoans
  Her heroines of Pilgrim stock,
Who heard fierce oceans' organ tones
  On bridal tours—to Plymouth Rock.

How hath the nation gone astray
  Where rotten monarchies have led;
What blood-bought rights have paved the way
  For greed and tyranny to tread.

How stands the contrast with that race
  Intent on building Freedom's shrine,
Whose women knew the martyrs' place,
  Lived, toiled and died in faith sublime.

Would sons as recreant robbers' band
  If daughters to Columbia turned,
Bewailing glory of the land
  That once beneath her banner burned?

Rise, women, rise! quench greed and pride
  Torch-lighted at the forge of hell,
For God's Republic now decide,
  Or shrink, and wait its funeral knell.

A LESSON.

ONCE I beheld—though years are long since fled—
   The sun come up out of the waters deep,
And, shrouded by the dream-haze of its sleep
Upon the snow-capped waves its rose-light shed,
And where was white foam, rubies danced instead.
   The winds bent low and gave their harp a sweep,
   The blue-keyed ocean did its rhythm keep
Until their songs seemed one, so closely wed.
And so I learned, it is not that things seem
   Just what they really are, illusions teem
From glass of different shades through which we look
To con the lessons given in life's great book,
   But we shall know and understand aright,
   If we but read them in the Truth's clear light.

MOTHERLAND.

DAUGHTERS of the nation listen!
   Liberty to you appeals!
Tearful eyes around you glisten,
   While she supplicating kneels.
To their homes your fathers brought her
   Through the flood and fire of war;
Through the thunderstorm and slaughter
   Rolled her fair triumphal car.

And they said, "All men are equal
   With inalienable rights;"
Little dreaming of the sequel,
   That has filled the land with blights.
For a while their sons defended
   That great heritage with power;
Sought the good that was intended,
   For the country's lasting dower.

But the demon, *slavery*, flourished;
  Half approved and half ignored;
At her founts his life was nourished,
  Till he grew to be her lord.
Boldly took not heavy duty
  On such articles as tea;
His, not taxes, but rich booty;
  Even pearls of liberty.

Then a lofty manhood crumbled,
  Like a soulless mass of clay;
For its spirit had been humbled,
  And its honor swept away.
Drooped the flag. the stars were broken
  As by clouds of inky hue!
And the stripes disclosed in token,
  Blood and tears that bondage drew.

When, at length, its folds were lifted
  By the soldier's dying breath,
Was the nation's harvest sifted
  From the bitter seeds of death?
Do not intrigue, sloth and plunder
  Still destroy her ripening grain,
While the world is struck with wonder
  At her turmoil, loss and pain?

Is there yet no hope for nations?
  Must all constitutions fail,
And the heart's uplifted patience,
  Sink and let despair prevail?

Safe between two veiling oceans
  God had kept a land to show,
When the Church and State commotions
  Blackened earth with crushing woe.
When the hells that *priests* created
  Lit the inquisition's flame,
And the flesh was satiated
  In the Holy Spirit's name.

MOTHERLAND.

From Republican Genoa
  To the tortured Spanish land,
Came a man, impressed like Noah
  With the rescue God had planned.
Europe had no aid to furnish;
  Tyrants heard no pleading tone;
They had thrones and arms to burnish,
  Schemes for prowess, all their own.

But a woman heard the story
  Of a land beyond the sea;
And bright visions of its glory,
  Gifted were her eyes to see.
She the jewel treasure offered,
  That adorned her as a queen;
And the gems thus freely proffered
  Bridged the waves to shores unseen,

Where shall be a declaration,
  That will make all *women* free!
Where our eyes shall see a nation
  That is fit for liberty!
Where the rights, divine and human,
  Shall forever be secure,
In the land first bought by woman,
  And by her made good and pure.

For a government parental
  Soon will bring true *order* forth:
Place whate'er is accidental,
  Build "new heaven and new earth."
Heavy is the task before us;
  But it takes no winding course,
Cloudless light is shining o'er us,
  In this day of vital force.

THE FAMOUS HUTCHINSON FAMILY.

THEY loved New England's rugged crown of pines,
    Her granite mountains and her storm-wrought strand,
Her thrifty homes—proud Freedom's lofty shrines
    That held the glory of that Sunrise Land.
They were such children as she well might own,
    For truth of heart had made their vision clear;
Their guileless souls could go with song alone
    To open siege where statesmen quailed with fear.
"Dear Abby," heiress to fair nature's grace,
    With subtle sweetness in her winsome ways;
The warmth of springtime fresh in heart and face,
    And voice attuned to gladsome forest lays.
What knew she there,'mid quiet native hills,
    Of cruel tyranny's encroaching claims?
The tinkling, purling of her playmate rills
    Told naught of wind that carried sleeping flames.
But as her brothers round the hearth-stone's glow
    Sent up the young Republic's noblest strains,
With heavy undertone of heart-wrung woe,
    And touching treble of appalling pains.
'Twas then her youthful, sympathetic eyes,
    Looked forth amazed o'er dark unfathomed wrong,
Like startled lark that sudden floods surprise,
    Her first affright broke forth in fluttering song.
At length; to them courageous impulse came,
    They took it as a mandate heaven-sent;
And all unstained with thought of wealth or fame,
    Like pleading angels trustingly they went,
Impressed that billows, black with threat'ning cloud,
    Illumed, would melt before their music sweet;
And Slavery with lash, with sceptre proud,
    Kneel humbly low at Freedom's sandaled feet.
As fearlessly resounding chords they swept,
    A thrilled world must at once to action rise;

And Honor's soul, that long supinely slept
   Awoke to shame and revolutionize.
Columbia clasped them in her loving arms,
   And let them sing upon her throbbing breast
Their prophecy, their vision of alarms,
   And wisdom's plan to banish wild unrest.
Full was their melody of daring thought,
   That knew not compromise in least degree;
Surpassed the laws the valiant fathers taught
   And claimed the nation wholly for the free.
'Twas for the captives tortured, bought and sold,
   Their pathos trembled on the waves of fire;
Then in unbroken utterance upward rolled
   To claim the golden harps and heavenly choir.
The stirring spirit of their heart found themes
   The breezes to the listening echoes bore;
There was a flash, with sharp portentious gleams
   And then the rude-mouthed vengeful cannon's roar.
Yet still devotedly with zeal they sung,
   And trusted the inspiring Muse alone;
To tocsin peals that Whittier loudly rung
   Their blended voices added victory's tone.
Not as he hoped in holy calm of prayer,
   The message of the great deliverance came,
But on the blast of battle-writhing air,
   And through the hissing sulphur's deadly flame.
Long years rolled on, that numerous household band
   Passed through the curtains of life's outer rim,
Save two, still earnest, journeying hand in hand,
   And oft intoning freedom's hopeful hymn.
But once when autumn's sumptuous gifts were cast
   In rich profusion over earth and wave,
With silvered hair, as from the far-off Past
   They came to stand beside their poet's grave,
In tender cadence, requiem to swell,
   Thus close their mission with events replete,
'Neath sunny skies to sing a last farewell,
   At Whittier's grave, 'twas strange and it was meet,—

For e'er hoarse winter struck his organ cloud
    And wild-wind music wailed on tempest's breath,
That brother's voice amid a solemn crowd
    Came plaintively for her the stilled in death.
Now when that solitary minstrel sings,
    Columbia views her realm from shore to shore,
As if she stood 'neath memory's brooding wings
    And gathered to her heart the days of yore.
And praying there with heavy tears like hail
    That for her cause another band may rise,
Strike mightily, the chords that must prevail,
    And sing new freedom to her shrouded skies.

LIFE'S TREASURE.

LIKE balmy south winds in the early spring,
    That help the myriad buds their sheathes to burst,
And like the perfumed freshness showers bring
    When earth is parched and nature droops with thirst,
        Pure love doth come to me.

Like warblers heralding the break of day,
    Cheering us on life's duties to pursue,
And like their pensive notes at twilight gray
    When falls on leaf and flower the cooling dew,
        Are tones of love to me.

Like violets abloom in tender grass,
    That brightly covers sere and faded sod,
Sweet violets that greet us as we pass,
    E'en though some heedless feet have on them trod,
        Is angel love to me.

And, like the fragrance of the opening rose,
    Whose subtle incense is so freely given,
Whose beauteous life that silently outflows,
    Reminds of ministrations borne from heaven,
        Love's breathings fall on me.

Each gentle deed and every kindly thought,
  Is to my soul a messenger of good,
For more than all the ties by nature wrought
  Is that blest gift of angel sisterhood
      Whose love encircles me.

I'll humbly walk the self-denying way,
  And oft will seek the silent vale of prayer;
Through earnest effort strive each coming day
  So true to be, as worthily to share
      The love bestowed on me.

A shield that from all harm my soul could keep,
  A light that guided through the shadowy vale,
A staff that helped me to ascend the steep,
  A living fount whose waters would not fail
      I've proved this love to be.

It giveth holy courage to the heart,
  And strength that crowns with victory its strife,
All radiant in the truth it doth impart
  A joy forever new in endless life,
      This power of love so free.

ALONE.

LINES SUGGESTED ON HEARING A ROBIN SING IN OCTOBER.

ROBIN red-breast, long ago I thought thy song was hushed,
  When autumn frosts thy leafy home with many tints had flushed,
And now the leaves upon the ground are rustling dry and sear,
Yet thy lone notes from yonder copse are sweetly quaint and clear.

Have thy companions left thee here to brave the wintry storm,
While they have sought the sunny skies of climate soft and warm?
Sing on sweet bird! the genial air of these autumnal days
Wakes in my heart a kindly glow responsive to thy lays.

I think of many hearts bereft, in this cold world of ours,
Who had their summer time of joy amid life's fairest flowers;
But when adversity's chill wind around their pathway swept,
The bloom of friendship withered, and streams of gladness slept. .

Averted faces smile no more as they were wont to smile,
And no loved song of cheerful hearts the weary hours beguile,
But, cloistered in the gloomy cell of bitter discontent,
Regretful of the past they sigh or wail a sad lament.

Misfortune's seal too oft is set on faces young and fair,
For lack of help the erring sink to misery and despair,
And darkning shadows forward fall on many a lonely path,
Where wayward feet unconscious, tread the downward course to death.

Oh, was there more of love divine on this broad earth below,
'Twould lume the gloomy haunts of sin with its celestial glow,
And many hearts now crushed by scorn —who to their fate were driven—
Would be reclaimed by love, that breathes the blessed word, "forgiven."

As He whose bright example gleamed adown the
   ages past,
Asked those who knew no sin, to first the stone of
   judgment cast,
But guilty hearts shrank from the deed, as ne'er they
   shrank before,
While He unto the erring said, "arise, go sin no
   more."

O words so full of charity! so rich in heavenly love!
More potent far than human law the sinner's heart to
   move;
'Tis Christ indwelling in the heart that prompts to
   noble deeds,
And meets with truth's exalted power the spirits's inmost needs.

Oh, blessed is the heart, that tunes its heavenly min-
   strelsy,
While drawing inspiration deep O fount of love from
   Thee!
Depending on the power that guides, through bright
   and clouded days,
At morn and eve it lifts the voice in hymns of grateful
   praise.

ADORATION.

I LOVE, I deeply love, there is so much
   My earnest heart embraces, and each day
Finds reason for true happiness. My mind
Springs up exultant every time I think
Of God's unfailing beauties, and my soul
Rejoices in His love.
                    Sometimes I think
To count the glories o'er, and blessings full,
And ever varying scenes before my eyes,

But find no good beginning, for around
And round, a perfect circle do they fill.

But be it first among my buoyant joys,
The winter time, with all its gale and storm,
And pearly snows and frosty air and chill;
Its radiant blue and clear and matchless light,
And glowing stars that gem the nightly sky;
These usher in the merry mornings of
The glad New Year, the season when old Time
Seems to have reckoned up his full accounts
And with new courage started out again.

I love the happy spring, and gleeful birds,
And myriad blossoms of the hill and dale,
Whose swaying censers perfume all the air.
The stream, its verdant banks and pebbly bed,
Whose varied coursing ends within the sea,
The great deep sea, the crystal ocean, where
Many millions have rendered up their souls,
And laid their bodies down among the strange
And countless wonders of its trackless vault.
I love the wave, the foam, the bounding shore.

I love the sunbeams gleaming through the blue,
And clouds that 'mid them sail, and all the gifts
They give throughout the year. The dews, the stars,
The breezes that make glad the summer time.
I love the daisied meadows soft and green,
The waving golden grain and tasseled corn,
And all the mellow fruits of harvest time.
How grand the thundering in the awful dark,
The vivid flash, and rolls of ebon mist,
And rainbows painted in the evening sky.
Behold the mountain-tops and sylvan slopes,
Fountains, cañons, cataracts, rocky cliffs, indeed
I cannot tell it all, but well I love,
Yea more, I fill with ecstasy, and pant
Amid the palpitations of my heart,

So awed am I, wondering how God could
Have made them so.
      I love the happy soul
Who walks and lives among these things, and loves
Them too; through them is known the great kind God,
His handiwork, omnipotence and power.
And 'mong them all, most dearly truly loved
Is my good *home, sweet home*, all circled round
With these unfailing lovely gifts.
       If things
External could the soul's *eternal* grace
Insure, and give to life below and life
Beyond, the joy and treasure it would gain,
Then would our living be complete; no sound
Of discord would there be, nor strife nor woe,
So perfect would the concord be. But sad
Enough, much evil born to mutiply
Has entered every human heart, and darkened
With its clouds and graceless images
The holy light, and robbed mortality
Of bliss, its just and rightful heritage.

I love the truth, the virtues every one,
The heart most honest, true to consciousness of right;
The brave, the noble, valiant in the cause
That will uplift to heaven all the race.
The ever gentle truly Christian spirit
That every day gives out its gifts of gold
In deeds and words refined, and coined within
The mint of faith, and scattered with kind care.
I love the wayward, erring, thankless,
With a pitying love that harbors no ill-will,
And fain would pardon those who do me wrong.
I prize my counselors, companions, friends;
The kiss that ministers sweet peace, and words
That teach the holy way of righteousness.
I daily pray that 'mong the many things
That *others* love, they may love *me*,
For I would win it by my toil, and strive

To recompense it by my humble gains.
I often pray for angel care and kind
Direction, and all that will redeem and
Make me worthy of a privilege to live
Upon God's earth, so glorious and great,
So beautiful, so grand and truly good.

THE PILGRIM AND THE MILE-STONES.

I AM a pilgrim, this is Christmas day,
   And I recall the Tyrian scenes of time;
Steal back in thought o'er memory's hallowed way
   Till I can hear the carol and the chime.
'Twas first through holly boughs and mistletoe,
   And clustering crimson berries hung o'erhead,
That I looked forth with wonder on the glow
   Which fell upon the path that I should tread,
Ah well! my heart, how strange, how strange it seems
   To musing wait till past and present meet,
To bring experience face to face with dreams
   And calmly taste the bitter with the sweet.
There stretched the spangled, twinkling world of snow,
   Then came the rain pellucid in its fall
That turned to velvet grass, soft, green and low
   Beside the road along the orchard wall.
The way was lengthy from the wee mile-stone
   Where violets wore spectacles of dew,
To that glist mark that reared itself along
   Where lovely school-bell morning-glories grew.
When reached 'twas further to the cross-road sign
   Beside the bridge where opening roses blushed,
Where trembling waters slid from shade to shine,
   Awoke the lilies white and onward rushed.
The stone half hid in sunset autumn leaves,
   In aster, ferns and feathery golden-rod,
Is just across the field of withered sheaves
   Where sunbeams bar the shadows deep and broad.

There is a snow space to the slab of moss
   Which stands beside the wall of gathered years,
Whereon is graved our varying gain and loss
   With glint of smile, with shimmering dew of tears.
That mile is shortest, for it melts in spring
   That overlaps chill winter's lowering gloom,
Shakes out the breath of fragrant blossoming
   And shows through mist-vales fair elysian bloom.
The pilgrim pauses, for the angels call,
   Life stoops and whispers, "come, I go before;"
From earth's great mile-stone crumbling linchens fall
   And lo! that tablet is the heavenly door.
Henceforth the road shall not be marked with stones,
   Nor fitful longings lure as here in time,
Glad crystal fountains shall divide the zones
   And life's sweet rhythm glide into its rhyme.

GRATEFUL THOUGHT.

NOT for a favored spot alone
   The sun its radiance gives,
But for the wide world's joy
   Its blessed influence lives.
The lone pine on the mountain top,
   The floweret in the vale,
The verdant grass and waving grain
   All tell the same sweet tale.
"Thou art my sun" is whispered softly
   From each living thing,
And day bears up this grateful thought
   Upon expanded wing.
So, with effulgence God infills
   This universe of life,
And none so low, or sad, or worn
   With time's embittered strife

But may look up with confidence
  To light and love divine
And say, O Father—Mother—God,
  I feel that Thou art mine.

UNREST.

Heave, heave, ye grand billows on Time's cradled sea,
  Tumultuous toss on its breast!
Break, break on its strand ye wild waves and free,
  Ye are emblems of human unrest!

The surging of thought from the depths of the mind
  Is swaying the nations to-day,
The tides that are rushing, what power can bind?
  Who, truth's potent forces shall sway?

There are prophets arisen as true as of yore,
  Apostles who hallow no creeds,
Who are waking to action as never before,
  To work for humanity's needs.

With new inspiration the people are stirred,
  How the old wrongs and new wrongs will quail,
Till righteousness answers to justice deferred,
  And the true golden rule will prevail.

While the voice of the throng loudly clamors for right,
  There are many who silently bear,
Awaiting God's time, and the arm of His might,
  To bring a response to their prayer.

The strong rule of centuries rises to sight,
  A castle, with battlements high,
Which the art, skill and valor of labor's bold knight
  With courage and patience defy.

Not force or blind passion will conquer' or win,
  Nor the red flag, defiant unfurled ;
Ope your hearts, O ye people, let Christ enter in,
  He triumphs o'er sins of the world !

The Master was greatest, yet humblest in name,
  No landed estate did He own,
No home, and no title to wealth laid He claim,
  By *love* was *His* mission made known.

The friend of the poor, the weak and oppressed,
  Reprover of folly and sin ;
The wrongs of the widow and orphan redressed,
  And strove all the erring to win.

Are ye his vicegerents, ye sceptered and crowned,
  Who rule with the pomp of a state,
Whom thousands of vassals with splendor surround,
  And homage receive from the great ?

Ah nay ! the cry passes from door unto door,
  From the temple whose service He loved,
The Saviour is found in the " Priest of the Poor," *
  His mission is blest and approved.

God sends through the lowly the means of His grace,
  Through hearts that are rich in His love,
Whose feelings go out to the whole human race,
  The worth of the gospel to prove.

Pride and power hath narrowed redemption's broad
      plan,
  The Church would extinguish its lights,
Its prelates deny the true manhood of man,
  And would wrest from him heaven-born rights.

Low arched are its portals, and dim are the rays
  That fall on high altar and aisle,
Or lume the deep transepts where worship and praise
  Resound through the time-honored pile.

---
*Dr. Edward McGlynn.

Shall he be disgraced whom the Lord would uphold?
   Who loveth like him to do good,
Whose teachings to-day, like the precepts of old
   By the selfish are not understood.

As multitudes listened in reverent mood
   To truths which the Saviour declared,
Nor went from his presence till comfort and food
   From his bounteous hand they had shared,

So the teachers of men must in sympathy blend
   With hearts that have one common need,
Equality, justice and mercy defend,
   The cause of the lowliest plead.

Then blessings will follow Religion's pure name,
   Its ministries truly divine
Will kindle anew its bright altar flame,
   And souls will return to its shrine.

TWO LESSONS FROM EGYPT.

O EGYPT! from thy land of sun and gloom
     We catch a gleam
Like rays reflected from a lighted room
     Across a stream;
Or like the hand that saves us from our doom
     In dangerous dream.

O Egypt! how the centuries have dealt
     Their withering blows
Against thy pride, and how thy soul has felt
     The pain that grows
More piercing as the tides of being melt
     In death's repose.

From thee mankind learned systems black with wrong,
    And learned from thee
How laws that foster vice protect the strong;
    How cruelty
And fraud condemn the weak; but ages long
    Thou'st bent the knee.

Thy masters came with Mammon's artful tricks
    That set aside
Thine ancient customs, and their interdicts
    Thy laws defied;
And where the Hebrews made the strawless bricks
    Thy princes died.

O Egypt! from thy misery and sin
    This truth is born,
That they who scatter thorns life's way within
    Must tread the thorn;
And they who hurl the deadly javelin
    By it are torn.

And Egypt, from thy gently flowing Nile
    Comes wisdom's creeds,
That they who sow in faith shall reap the while
    The precious seeds;
That yet where tyrants fall, shall sweetly smile
    More holy deeds.

For at the yearly flood-time of the waves
    Thy children cast
The lotus seeds, and from their hidden graves
    They rise at last
Strong in their moorings as a ship that braves
    The sweeping blast.

And so with sun above and waves around,
    And Nature's praise
Forever urging them with cheerful sound
    And pleasant ways,
They yield a plenteous harvest to abound
    Through many days.

Thus from thy lotus blossoms we have learned
    A lesson true,
To plant in season though by many spurned,
    Or praised by few,
And wait in patience till the seed is turned
    To beauty new.

WILLIAM CULLEN BRYANT.

BORN NOVEMBER 3, 1794.

A CENTURY'S close dims not thy glorious fame,
  Thou loyal son of brave New England sires,
  Who at their hearth-stones kindled freedom's fires
And won by valorous deeds an honored name.
A noble lineage holds thee in claim ;
  Thy soul was cradled 'neath these forest spires
  Where "God's First Temples" wakened high desires,
And inspiration fanned Faith's sacred flame.
  Thy dream of youth in " Thanatopsis " given
Into thy closing days its beauty wrought,
  And gave thee access to a loftier heaven
Than is by creed or cringing error brought.
  All honor to thy blessed memory,
  Long live the praise of thy sweet minstrelsy.

BETHESDA.

WITHOUT the Holy City's pond'rous gate,
  There calmly lay Bethesda's healing pool,
  Whose waters gushed from hidden fountains cool.
Beside its curb were stricken ones, whom fate
Had made to suffer, there to watch and wait
  Till God's dear angel came, as was its rule—
  To bring the gift unknown to man or school
That would restore the sick and desolate.

We all have errors, illness and distress,
Which like a weight upon our spirits press,
   That need the cleansing of the crystal wave,
   That need the power to strengthen, help and save.
From every sin we long to find redress
Through the redeeming life of holiness.

THE HUMMING-BIRD.

WEE jeweled beauty of the summer fair!
   How love our hearts such pretty little things,
  Like feathery mist appear its lightning wings
Wrought like the rainbow sunset, sky and air.
With weight that scarce would balance with a hair
   It visits 'mong the flowers, unpoised it clings,
   And from deep nectaries rich sweets it brings
With matchless speed and most exquisite care.
It darts between the breezes without fear,
   And dances on the sunbeams every way;
Is still as gay when stormy clouds appear
   As when a star lets down its silvery ray.
Think of its tiny nest and nestlings dear
   'Mong green moss sheltered where the shadows play.

HYGEIA.

FAIR goddess, thou wingest through every land
   To paint bright roses on each smiling face;
  O leave some symbol of your matchless grace
Where'er you linger, and with steady hand
Renew the weak and fainting with your magic wand;
   Though far you roam yet still in every place
   The artist's skill in beauteous forms we trace
Like gleaming pictures of a fairy band.

Pure health, we prize you for the wealth you bring,
    For strength and blessing crowning all our days,
And may the youthful voice with merry ring
    Make all the woodlands sound with loving praise
For your rich gift, your lovely offering
    To human hearts who walk in righteous ways.

COMPENSATION.

NATURE is strange, but meets the great demand,
    She has a substitute at every hand;
If blind, our sense of touch will keener grow,
    If deaf to sound, our eyes will motion know,
If numb our feet, the brain will help contrive,
    Our hands will prosper us, and hopes revive;
But, if it be perchance we lose our breath,
    Her only offer, is the boon of death.

DEATH OF THE PHARISEE.

PASTOR and deacons, and members were there,
    The church tower was just in sight,
And the Pharisee gave them his last proud prayer
    From lips that were deadly white.
He spoke of the good that the blood had done
    That dripped from Calvary's tree,
Of the godly race which his feet had run,
    Of his deeds of charity.

And he thanked the Lord again and again
    With a pious befitting look,
That he was not like unto other men,
    But followed the Holy Book.

And pastor and members and deacons groaned,
    And murmured, "let praise be given,
The crucified also for us atoned,
    With him we shall share in heaven."

But the Pharisee saw through veil of death
    An angel of truth draw near,
And he wildly struggled and gasped for breath,
    For his soul was struck with fear.
And the angel said with searching voice,
    "Do you think that your shams will win?
Can your spirit in light of life rejoice
    When it hath a burden of sin?"

They kindly bolstered the Pharisee up
    To give him the holy bread,
And brought with care the communion cup,
    Then stood amazed at his dread.
"Oh, why do you bring me the wine," he said,
    "For drunkards my eyes can see,
That unto its treacherous tide have fled
    From a woe that was wrought by me.

"Ah! they were the trustful, hopeful men
    Who thought my profession true,
But just by the turn of my crafty pen
    Black ruin their fortunes knew.
And oh! from my sight take the children's food,
    That I stole from the widow's hand,
Their father had called me his kinsman good,
    And left me his helpless band.

"But now I must meet with that humbled race,
    Distorted by want and crime;
Their deep, hidden misery and anguish trace
    In passing from shores of Time.
And look! do you see in yon crowded street
    Lone outcasts that wander there?
Do you know that their hearts once pure and sweet
    Were wreathed with parental care?

"I gathered them into my lustful arms
   By wiles that a fiend might hate ;
I robbed them of more than youthful charms,
   But repentance comes too late."
And the angel said, with uplifted hands,
   "Oh ! would that they all might hear,
For that is the guilt that ensures the brand,
   Which will hardly disappear."

Then the Pharisee raised his dying head,
   And said in a bitter tone,
To those who were shrinking round his bed,
   "Can anyone cast a stone?
For we are alike in our worldly pride,
   Alike in the angel's eye,
Alike in the sins I strove to hide,
   And alike we all must die.

"Then give to the flames my vain, pompous will,
   And know you are dispossessed,
For gain that was gotten by means so ill
   Belongs to the sore oppressed."
And pastor and deacons and members said
   With many a knowing shrug,
"Our brother is fevered, out of his head,
   Physician, where is thy drug?

"Or where thy balsam of acid and gall,
   That was a last drink of old?"
But e'er he could answer their urgent call
   The Pharisee's heart was cold;
And they gave the Pharisee burial grand,
   Griefless as ever was given ;
Published his righteousness over the land,
   Yet knew he was far from heaven.

THE RAINBOW OF THE MORNING.

A SOB, a moan, and then a burst of tears,
  All through the night the spirits of the air
Spoke grief like lost souls smitten with despair,
In wail and groan.

A shaft of light, the first glad morning sign,
Then grand and swift through ragged rift
Bright golden wedges pierced the misty hedges
That hid the valley's line.

And up the hills like shadowy ghosts
Advanced the morning's phantom hosts,
The spectral shades that warm the glades
When dew distils.

The east was blue,
But in the west a cloud hung like a mourning shroud,
Then silvery streams that caught the beams,
The sun sent forth from south to north,
Stretched o'er the shaded plain and draped the golden
    grain
Like beaded fringes new.

Then sunlight struck the form of fast retreating storm,
And from its web of mist spun out a shining twist,
Whereon with magic thread of gold and blue and red
It wove a fabric old; and yet as new as when
God sent His sign to men that He would ne'er again
Destroy His works.

And so when friends inquire
What lovely scenes inspire
The soul to marvel at the earth's adorning,
I say that to my mind
The best that God designed
Is perfect in the rainbow of the morning

THE GROVES.

WE love the groves, the groves of leafy green,
    Where cometh many a beauty of the year,
Where lingereth not a shade of gloom or fear,
For sunshine rays come every bough between,
And waves of summer air pass through unseen.
    From topmost heights that in the blue appear
    Swell happy matinees glad, full and clear,
And all day reigneth peace, calm and serene.
The Dryads love the groves and in them stray,
    And Flora takes her vines to blossom there;
E'en Boreas—though in wild tumultuous way—
    Leaves pearls and stars among them everywhere.
Who loves the flowers and grass and summer day
    Must love the sylvan isles with thought and care.

PSYCHE.

O SOUL! in smallest globule sent
    From the innermost Soul's bright Portal,
With infinite purpose and life intent
    When fledged are thy wings immortal.
No folding thy powers when once they have sprung
    From the chrysalis that confined thee,
From life's first note is the paean sung
    Of the ages that enshrined thee.
Thy breath in the atom first is felt;
    Rock, grass and tree enfold thee;
Dissolving matter may fuse and melt,
    Yet its various forms all hold thee,
Progressing toward the destined height
    Through mineral, plant and creature,
Till man appears as a God of Light
    Perfect in form and feature.

FAITH.

INTO the solemn silence of the night,
    We lift our hands in confidence, not fear,
    We feel the strength of unseen forces near;
A sheltering love encircles with its might,
A light shines out upon the inner sight.
    The outer darkness may be dense and drear,
    Yet even then we feel that God is here,
And with a childlike trust we seek the light.
Until by *faith* anointed, eyes were dim;
    We blindly groped the valley's shadowed way,
Nor saw the glory of the mountain's rim,
    Nor blessed the hand that led from night to day.
The stars may pale, but faith's clear flame shall rise
Refulgent as the glow of noon-day skies.

BY THE SEA.

I LINGERED alone on the shore white and still,
    Close by the grand, great and wonderful sea,
    While foam-crested waves, high-rising and free
Surged inward and outward as ever they will.
I saw the sea nymphs in fanciful drill,
    My ear caught the notes of their sweet melody;
    My spirit transported with glad ecstacy
Forgot every dread and deep-hidden ill.
High up from the waves I watched the sun rise,
    And gathering its rays, again hide its gold;
O'er the swelled waters with forceful surprise
    I saw the wild storm its terrors unfold,
Then pass; and a mirror unchanging it lies
    Where heaven's bright image is fair to behold.

WRECKED.

WHAT more could have been done for thee O soul!
  Whose plighted faith and broken vows, now lie
Like empty shells upon a foreign shore.
Where hast thou drifted? Down a dangerous tide,
Till thou art stranded on those hidden reefs
That skillful mariners with care avoid;
But which the incautious dash upon
With all the fury of the surging waves.
Wrecked! alas! the very thought brings grief.
That barque, whose sails, spread to the favoring
   breeze,
Braved tempest, storm and tide full many a year,
While faith stood at the helm, and marked her course,
And every virtue, bore a noble sway
At all the posts of duty and of trust.
But lo! a dead calm rested o'er life's sea,
The white sails, reefed, unto the topmasts clung,
The pilot slept, and all on board reposed,
Nor ever thought of danger brooding near.
E'en conscience failed her vigils true to keep;
So, lulled to rest secure, they sweetly dreamed
Of quaffing pleasure from life's gilded font.
But, from below, up sprang a treacherous crew,
As unperceived before; weak in their strength
When all the higher powers held firm their sway
Nor parleyed with a spirit mean and base.
Bold unbelief, at first possession took,
Desires unhallowed followed in its wake,
And bound were all the safeguards of that soul.
They loosed the anchor, spread the outmost sail,
Threw out the ballast, and in reckless haste
Sped on, they cared not where they went.
The captain's voice was dumb, and mute the sighs
Of all the former guardians of that barque.
And now aground on shoals and sands of time,
O who shall rescue? Is there none to save?

We leave it in the hands of Him, who rules
The destiny of souls, and giveth charge
Unto the angel world concerning them.

FORGIVENESS.

A BLOOMING rose, with matchless beauty flushed,
    Swayed in the breeze its censered fragrance rare,
Each passer by thought it surpassing fair.
The noon-day sun glowed bright, it deeper blushed,
The dews at even-tide came still and hushed;
    But ere the light had flown, O want of care,
    A thoughtless hand had snapped the beauty there,
And in the path it lay all torn and crushed.
Then, did it tear with thorns the ruthless foe
    That flung unto the winds its wealth of bloom?
It blest the hand that laid its beauty low,
    And with its dying breath gave sweet perfume.
O, Christ-like love! Shall human hearts do less?
Then render good for ill, the smiter bless.

PATIENCE.

NOT unto every one comes wealth or fame,
    The pomp of triumph, and the gift of pride;
Not unto all comes glory's wondrous name,
    Whose throne and altar have been deified.

All may not wear the martyr's cloak of fire,
    Nor clasp with fervent arms the burning stake;
All may not feel the prophet's high desire,
    Nor drink the poison cup for conscience sake.

These call for courage which to few is given,
  But humble martyrs meet us every day,
God's patient ones who steadfastly have striven
  'Gainst foes within, and kept them far at bay.

Still all sometimes may feel the stress of toil;
  The disappointment that has failed to win;
All may with sorrow burn the midnight oil,
  Alone with trouble, doubt, distrust and sin.

All may be tried as never soul was tried;
  For so I know, no two can feel alike;
No one can die the death another died,
  No one has struck where you and I must strike.

No one has felt the triumph we may feel,
  Nor seen the light that yet may flood our eyes,
No one has heard the music grand and real
  That still may come to us from paradise.

But hearts that suffer secretly will know
  That Patience with her gentle touch is near,
With balm to soothe the spirit's inmost woe,
  And heal the wounds of bitter doubt and fear.

Then take new courage where before you failed,
  Guard well your life with watchful faith and prayer,
And when your eyes with falling tears are veiled
  Look o'er the mist, the Patience-bow is there.

MY CONCLUSION.

I SOMETIMES deem good fortune
    Has come with me to stay,
  For shadows seem to turn about
    And go the other way.

The clouds disperse, the sky grows bright,
   Despair is lifted up,
I find success in everything,
   I read it in the cup.

I gather up the ills of life,
   I'll never have them more,
And put them in the wheel of fate
   Revolving at my door.

But consternation, what dismay,
   What disappointment, when
The wheel of fortune turns around
   And spills them out again.

O I'm forever baffled
   With the ups and downs of life,
And ceasing will be never
   Till ends this mortal strife.

But life's gray skein and threads of gold
   Are tangled into wit,
And if this world is good for me
   I still am good for it.

TO OUR HONORED FATHER,

DANIEL BOLER.

O SOUL colossal! loving fountain heart!
   O spirit clothed with heavenly holiness!
A wisdom that was wise in every part,
   A charity revealed in lowliness.

We stand before thee, children of thy care,
   Whom thou has guarded thro' the changing years,
Taught by the counsel, shielded by thy prayer,
   That circling bond that gathers and endears.

Thy foresight that o'erlooked the battle-cloud
   Heavy with thunder-bolt and black with doom,
Saw still that God was where the tempests crowd,
   And Zion should preserve her pristine bloom.

Calamity was powerless to dismay,
   Nor could emergency o'erthrow thy trust,
That searching vision in its grand survey
   Beheld life's trials but as desert dust.

Thy love was an oasis, restful, calm,
   And cooling springs the weary pilgrims found,
The breath of balsam and the touch of balm
   That banished grief and healed the sharpest wound.

A shepherd, father, saviour, true from youth,
   Then God's Annointed, called to comprehend
Unfoldments vast from occult realms of truth,
   And yet to lowliest, blindest souls descend.

Tho' thistle-hearts wore armor barbed with sin
   That tore thy tender heart and made it bleed;
Thine eye discovered soft, white love within,
   Above wild nature's rank and cruel seed.

What joy, what anguish quivered in thy breast
   Like arrow-heads and sunbeams on a tree,
The heavenly host and Zion's faithful, blest,
   While rabble passion shot askance at thee.

Within Christ's sufferings thou hadst learned to live,
   Until beatitudes thy spirit knew,
And thou couldst say, "My Parents, O forgive!"
   The undeveloped know not what they do.

We heard thy eloquence for Zion roll,
   And bear conviction to invade the heart,
Exalted messages that thrilled the soul,
   And gave it courage for an upward start.

There was a grandeur not to be described
   In thy integrity's pervading grace ;
The immortality thy life imbibed
   Gave strength and glory to thy noble face.

Our thoughts, our memories like the swelling sea
   Whose loud-voiced billows sink in music sweet,
Lift up their waves of gratitude to thee,
   Then murmuring melt in tear-drops at thy feet.

Like birds of passage, resting from the wing,
   The words that we would summon take their flight ;
But what are words before the offering
   Our innmost souls bring to thee as thy right.

DUTY.

A NARROW mountain pass my feet must go ;
   A steep declivity, a rugged way,
My back must ache with burdens of the day,
Stern cragged rocks their darkening presence throw,
The mists rise up from valleys dim and low ;
   O'er thorny paths, through shadows cold and grey,
   Still on I press, nor pause in dread dismay,
For it is duty's path full well I know.
Still will I climb, and climbing, gain the height,
   Worn are my sandals, peace my feet has shod,
While hope beholds the shining Tabor light,
   And love forgets the road my feet have trod,
And from the mount of vision, on my sight
   Gleams the bright vernal table-lands of God.

TRIBUTE OF AFFECTION TO ELDER GILES B. AVERY.

O WE bewail thee! yet with sorrowing trust
    Reach through the darkness for the helping hand,
For God will succor, yea He will, He must
    Relieve the anguish of this smitten band.

O we bewail thee! on the mountain height
    Thy spirit like a quenchless signal gleamed,
Inspiring to a freer, loftier flight,
    To that full good whereof the world hath dreamed.

Thou were to us an angel in the form,
    Thy love encircled Zion in its sheen,
To temper e'en the passing of the storm,
    And make her vineyards flourishing and green.

A soul transparent, yet not sun nor moon
    Made of thy righteousness a beacon tower,
The light of God was in thee at its noon,
    His attributes unrivaled gave thee power.

O patient loving one! O martyr soul!
    Beside the altar standing in thy lot,
How oft ingratitude made thee its goal,
    And all that sin produced with venom brought:

But virtues held the temple of thy life,
    Serene forgiveness kept the pearly gate,
And looked with pitying eyes upon the strife,
    And but deplored the fallen human state.

Thy triumph here, an altitude sublime,
    Ambition dead and crumbled into dust;
Thy spirit roused to teach the weak to climb
    To where thy treasures were secure from rust.

Thy wealth of kindred o'er the opal tide,
   A shining host, by far too vast to view;
Thy loved companions on the shadow side
   As bright, as trusted, but alas, so few.

With them thy interest and thy strength will be,
   Fair courts could not entice nor death debar;
As well set back the limit of the sea,
   Or from its orbit drive the polar star.

Thy dauntless words still ringing in our ears,
   "Alone!—not so; the heavens are on our side,
The work of God is thrilling! and appears
   In endless magnitude, all glorified!

"The numbers may be few, the remnant small,
   We do not see the hosts that for us fight,
Discouragement nor evil, ne'er befall
   The faithful souls who travel in the light.

"The work of God His legions will sustain,
   There is no such thing as failure, Truth is sure;
The cross wins what the sword can never gain,
   Faith! living faith! the victory will secure."

O words of prophecy! your import grand
   Break our bereavement with a sense of cheer,
For he who bore them, now in spirit land,
   Will he not make our duty still more clear?

Did he unmindful from his burden go,
   And leave to bleeding hearts his life-long care?
Nay, he will enter heaven's immortal glow
   With lips of eloquence, with heart of prayer.

Our own ambassador, gone up to plead,
   Appeal, implore and crave for aid divine;
Who better knows our urgency and need
   Than he whose soul was prayers, perpetual shrine?

The supplications often sent, he takes,
  Goes with them now to advocate their claim,
His hidden fire in Zion, smolders—wakes—
  And bursts in shafts of sin-consuming flame.

Home questions rise, and in the honest soul
  The answer follows with unswerving zeal,
For they who seek the cleansing waves that roll
  Pause not to cavil, nor uncertain feel.

What is my aim, my purpose, slow or swift?
  My love, my loyalty to Zion's laws?
Abjuring self, submission to the gift,
  Full dedication to her sacred cause.

And whatsoe'er is less than this is sin,
  The Judas spirit that would still betray;
The coward—traitor—that would seek to win
  Some vile advantage in the adverse day.

The brave support the lasting work of God,
  And to the rock-bed of their faith go down
To find its strong foundations firm and broad,
  Whose superstructure shall the ages crown.

In Zion's tribulation none are small;
  From out of sorrow heroism springs;
Integrity is more than mounted walls,
  And sweet obedience draws protecting wings.

Calamity unmatched hath dealt its blow,
  And smote the Shepherd, and our eyes are dim,
While they whose balsam healed our every woe,
  'Tis ours to solace in their grief for him.

The mantle of his suffering must descend,
  Some back must bend its heavy weight to bear;
But send by whom thou wilt, O Mother send!
  And Zion's borders will respond with prayer.

Affection's sheaves—the garnered good in store—
　The first fruits and the last—the blossoms new—
Afflicted parents, at your feet we pour,
　For Zion's heart of hearts would comfort you.

A HOLY STILLNESS.

O CALM, clear morning air! all earth is still
　With sweet serenity of Sabbath day,
The early light of morning's golden ray
Rests like the smile of God on plain and hill.
Subdued the songster's lay, and babbling rill;
　The grasses, glittering in their gemmed array,
　Wave low, as if an angel passed that way;
This holy stillness chides each erring will.
Calm us, O God! and let Thy balm of peace
　Drop soothingly, as dew drops on the flowers;
And may Thy love our aching hearts release
　From the harsh tumult of life's weary hours.
For in Thy peace our fevered longings cease,
　And in Thy love, strength, rest from toil are ours.

ELDER RICHARD BUSHNELL.

HE brought a glorious manhood to the strife,
　And gave it freely, with a noble will;
He made a consecration of his life,
　And bade ambition's trumpet-voice be still.
For he had powers that would have gained the fame,
　The wealth, the honors, that the *world* bestows.
But better far, to him, was lot and name
　Among the people that his conscience chose.
He came to them with zealous heart and hand,
　Made all their interests his absorbing care;
Strong in his faith, met persecution's band,
　Yet held his heart in lowly strains of prayer.

The clash of elements that round him rung
    Awoke his energies to fight within,
To strive for conquest while his life was young,
    And evermore to wage a war with *sin*.
In thought, and power to *sway*, he was a king;
    He won a royal priesthood by his zeal;
His soul was gentle as an angel's wing,
    Yet it was keen as Truth's incisive steel.

Before him, malice (supplicating) knelt,
    And bitter envy laid her face in dust,
While bold assailants lost the rage they felt
    And sought for pardon, half convinced they must.
He gave forgiveness as the morn gives light;
    He gave his love as seasons give their fruit;
He blessed with tenderness, rebuked with might,
    Quelled human passions till their waves were mute.

And when his autumn crimsoned to its close,
    We saw the garnered treasures he had found;
We felt his soul's unspeakable repose,
    And knew his spirit was with vict'ry crowned.
We'll miss his cheery voice, and kindly smile;
    We'll miss the hands whose industry we prize;
We'll call him often, in the little while
    That from *our* home to *his* so misty lies.

O *father*, as we bid adieu to thee,
    Our heart-strings vibrate with a plaintive swell;
Our love upwelling, gushing warm and free
    Shall reach thy spirit wheresoe'er it dwell.
What though the years made halos in thy hair,
    And carved their furrows on thy open brow;
They could not give thy heart one rankling care;
    Thy life was true, and thou art blessèd now.

FIELDS OF HEAVEN.

HE has gone to the broader fields of heaven,
    To reap fruition of his earthly toil,
No more for sustenance to strive and moil
For which his mortal strength and life were given;
For simple good his soul has wisely striven,
    And not for greed of wealth or worldly spoil,
    Acquired by means from which true hearts recoil.
O, hang his scythe upon the willow bough
    The old-time friend of more than forty years,
With laurel twine the faithful farmer's plow,
    Nor weep, nor sigh with many bitter tears,
For he who passes from our vision now
Hath wrought with honest aim and noble vow;
    His sterling worth a shining shaft appears.

TO OUR FATHER,

ELDER FREDERICK W. EVANS.

ONE OF THE IMMORTAL NAMES THAT WERE NOT BORN TO DIE.

HONOR in life to whom is honor due;
    O gladly do we bring the pearls of praise,
And flowers of gratitude profusely strew
Upon the pathway of thy autumn days.
Why should we wait until the earthly end
To blindly reach across the jasper wall,
The wealth, the blessing that should now descend,
The benedictions that should on thee fall?
Affection's tokens fill each rolling year,
They come like planets fair to gem thy dome,
The true, the just thy uprightness revere;
But more than fame to *thee*, is love of home.
From east and west, from islands of the sea,
From lands afar beyond the belt of waves

Come messages of love and thanks to thee
For nobly sending forth the word that saves.
True to thy call to preach unto the world,
That place of bondage and of spirit needs,
To show the serpent in the roses curled,
And hurl swift thunderbolts against the creeds;
No fear, no tie, no favor could deter
Thy valient spirit from the conflict strong,
Unflinchingly it faced the powers that were,
And bravely used its sword on ancient wrong.
Integrity and zeal perhaps are stern;
They are thine armor, warm the heart below;
Up through thine eyes we see its home-fires burn,
And in thy kindliness we feel their glow.
The earth demands such saviors as thou art;
Myrrh and frankincense will not banish sin,
'Tis fire from heaven that will cleanse the heart,
And consecration, life anew begin.
'Twas work, 'twas battle that thy ardor taught,
'Twas deep repentance where God's mercies flow,
'Twas Babylon's confusions brought to naught,
Ambition, pride and selfishness laid low.
'Twas angel purity, pellucid, bright,
The word of life revealed, not man-construed;
The dawning of the *day*, not *sunset light*,
The large unfathomed faith that still renewed.
The hope that on the present laid its balm,
Healed the dull wound and soothed the rankling pain,
To grief's wild tempest gave the magic calm,
And soaring, breathed a full triumphal strain.
That hope, no storm-glooms could obscure or dim,
It cleft the darkness with its sabre rays,
And gave the future's broken, distant rim
A coronet of jewels all ablaze.
Dear father, how we prize that glorious hope,
That chieftain spirit, that the heights would scale,
That never stooped in fallacies to grope,
And never knew the coward's watch-word, "fail!"
Swift as the eagle's glance o'er cloud or fen,

Thine eyes discerned the work that was of God,
And knew the structure that was reared by men,
And smote it with the angel's gifted rod.
Whate'er of Christ or holiness the claim,
Lofty in *whiteness*, or in *whiteness low*,
Thy test of purity was still the same,
For loathsome leprosy is white as snow.
The test was in thy soul, the work it did
Gave doctrines by the dual-Christ revealed,
Henceforth in thee were treasures shown and hid,
Because thy call by sacrifice was sealed.
What is the mountain's crest above the storm,
And what the seaward river's constant tide,
Or mellow autumn sun diffused and warm,
Compared with lives by travail glorified?
Think not our love has placed thy worth too high,
For thou art Zion's, none can swell the claim,
And long as truth is blazoned in the sky,
Bright in her galaxy shall glow thy name
With those of *saints* who suffered. Earth may pass,
And heaven be brought together like a scroll,
Yet shall *they* shine above the sea of glass,
Within the deathless region of the soul.

PLEASURE.

<blockquote>
Can pride and sensuality rejoice?
From purity of thought all pleasure springs,
And from an humble spirit all our peace.
— *Young.*
</blockquote>

O, VAIN and empty is the human mind
   That seeks for happiness in sensuous things,
That drinks of pleasure's bubbling surface springs,
And thinks therein to satisfaction find.
True joy is born within the soul's calm deep,
Where lofty aspiration plumes her wings,
Where wise reflection all her treasure brings,
And sweet contentment ever dwells enshrined.

Gay throngs and giddy crowds may onward sweep
Along life's path with passion's blinding force,
But they who in love's lowly valley keep,
Shall join with angels in an upward course,
The rich reward of conscious blessing reap,
And draw their pleasure from a heavenly source.

JOINED THE IMMORTALS.

IN earth we lay the manly form away,
    But who can hold the spirit bold and free?
    It soars to broader life and liberty
Where noble powers of heart and mind bear sway.
With conscious strength of will he held at bay
    And conquered truth's most subtle enemy,
    He magnified his soul's divinity
And lived beyond the progress of his day.
    Prophet and priest, perhaps of eons old,
Inhabitant of world's advanced in light,
    Incarnate, that his spirit might unfold
Unto the race the higher law of right.
How true his purpose, and how keen his sight
    That through time's vista pierced the gates of gold.

GRATEFUL TRIBUTE

To a beloved father in Israel, Elder Joseph Bracket, of West Gloucester, Maine, for his beautiful soul-inspiring words contributed to our monthly paper, *The Manifesto.*

AH! words of truth from living springs sent forth,
    A father's blessing mingled with his love
Are to the soul what light is to the earth,
    Or dew and shower distilling from above.

Baptized, regenerate and exalted soul!
   True to the virgin principle, that gave
Thy early manhood power of self-control,
   And bore thee safely o'er sin's tidal wave.

All glorious in the resurrection life!
   A savior risen on Mount Zion's height,
Where earth, tumultous in her surging strife
   Can never wreck thy battlements of right.

A happy greeting from unnumbered hearts
   Flows forth like ripples on a summer sea;
The tide of loving feeling outward starts,
   Moved by the weighty words there dropped by thee.

The golden sheaves of ripe experience
   We gather in the storehouse of the mind,
And realize the goodly recompense,
   The faithful through obedience may find.

Thy four-score years to holy service given,
   Thy consecration to a noble aim,
Have made a record in the higher heaven,
   And placed among the saints thy hallowed name.

Just like the worthy patriarch of old,
   O, may the mantle of thy blessing fall
On those who now thy pure example hold,
   And on truth's altar sacrifice their all.

Ah! selfish loves and vain ambition draw
   Too many souls from purposes of right;
The carnal life all good would over-awe
   And dim the brightness of fair Reason's light.

The cross forbidding seems to those who seek
   The charms of pleasure's evanescent day;
But to the innocent, the chaste and meek,
   'Tis wreathed in flowers that never fade away.

Not vain shall prove thy labors in the Lord,
   Though souls—unwise—the way of life shall spurn,
Thou wilt enjoy thy merited reward,
   And many yet to righteousness will turn.

O, may thy few remaining years be crowned
   With peace and rest, angelic and serene,
And heavenly glory to thy soul redound
   When no dark clouds or shadows intervene!

With thee our prayer of faith shall never wane;
   The good thou'st prophesied we know will come,
And rich will be the spiritual increase
   That yet shall bless each happy Zion home.

DAY AND NIGHT.

ONE mass of gems the arching dome,
   One mellow twilight way,
A burst of morn's effulgent light,
   And night is lost in day.

The lengthening shadows circle round,
   The sunbeams glide from sight,
Far westward spreads a lake of gold,
   And day is lost in night.

An opening bud—a full blown rose,
   The sands of life are run;
Death clasps time and eternity,
   And day and night are one.

NOT DEAD.

IN MEMORY OF BROTHER DANIEL FRASER,
OCTOBER 10, 1889.

PASSED from our mortal vision,
    Stamped with the seal of death;
Not dead, but in homes elysian
    Breathing immortal breath.

"Not dead," I hear him saying,
    "For in these realms sublime,
Those who are truth obeying
    Find death life's blossom time."

The floweret of the summer
    Lies cold in autumn's tomb;
But soon the soft May breezes
    Revive the bud and bloom.

And thus the spirit groweth
    Through all life's toil and pain,
Its essence upward goeth,
    To bloom in spring again.

So our beloved has left us,
    Yet mourn we not in grief,
The angels have bereft us
    To claim the ripened sheaf.

Yea, ripened by the doing
    Of deeds of godliness,
By duty's path pursuing
    That leads to righteousness.

No good thing ever dieth,
    And they who rise from loss,
Will find earth's struggles brightened
    By the halo of the cross.

The tribute that we bring thee
  Our heart's affections hold;
Through all thy life there runneth
  A thread of purest gold.

For lowly one benighted
  Thy pitying heart was stirred,
No cause by justice lighted
  But thy strong voice was heard.

No monument we rear thee,
  No costly work of art,
Thy works and life endear thee
  Unto each loving heart.

Blest is the soul that giveth
  Its all in sacrifice;
Not dead, that spirit liveth
  In heaven's own paradise.

Not dead but only drifted
  A little farther on,
To where the veil is lifted
  In the summer land of song.

I catch the strains of gladness,
  Rung from the harps of gold,
Released from mortal sadness,
  What glories now unfold.

O spirit blest, immortal!
  Yea, pure and holy one,
Gained is the pearly portal,
  Thine are the laurels won.

Harken, sweet angel voices
  Float from the azure height,
"Not dead, his soul rejoices
  In heaven's eternal light."

MOTHERHOOD.

WHO is a mother? She who strongly holds
    A little group of ties of kindred blood;
Whose dearest treasures are the hearts she folds,
    Whose one ambition is their joy, their good.

Her deep, deep love knows not the ebbing wave
    That wrecks the heart on life's dark treacherous
        tides;
She takes the path that leadeth to the grave
    If on it duty to her loved abides.
Her self-forgetfulness is still the same,
    Affection prompts her ever helpful hand;
From childhood's foible unto manhood's aim
    She patient suffers for that little band.

Yet she is only like the brooding bird
    That spreads her breast against the coming storm,
That trembles not when thunders loud are heard,
    But self-reliant, keeps her fledglings warm.
From fierce gorilla down to sightless mole,
    The female loves and cherishes her charge,
Then cannot woman with immortal soul
    That narrow scope of motherhood enlarge?

If she have children, they should bind her heart
    To sympathize with every child on earth;
To make all mothers' care of her's a part,
    And claim her hand to sow the seeds of worth.
And happy she if none around her cling,
    And she is free where childrens' need is great,
To gather orphans 'neath her sheltering wing
    And be an angel in the way of fate.

O she whose mind may tread a path of stars,
    Whose aspirations heavenly circuits take,
Shall pass with seraphs, through all bolts and bars
    Till fettered captives learn their chains to break.

And wrongs that now cry loudly unto God,
  Will sink in silence and dissolve in air,
When the weak victims that oppression trod,
  Shall rise to freedom and develop there,
No more will they the crystal goblet fill
  With crimson serpents to infest the brain ;
No more will they the unborn infant kill,
  Nor blight its life with sin's corroding stain.

And draining luxury (death's haughty aid),
  That slays with famine and with overflow,
With all injustice will be lowly laid
  Where cold oblivion's misty waters flow.
When mortals feel that God created them
  In that grand "image," *male* and *female* too,
Maternal love shall like a diadem
  Enwrap the soul and give it impulse new,

THE MEMORY OF OUR OWN DEAR MOTHER.

OH ! must she leave us ? Yea. Time's dial hand
    Points to the number that marks off the years
Allotted to her mortal life, and vain
It is to wish it were not so ; but sad
Indeed becomes the circumstance and sadly
Do we bow to the inevitable.

Why so much grief ? Ask each and all her dear
Confiding children, they who have sought her
Constant care, and gained it at her generous
Hand for many, many years ; they who have
Known full well the virture of her love,
And felt the pure affections of her heart ;
They who have heard her counsels true, in words
That sounded forth the oracles of God,
Which bade departure from the paths of sin
And taught the holy way of righteousness.

How often in her gentle mercy has
She called the erring back to Christ, and even
Wayward prodigals forgiven, and made
For them a fullness of good things.
      Firmly
As the mountain rocks that have lain unmoved
Amid the storms of ages, has she stood
Against the tide of nature, persistent
In the right which triumphed in her soul,
Guided by truth that led her calmly on.
Temptation could not turn, nor art deceive,
So perfect was her life, so keen her sight.

Yea our dear mother,—and must she leave us?
Must we behold no more her mortal face,
Nor meet the tender greetings, nor the smile
That let to us the sunshine of her soul?
The spirit world is not afar, and though
We see her not, she will be with her own
Dear children, still to comfort, still to bless,
Still to teach and lead, and save from harm.

O mother! we behold thee passing through
The pearly gates of heaven, not the vale
Of death, crowned with the golden crown of life,
Brightly set with royal gems of virtue,
Robed in fine raiment, white and spotless
As the crystal snow, haloed with the fullness
Of the glory of thy inward being,
And circled with the beauty of the spheres.

Choirs of thy early friends sing happy
Welcomes unto thee, and loving hands
Will grasp thine warmly, and with gladness
Lead thee to sweet rest; rest from earthly toil
And care, within some mansion all prepared
In thy fair heavenly home, where thou may'st
Claim in peace the harvest of thy toil.

O let us live as she has lived, that with
A record pure as her's, *we* too may meet
Our God, and share His boundless grace.

Sing! sing! ye holy ones your *welcome* tunes,
But *we* must sadly chant the *requiem*.

"WE RISE TO CALL HER BLESSED."

AS melt the stars before the morning's light,
    As fade the sunset beams in dusk of even,
So hath her spirit, radiant and bright,
    Passed from our sight to brighter shine in heaven.
Departed from us as a tower of might,
    Based on a rock unyielding, firm and sure,
Gone from our midst, an angel of God's light,
    To wear the star-gemmed crown and robes so pure.

She knows no death, 'tis lost in victory,
    She sleeps to wake to everlasting peace;
With conscious joy she crossed the narrow sea,
    To find from earthly cares a long release.
We ask, what maketh death so calm, sublime?
    She wears the light of triumph round her brow,
Hath she not lived to God the life divine?
    May she not yield with joy the conflict now?

In early youth she heard the angels' call,
    With heart sincere she hastened to obey,
Left father, mother, brothers, sisters, all,
    To find in Christ the life, the truth, the way.
And backward thro' the mist of by-gone years,
    We see her strive each duty to fulfill;
She stood for right through all opposing fears;
    In faith she calmly sought to do God's will.

O, we shall miss her in that holy hour,
    When saints and mortals in communion meet ;
Yea, miss those thrilling words, those tones of power,
    That voice of tenderness and love so sweet.
Yet, mourn we not as those bereft of hope,
    Full well we know the goal is nobly won ;
An angel band the pearly portals ope,
    To greet her at the setting of life's sun.

I see her now all robed in white, her soul
    Enhaloed by the light of Christ-like love,
Distilling power that tells of self-control,
    That raised her spirit from the earth above.
No earthly passion mars her soul's retreat,
    No blight of sin her spirit form doth wear,
For *purity* hath made its impress sweet,
    And left its everlasting signet there.

We'll waft to her the fragrance of our love,
    And thank her for her long untiring zeal,
And pray that from her heavenly home above
    Her angel benedictions we may feel.
So fare thee well, in peace we let thee go,
    And lay thy dust beneath the frozen sod,
And say, the spirit is not there ; for lo !
    Her resurrected soul mounts up to God.

IN MEMORIAM.

FOR A DEPARTED SISTER.

CLOSED is the beautiful day-lily's dream,
    Wrapped were its petals at sunset's last gleam,
Spirit of incense to ether realms fled,
And the white casket found earth's lowly bed.

Thus hath the soul of a lovely one flown,
Bearing a beauty and glory her own;
Chaste as the lily-cup, crystal and white,
Bathed with the dews and heavenly light.

Deep in her soul-chalice nectar was stored,
Finer than blossoms of earth could afford,
Aura of purity circling her sphere,
Blest every spirit who to her drew near.

Peace like an angelic presence sent down,
Placed on her life-brow a star-jeweled crown,
Wrought in her spirit that heavenly grace
Time in its changes can never deface.

Wisdom her seal on those hallowed lips set,
No vain words or folly her heart needs regret,
No bitter invective found utterance there,
But only the sweet voice of meekness and prayer.

Large was her charity, broad her good will,
Of brother, or sister she never spoke ill;
But Christ-like in spirit, imbued with pure love
Strove ever the causes of wrong to remove.

How true to God's Order, and counsels there given,
The main spring creating the kingdom of heaven;
Submissive in spirit, through sacrifice blest,
She shared with the faithful soul, comfort and rest.

O sainted one! faithful thy travel has been
Out of the wilderness places of sin;
Called in thy early days, wise was thy choice
In following ever the angelic voice.

For country and kindred, O what is a name
To the soul who with truth's sacred fire is aflame!
Whose vision expands to a life that's above
The narrow relations of earth and its love.

How nobly and well thou hast fought the good fight
Of faith that exalts and enshrines thee in light!
Thy name in Mount Zion an honor shall be,
When numbered thou art in the ranks of the free.

Farewell, blessed spirit! the love-chords are thrilling,
'Tis but for thy good that our hearts are made willing
To part with thy presence and aid to us here,
Yet oft in our midst may we feel thou art near.

No dark thought of death in thy exit we cherish,
While we give unto earth all of earth that will perish,
Thy spirit immortal, all conscious of gain,
Mounts upward triumphant o'er weakness and pain.

Afar? not afar, are our loved and our dearest,
But when we seem blindest, e'en then they are nearest;
O happy the thought! to that future we tend,
When heaven and earth in communion shall blend.

REST IN PEACE.

READ AT THE FUNERAL OF SISTER EMILY SEARS.

CALMLY as melts the dark shadows,
   In the clear sunlight of day,
So hath thy spirit arisen
   From earthly turmoil away.
In pure affection we hold thee,
   Friendship that never will cease,
'Neath the sweet care of the angels,
   Rest, O beloved, in peace.

All for the right thou'st forsaken
   Kindred and all earthly gain;
Thine was a life of devotion,
   Free from remorse and from stain.
O sainted one! we behold thee
   Sharing a happy release,

And with rejoicing and gladness
  Gathering laurels of peace.

Bright is faith's star that hath led thee,
  Guiding thy footsteps aright;
Unselfish toil hath thy spirit
  Clothed in pure vestments of white.
Earnest in all thy endeavor,
  Working for Zion's increase,
Death brings to thee naught of terror,
  For thou art resting in peace.

Life with its care and its burden
  Often thy spirit weighed down;
Thine was the cross and the conflict,
  Thine is true joy and the crown.
Love unto thee brings her tribute,
  Freely the promised reward;
Sweet is the peace of the faithful,
  They who find rest in the Lord.

O dearest one! shall our spirits
  Share of thy blessings no more,
Lessons of wisdom and virtue
  Given from thy garnered store?
Yea, we will watch for thy coming,
  Seek in thy presence to be;
While these as fruits of thy labors
  Cluster round life's memory.

Home to the realms of the blessed,
  Free from all sadness and gloom,
Voices 'mid songs of rejoicing
  Bid thee, beloved, to come.
Blest by thy friends tried and faithful,
  Blest by the angels above,
Take the pure gems of affection
  Placed in a casket of love.

THE REWARD OF A DEDICATED LIFE.

TO SISTER RHODA R. HOLLISTER.

IS not the hour of pain the hour of balm
   When love's sweet solace drops upon the soul?
When comes the unction of sustaining calm,
   Tho' tidal waves of sorrow swell and roll.
The drift-wood and the sea-weed cast aside,
   The pearls thy spirit won from life's great deep
Will gleam in beauty that shall e'er abide,
   For they are treasures which thy soul can keep.
Proud was thy spirit when it rose and smiled,
   Intent to reach its own ambitious height;
The voice Maternal, bade thee be a child;
   Was not the Heavenly Mother's mandate right?
Thy heart of faith hath e'er proclaimed, "It was;"
   Thro' cross and trial, steady was thy aim,
Thy soul's devotion centered to Her cause,
   And to Her love confidingly laid claim.
Her people were thy kindred, in their hearts
   Thy home of homes was found and made secure,
The mocking enemy sent poisoned darts,
   But thou wert shielded by an armor pure.
Not through the lenses of to-day we view
   The worth which we have counted year by year,
Not in the tearful time when flowers we strew,
   Do we first learn to prize and hold thee dear.
Could gold of Ophir buy thy loving toil
   Or prompt the hand so ready to bestow?
Could station give the balsam and the oil
   That thro' the soul's affections had their flow?
Half o'er a century the field extends
   Whereon broadcast thy glorious deeds were wrought,
Where sainted, hallowed souls became thy friends
   And blest thee with the love thy spirit sought.
Then what to thee was all the world's false show?
   Its aspirations were the tempest's breath;

When once thy feet had found the valley low
  The road to glory was the path to death.
Thy faith had tests severe, when kith and kin
  And comrades loved and cherished in the way
Turned from the fold to devious wiles of sin,
  Thy choice was heavenward, where, O where are they?
Immortal life is thine; thy soul is strong
  To bear the changes of the transient state;
Thou hast a trust, a triumph and a song,
  With which to enter at the Morning Gate.
The flowers of earth to thee were more than fair,
  They were the gifts of God so freely given
In answer to the world's sick, yearning prayer,
  When mortals craved some token — boon from heaven.
There in that land where all the bloom is sweet,
  Beyond the loveliness of which we dreamed,
Shall Zion's faithful ones united meet,
  And by her laws refining be redeemed.
The opaque pebble-crust from souls removed,
  The diamonds polished by the life divine,
Shall blend their luster with the hosts beloved—
  God's living jewels, evermore to shine.
Such is the end of faith to us revealed,
  However much to do or long to wait;
Through labor are the promises unsealed
  That bear the glory of the holy state.
There is one baptism, above, below,
  One way, divided by a mountain cloud,
We climb the steep up which thy feet must go,
  While only silvery screening mists enshroud.
But we shall miss thee from *external* sight,
  Our *outward* senses oft will feel a void,
Yet from earth's shadow to eternal light
  The bond of union cannot be destroyed.
We give thee thanks for the unmeasured good
  Which in thy consecration had its root;
We give thee blessing, that will ever brood

Upon a life that bore unselfish fruit.
The ministrations coming from the gift
   Bring fortitude and courage to us all ;
Dear angel-hands the burdens help to lift,
   And angels' soothing accents gently fall.
These spirit friends that now our numbers swell,
   Are from our Zion home that is above ;
We dare not *emphasize* the word, Farewell,
   But we have clothed and crowned thee with our love.

CROSSING LIFE'S TIDE.

THE loved, and the dear ones, are passing from me,
   One by one they are crossing life's tide ;
They're borne from my vision like ships on the sea,
   To the shore on eternity's side.

The spring time of childhood, and bright years of youth,
   Were blest by their kindness and care ;
Their spotless example, of virtue and truth,
   Gave strength every conflict to bear.

O precious the memories, twining my heart,
   Like tendrils of summer's fair vine !
A new thrill of life to my soul they impart,
   For sweet recollections are mine.

The faces that beamed with the sunshine of love,
   The hands that with mine were employed,
The feet that were wont in my pathway to move,
   And hearts that life's pleasures enjoyed.

Though now in the immortal regions beyond,
   And toiling in new fields above,
Yet sacred and precious I hold the pure bond,
   That links me to kindred, in love.

For heavenly communion, my spirit oft yearns,
  I'll draw from an angelic sphere ;
I know there's a land whence the trav'ler returns,
  To gladden our pilgrimage here.

Then come, O ye dear ones, who love as of yore,
  Add strength to the faith that we hold ;
Bring gifts that are new from the evergreen shore
  And treasures that will not grow old.

RECOMPENSE.

I WOULD not ask O Lord, for more of good
  Than Thou hast given through Thy Fatherhood ;
Nor even seek that Thou should'st longer be
The debtor for my soul's security ;
For undeserved, the gifts that come from Thee
Fall on my path of life continually,
And in them all I find a sweet content,
A blest retreat, a safe environment.
Yet somehow 'mid them all I fail to find
The perfect peace, the spirit all resigned.
The finite part so weak and insecure
Struggles to know Thy purpose wise and pure,
But still at times when life seems smooth without,
I feel an inward dread akin to doubt,
A wavering, like one who treads alone
The mazy pathway of a land unknown,
A vagueness of the mind one feels when lost,
With dangerous ways before, that must be crossed.
And yet I *do not doubt*, but keep a sense
That waits to know the ways of Providence,
That longs to hear Thy laws interpreted,
And learn the answers to the prayers once said.
I dare to think from lessons Nature gives,
That somewhere else the vital Spirit lives,

As storm and shadow eagerly declare
That calm and sunshine surely reigns elsewhere.
So, when my soul sinks deep in questionings,
I trust there is an answer to all things,
But fail to find the nicely fitting key
That turns the temple's lock still closed to me;
Cannot discern with reason's optic glass
The path o'er which Thy bright-gift angels pass;
But hold in faith to intuition's thread
That runs along the complex way I tread,
Still careful not to blind my soul through dread,
Nor through erroneous ways to be misled;
My trusting heart gives o'er its task to Thee,
It fails in all to solve the mystery.
Still I will struggle on and hope and pray
Nor courage lose through danger or delay.
If when I enter Thy white temple's gate,
I may be taught the laws for which I wait,
And having learned what life has dreamed of here,
That time will be my spirit's festal year.

YOUTHFUL PETITION.

WHEN with the saints assembled
   In worship's holy hour,
Where unseen hosts have gathered
   With blest redeeming power;
Where offerings of the faithful
   With fragrance fill the air,
And angel gifts are falling,
   O, breathe for me one prayer!

When round the holy altar
   Where sacrament is given,
The wine of truth eternal
   And living bread from heaven;

And you with dearest kindred
  In soul communion share,
Some crumbs for me, O gather
  And think of me in prayer.

I know I am dependent,
  My soul would famished be,
If that I only merit
  Were given unto me;
And meager be the raiment
  My spirit form would wear,
Without a woven garment
  Of charity and prayer.

Though shadows of affliction
  My pathway now have crossed,
The light that shines above me
  Can ne'er be dimmed nor lost;
If I in spirit lowly
  Will seek the angel's care,
And you my precious kindred
  Remember me in prayer.

I'll seek the flowing river,
  And wash my soul from stain,
I'll prove the heated furnace,
  Until no dross remain.
And when the clouds are breaking,
  And lightnings rend the air,
To gain a new baptism,
  O help me by your prayer.

I'll arm my soul for contest,
  'Gainst selfishness and sin,
Will list to wisdom's counsels,
  And bear the cross within;
I would not shrink from duty,
  But toil and trial bear,
That healing power be given,
  Remember me in prayer.

Oh then with soul and body
    Renewed for toil and strife,
Thank offerings I will render,
    In fruits of holy life ;
And thus to those who've blest me,
    With patient, loving care,
Through consecrated service,
    Give recompense for prayer.

CULMINATION.

THERE comes upon our life-day
    The gloom that autumn weaves,
There falls upon our pathway
    The golden harvest leaves.
And shades that dip at evening
    Predict approaching night,
The soul that meets its darkness
    Looks forward to the light.

There is a spell of gladness
    Before a time of pain,
The harp attuned to sadness
    Holds yet a brighter strain.
The pearl that drops at night-fall
    In morning light is fair,
The rose that holds the tear-drop
    Sends up an incense prayer.

There comes a time when freshness
    Makes all the woodland bright,
But circling of the seasons
    Brings to its greenness blight.
The sun will light the morning,
    And gray of winter's night
Will open of its purity
    To robe the earth in white.

There comes a time of sunset
   When day-beams lie aslant,
And shades of deepening night-fall
   Will lingering days supplant.

When life of youth's fair morning
   Returns to Him who gave,
And lengthening of the shadows
   Are stretched upon the grave.
The song that's almost ended
   Will rise in sweet refrain,
The hope-star that is dimming
   Increase its light again.

As fragrant breath of incense
   Exhales from fading bloom,
The tired passing spirit
   Escapes as from the tomb.
For love that buds the flowers
   On lonely desert sand,
Will cull the spirit blossoms
   To bloom in summer land.

www.ingramcontent.com/pod-product-compliance
Lightning Source LLC
Chambersburg PA
CBHW030020240426
43672CB00007B/1020